BE THOU MY VISION

Be Thou My Vision

Daily Inspiration from the Greatest Hymns of All Time

John Fischer

Servant Publications
Ann Arbor, Michigan

Vine Books is an imprint of Servant Publications especially designed to serve evangelical Christians.

Published by Servant Publications
P.O. Box 8617
Ann Arbor, Michigan 48107

Cover design by Multnomah Graphics, Portland, Oregon

95 96 97 98 99 10 9 8 7 6 5 4 3 2 1

Printed in the United States of America
ISBN 0-89283-924-4

Library of Congress Cataloging-in-Publication Data

Fischer, John.
Be thou my vision : daily inspiration from the greatest hymns of all time / John Fischer.
p. cm.
ISBN 0-89283-924-4
1. Hymns—Devotional use. 2. Devotional calendars. 3. Hymns, English—History and criticism. I. Title.
BV340.F57 1995
245'.21—dc20 95-22882
CIP

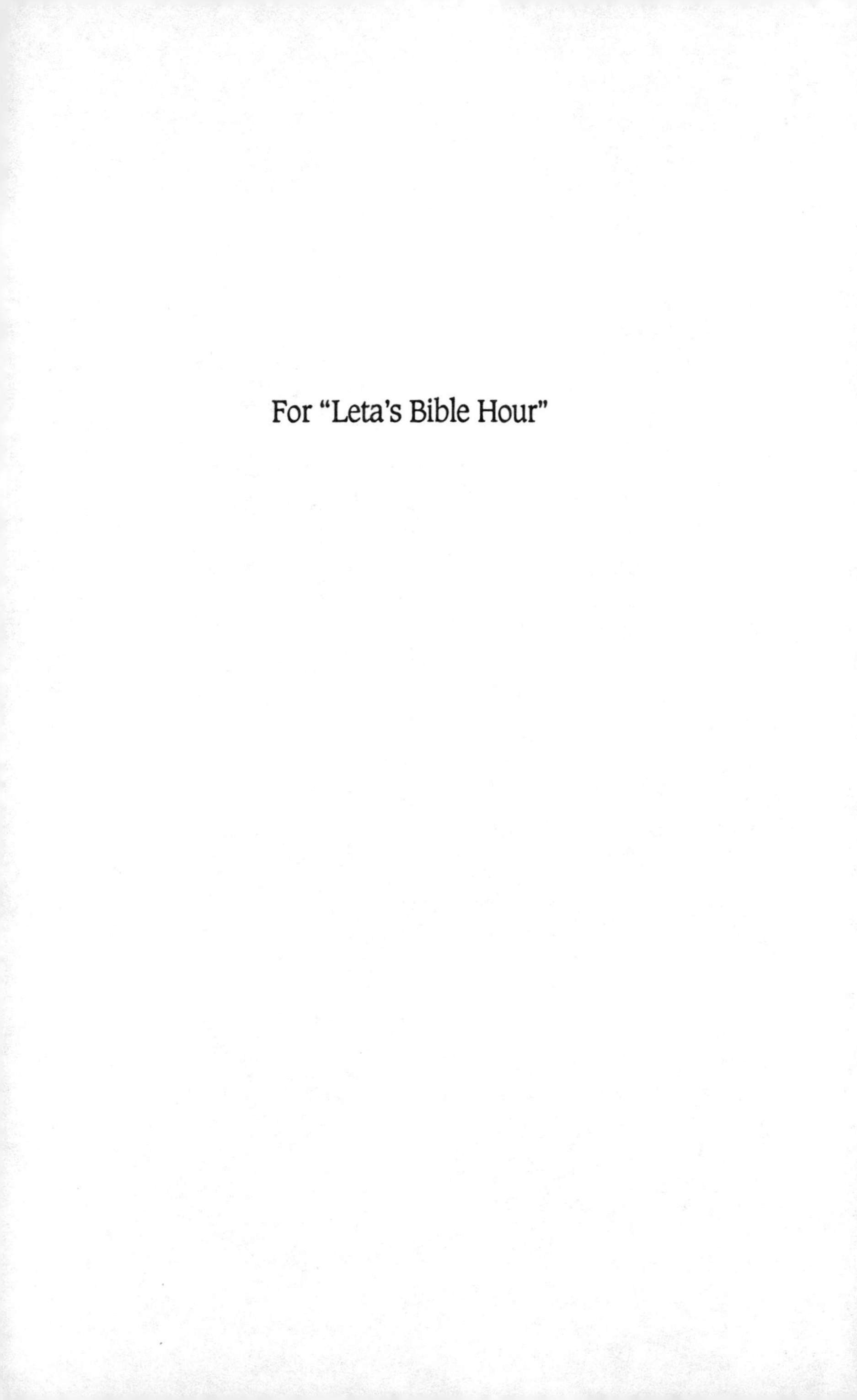

For "Leta's Bible Hour"

Therefore, since we are surrounded by such a great cloud of witnesses, let us throw off everything that hinders and the sin that so easily entangles, and let us run with perseverance the race marked out for us.

Hebrews 12:1

Introduction

Deep calls to deep
in the roar of your waterfalls;
all your waves and breakers
have swept over me
—Psalm 42:7

I grew up on hymns. My father was the part-time choir director of our church, so church for us was more than just a Sunday habit. It was a vocation. When I think of the word *church*, I think of it in Gothic print, the way it appeared on the outside of our *New Church Hymnal.* They were gold letters that were slightly indented. You could press a blank space of the bulletin into the letters and pencil them in perfectly, like a stencil.

I often occupied myself during the sermon doing things like that. I would also draw geometric, snowflake-like patterns on the backs of the three-by-five registration cards, folding them in half and making the patterns identical—a kind of Rorschach Test, before I knew what one was. The hard cover of the hymnal made a perfect portable desk to draw on. It also put in my hands a good, hard surface to crack over the top of a friend's head after the service.

I came to know many of the hymns by heart, strictly through singing them over and over. This was before there were any contemporary songs in church. The most contemporary we got was when we sang "choruses" on Sunday night. My father would usually lead the congregation in a lively hymn sing that featured more informal songs, such as

"He Lives," "One Day," and "Count Your Blessings." For these the congregation was usually accompanied only by piano. The church organ was reserved for Sunday morning, as were the more staid hymns, such as "Glorious Things of Thee are Spoken," "Crown Him with Many Crowns," and "Lead On, O King Eternal."

I used to think hymns were merely old, outdated ways of saying the same things a believer might say today. Flip-flop the word order and throw in a few "billows rolling" and "fears assailing," or beat on a "troubled breast" or wave a "festal banner on high," and you had a hymn.

I've since found out that this is not so.

Sometimes, it takes a little growing up—that, and perhaps a few years' hiatus from the hymnbook—to see something more. In the past twenty years, we have had a tendency to relegate the hymnal to the rack behind the pew—or even the closet—in deference to the more singable, repetitious contemporary choruses that continually replenish Sunday morning worship, Christian conferences, and religious radio waves across the nation.

However, many are discovering—with fresh zeal—the treasures hidden in the average church hymnal. To some—those new to the family of God or simply new to the family of life—these songs are uncharted territory. To others, like me, they are like awakening a call from the deep. They are like finding a familiar buoy in the midst of a treacherous ocean—a place to cast a line and know I can secure it once again to the truth.

Hymns are deep in doctrine. Almost every hymn is about the gospel in some form. And those that are praise-oriented are never free-floating, repetitious praise words, like many of our current praise songs. Rather, they are eloquent reminders of the character of God and what He has done in history, what we can count on Him doing in the present, and what He will do in the future.

But hymns are deep in emotion, too. This aspect of hymns surprised me during my current re-familiarization with the hymnbook. Hymns are passionate. They capture depths of the human spirit as well as the deep truths of the gospel, as in this fourth stanza of Charles Wesley's "And Can It Be That I Should Gain?":

Long my imprisoned spirit lay
Fast bound in sin and natures night;
Thine eye diffused a quickening ray,
I woke the dungeon flamed with light;
My chains fell off, my heart was free;
I rose, went forth and followed Thee.

Though they are personal—when they need to be for intimacy's sake—hymns are quite often corporate in focus. These are hymns not just for me, but for the church in history and in time, and thus they are reminders of my place within the grand scheme of things, identified as God's work in the world.

But most importantly for purposes of this daily devotional, hymns are just old. This is not to say that old is necessarily better. But in that these hymns are, for the most part, a hundred or more years old, they stand outside the influences of our present culture. Getting close to the hymns is getting to know believers from another part of time who were immersed in a culture that is foreign to us. What translates from them to us, therefore, is most often that which is universal about our faith. These statements of faith and devotion are refreshingly free of the pop psychology and political grandstanding that so often accompanies at least the grid out of which contemporary Christian music is created today. In one sense, then, they are culturally unconscious and able to illumine blind spots in our current theology by merely being what they are.

Thus, the hymns are personal encounters with God and biblical truths of the gospel that stand outside of time and have been preserved for us today. And because of this, they are a rich source of devotional reflection. Though many of them are solid enough for biblical teaching, that is not the primary purpose of this book. The purpose of this book is to inspire and deepen the believer's walk. To do that, I have chosen only certain words, lines, and phrases from these great hymns. This is to give us a point of reflection—to draw a line along the straightedge of history to a point somewhere in our daily lives that will help you and me in our walk of faith.

In the expressions preserved on the pages of a hymnal I have often discovered doorways to a spirituality that might have otherwise escaped me. It is my hope that encountering theology and spiritual experience by way of this oblique, anachronistic route will surprise, deepen, and broaden the paths of many people.

It certainly has mine. That's why I am genuinely sad to see this project completed. I have grown intimate again with the hymnbook. It has become a kind of personal friend. I have decided that when this devotional book is in my own hands, I will probably read it daily, as I hope you will, so I can remember the joy it has been to create it, and continue to hear along with you these ancient voices of faith comforting, prodding, and encouraging us on.

JWF
1995

P.S. Before jumping into my entry for each day, let the hymn selection soak a little while into your heart and mind. I have captured only one small facet of the many things I believe the Holy Spirit can reveal through these great lyrics. Allow some time for your own insights before you check out mine. Your own are usually the best.

From *Close to Thee* by Fanny J. Crosby

A Hungering Heart

Not for ease or worldly pleasure,
Nor for fame my prayer shall be;
Gladly will I toil and suffer,
Only let me walk with Thee.

Do you want this? More than anything, do you want to walk with Him? To hear Him speaking and know the voice is really His and not someone else's—even your own—ringing in your head? Do you want to hold onto Him when everything else gives way?

Then take heart, because this desire is born of the Spirit. God put it there. It is the child in us calling out the "Abba" to its Father. Our spirit bears witness with His Spirit. The first-fruits in us groan for the second, third, and fourth fruits (and so on) to be revealed.

That we have this desire tells us that God has indeed been born in us. "Everyone who believes that Jesus is the Christ is born of God" (1 John 5:1). That's because it is God in a person that gives someone the ability to believe in the first place.

This hunger will not go away. Nor will it be completely satisfied in this life. "Blessed are those who hunger and thirst for righteousness, for they will be filled" (Matthew 5:6). Jesus promised us that those who hunger for Him will be filled. But God will never fill us to the point that we are no longer hungry and thirsty for more.

From *This Is My Father's World* by Maltbie D. Babcock

Singing Planets

All nature sings, and round me rings
The music of the spheres.

Has anyone ever heard the planets sing or the mountains break out in full chorus? If someone claimed to hear such a thing, most people would no doubt think this person was not playing with a full deck. But then again, when the Creator of the universe fills all your vision, there's no telling what might happen.

Years ago, my children learned to lip-sync a humorous Chipmunk version of the pop song *There's No Rock and Roll on Mars*. It talked about whether there was a rhythmic beat among the stars. That song got me wondering if the universe isn't virtually throbbing with music.

"The heavens declare the glory of God," says the psalmist, "the skies proclaim the work of his hands. Day after day they pour forth speech; night after night they display knowledge" (Psalm 19:1-2). All this proclaiming and pouring forth—I bet if we could actually hear it, it would be music to our ears. Why couldn't this be music? Why couldn't the skies be full of something that, with the right set of ears, you could hear?

All human beings are fascinated with outer space. This came home to me vividly when I saw *Close Encounters of the Third Kind*. At the conclusion of the movie, which presented the possibility of a pleasant encounter with an intelligent, non-human extraterrestrial life form, the camera simply stares out at the beauty of a night sky. No one leaves the theater. They're looking, listening.

Maybe they can hear the music of the spheres. Maybe, for just a moment, whether they believe or not, they are hearing the song of God's creation from a long way away.

From *This Is My Father's World* by Maltbie D. Babcock

The Big Surprise

This is my Father's world,
He shines in all that's fair.

We've all asked for signs from God, asked for Him to allow us some miraculous visitation. All we want is just one glimpse of His supernatural presence in this world. But our requests are usually denied.

At times I am reminded of God's presence and evidence everywhere in the created world. Then I wonder how silly my request for a personal visitation must sound to Him. It must be as if I were standing in the middle of a gallery of the works of major nineteenth-century French impressionists, and asking Claude Monet to please reveal himself in person. On the wall is more access to the man than I would have if he were there to talk with me face to face.

God's shining evidence is constantly being displayed in all that's fair. Not just in all that's "Christian," but in all that's fair and true and right and beautiful. The "Christian" category is much smaller and less accessible than the others. It is dependent on spiritual "policemen" to sanction it for us, and it leaves us without enjoying the search and the privilege of discovery.

God's work is everywhere. Come, see Him shine. Don't wait for anyone to tell you "He's over here," or "He's over there." You can see Him yourself. He has written His law on your heart and left His mark on everything that is beautiful. Open your eyes and get ready for a big surprise!

From *This Is My Father's World* by Maltbie D. Babcock

Crazy for Him

In the rustling grass I hear Him pass—
He speaks to me everywhere.

Shhhhh! What was that? Did you hear it?

Hear what?

That sound.... There it is again!

I don't know what you're talking about. It's just the wind.

No. It's more than that. It's the sound of someone passing. Someone invisible.

You're crazy.

And you're boring. Wait! There it is again!

Look, I don't know what your problem is. But there's nothing out here but sky and trees and grass and wind.

Trees? Did you say trees?

Oh no...

Yes! There they go; they're clapping their hands! They must have heard Him pass too!

You keep on like this and they will have to come and put you away.

Really? Do you think they might? I would like that! Then I would have nothing else to do with my time but listen for Him everywhere.

Well, old friend, I'm going to leave you out here to your madness. I don't want to be around when you start seeing stars.

Stars? Did you say stars? Of course! It's the morning stars singing! Come on, you'd have to be deaf not to hear them....

From *My Saviour First of All* by Fanny J. Crosby

Dinner Immediately Following

In the glad song of ages I shall mingle with delight;
But I long to meet my Saviour first of all.

I can see it now. Prior to the biggest banquet of all eternity, we're mingling around a huge parlor. Name tags are unnecessary—we've known everyone here forever. We know things about them and they know things about us that we've never communicated before. We don't need any get-acquainted time—no mixers.

Instead, our conversations with "strangers" begin at a level deeper than anything we knew on earth, even with our closest friends. We talk about God and His Son and Holy Spirit, and we share our delight at the amazing events that have brought us to this place.

And then the wide double doors swing open, and we are bathed in the light of His glory as He invites us in to sit down at the marriage supper of the Lamb. Each of us has a place reserved, and we find it easily because we know where it is. And once we are seated, He begins to speak to us. But when He speaks, He is in some miraculous way speaking to all of us and each of us at the same time. It's as if He were sitting right next to us, having a private conversation. It is then that we will look into His face.

From *Jesus, Joy of Man's Desiring* by Johann Sebastian Bach

Out and Up

Drawn by Thee, our souls aspiring,
Soar to uncreated light.

God tantalizes us. He gives us glimpses of Himself, and then He shrouds Himself in mystery. I actually think He delights in this—it's like a game in some ways—but He doesn't toy with us for His own amusement. He has too much respect for His own creation to do that. But He created us to seek after Him "and perhaps reach out for Him and find Him" (Acts 17:27).

As He tantalizes us, He is pulling us higher, stretching us. He will not force Himself on us, but He draws us out and up, so that we discover our higher value in discovering Him.

In a time when worship is becoming more and more contemporary—appealing to our familiarity with popular culture—we need to be careful not to abandon high art, high praise, tradition, hymns, and worshipful architecture that pulls us out beyond where we live—out and up to higher places of contemplation and glory. If we make our worship too familiar, we will forget about its mystery. We will think we have it all when we don't. We need to be challenged to go beyond the spotlight to uncreated light—light that is God Himself, since He alone is uncreated.

From *He Hideth My Soul* by Fanny J. Crosby

Rock Doves

He hideth my soul in the cleft of the rock
That shadows a dry, thirsty land;
He hideth my life in the depths of His love,
And covers me there with His hand.

In the Holy Land there is a species of dove that is named after the rocky terrain in which it makes its home. The rock dove builds its nest in clefts in the rock that shield it from wind and rain of winter and the sun and heat of summer. The Lord refers to this image when he said to Moses, "I will put you in a cleft in the rock, and cover you with my hand until I have passed by" (Exodus 33:22). This is also echoed in a number of hymns, including this one.

The image is a striking one that bears some reflection. Something as delicate as a dove seems out of place in such a hostile, barren environment. Unless this is the whole point. This dove could have been put in this rocky environment by its Creator to be a picture of believers in the world. (Why couldn't God have designed elements in nature for the very purpose of being visual aids to us?)

The world is a dry and thirsty land for believers, and it's not going to get any better. According to Jesus, it's only going to get worse (see Matthew 24:21-22). Yet this is our home, if only for a season, and God is going to look after us while we are here. He's going to do that by tucking our souls away in a safe place right in the middle of the desert.

This doesn't mean things will get better for me. It means that whatever happens, God is protecting my soul.

From *I Want to Be Holy* by Albert B. Simpson

Dealing With Myopia

I want to be patient and gentle,
Long-suffering and loving and kind,
As quick to acknowledge my failings
As I to another's am blind.

I want to be as good at spotting my own faults as I am bad about spotting the faults of someone else. This will take some doing because human nature is set up to do the opposite: I'm naturally more adept at pointing out everyone else's flaws.

When it comes to others, I have X-ray vision. I see my friends so well that I am the resident psychologist. But when it comes to my own problems, I complain of being short-sighted. I claim to need glasses in order to see myself objectively—and I *do!* All of us are myopic when it comes to seeing ourselves.

We should take note of what we spot in others, as this almost always shows us what we cannot see in ourselves. Judging others always works this way. This is why Jesus said we are all judged by the same judgments we give out.

What really bugs you about other people? The answer to that question should be very self-revealing.

From *Ask Ye What Great Thing I Know* by Johann C. Schwedler

Ask Me

Ask ye what great thing I know
That delights and stirs me so?
Whose the name I glory in?

Go ahead, ask me. Ask me what great thing I know that stimulates my mind and makes all things worth knowing. Ask me who speaks to me in the morning sun that streams through my window. Ask me who rides on the wings of the dawn and touches the flowers with dew. Ask me what great thing I see in the headlines of the newspaper.

Whose hand can I see shaping and taunting the longings of men and women? Who can I find hidden in the shelves of the library? What protagonist peeks through the holes of novels and stays on the screen at movie's end? Who inhabits the hopes and dreams of artists, and who dances with the muses of the philosopher? Who mocks the theologian and hides from the pen of the reporter? Who escapes the scrutiny of the calculating eye and shines in the smile of a child? Who comforts the aged when visitors don't come anymore? Who wakes me up in the morning and keeps me up at night?

Ask me what great thing I know that sets me searching, asking questions, and knocking on doors. Ask me what makes me search for what I have already found, what makes me ask what I already know, and sends me knocking on doors already open.

Go ahead... ask me!

From *Hallelujah! What a Saviour!* by Philip P. Bliss

The Incomprehensible Transaction

Guilty, vile, and helpless, we,
Spotless Lamb of God was He;
"Full atonement!" Can it be?

These words fall hard on the ears of any generation, but none more acutely than ours. How can we call ourselves these awful things? This has got to be bad for our self-image! I know I've got some problems, but I am redeemable, aren't I? Isn't that why Jesus died on the cross for me—because I was worth it?

On the contrary! Our worth comes as a *result* of Christ's dying for us, not as a *cause* of it. It's not that God got a good deal here, that He purchased us because we were so valuable. And it's not that He negotiated the price as being the death of His Son. (Would that we could be considered so priceless as unredeemed humanity!) No, it is actually the other way around. We *became* valuable at the cross, and not a second before. We were not worthy *of* this death. He made us worthy *in* this death. He put the value on us when He redeemed us by His blood. He didn't have to do this.

No great law of the universe would have held God in court for permanently doing away with His fallen creation. The potter making the vessel has every right to destroy it if it does not match up to his standards.

Jesus was the spotless Lamb, and we were the guilty sinners. In this incomprehensible transaction at the cross, He gave us His righteousness and took on our sin. In the cross alone I am righteous. I am worthy to be called His because of what He did, not because of what I am. His death on the cross bestowed this value on me.

Without that sacrifice, we are nothing but guilty, vile, helpless sinners, whom God would have had every right to destroy.

From *Hallelujah! What a Saviour!* by Philip P. Bliss

Sealed in Blood

Sealed my pardon with His blood;
Hallelujah, what a Saviour!

To seal something is to determine irrevocably that it is authentic. A king puts his official seal on royal messages and announcements to guarantee their authenticity. A seal is also a means of closing something and protecting it from intrusion. They sealed the tomb of Jesus to protect His body. It never occurred to them, of course, that the real threat came from *within* the tomb.

Now consider that it is the blood of Jesus that authenticates your release from guilt and sin. It is the blood of Jesus that guarantees the royal decree of pardon. Not only does this ensure your freedom, it also protects against anyone getting in and messing with it. What has been given to you cannot be taken away, not by anyone or anything.

When we were kids, we used to prick our fingers with a pin and touch our little bead of blood to that of a friend, making us "blood brothers" or "blood sisters" forever. (Well, almost forever. At least until we were in high school.) Little did we know that God would take His Son's blood and stamp a royal seal on our lives, making us irrevocably His—forever blood brothers and sisters of Jesus, and sons and daughters of God.

From *A Charge to Keep I Have* by Charles Wesley

Fit For Both

A charge to keep I have,
A God to glorify,
A never-dying soul to save,
And fit it for the sky.

As believers, we don't get any time off. We have a charge to keep. First, there's a God to glorify. This shouldn't be too difficult if we just keep our eyes out for Him behind the scenes of everything. We glorify Him when the sun comes up and when it goes down. We glorify Him when we go to work because we see our work as sacred. We glorify Him when we see an exceptional piece of art or hear beautiful music. We glorify Him when we witness a superior physical feat, realizing that God gave men and women the ability to do things that glorify Him. The people doing these things may not give God the glory, but you and I can.

Most of this won't take extra time, either. What it takes is a heightened awareness of Him all the time.

There's also our never-dying souls to save and get ready for heaven. While we're busy turning everything we do, hear, and see into worship, we're also getting our souls in shape. We were created to glorify God, and we need to start early at this endeavor: the better we become at glorifying God here on earth, the more ready we will be for heaven.

As we prepare our souls for heaven, we will also find more meaning in our stay on earth. Remember, His will is for things to be done on earth as they are in heaven. So if you're getting fit for heaven, you are automatically getting fit for earth, too!

From *A Charge to Keep I Have* by Charles Wesley

My Utmost for His Highest

To serve the present age,
My calling to fulfill,
O may it all my powers engage
To do my Master's will!

God wants our total commitment toward accomplishing His will for our lives. As Charles Wesley wrote, fulfilling God's will requires all the power we can muster. But we don't do this alone, as Paul wrote: "To this end I labor, struggling with all the energy he so powerfully works in me" (Colossians 1:29). His power demands ours, too. It is a 100 percent investment from both sides—all He has for us *and* all we have for Him.

It really wouldn't be fair for it to be any other way. It wouldn't be right for Him to give everything He has—His very Son on the cross and His Holy Spirit on a daily basis to help us live—only to have us put forth a weak, ambivalent effort at following Him.

Anyone would agree that such an arrangement wouldn't be fair. It would be a mockery of His gifts. It would be a cheap trick for us to take *all* that He has, only to give Him *part* of what we have. Maybe we think He has so much more than we do that He can afford to pay more than us. We tell ourselves that He won't miss a slack in our already meager contribution. After all, our debt is so small compared with all He has.

But our logic here is faulty. It doesn't take a genius to know that we get *out* of something what we put into it. His efforts demand all of our own efforts.

Oswald Chambers' famous devotional title says it best: *My Utmost for His Highest*. God made everything He has available to me. How can I, even with my minimal earthly resources, give back to Him anything less than everything?

From *At Calvary* by William Newell

So Near But Yet So Far...

Years I spent in vanity and pride,
Caring not my Lord was crucified,
Knowing not it was for me He died...

A lot of people live within earshot of the gospel, but they don't hear it for themselves. Something doesn't click. This is especially true in countries where Christianity is common. For instance, Christianity is the state religion in many European countries. Though few people actually attend church, many assume they are a part of it. (Just as they are a part of the state, though they might never enter a state building.) In the United States, Christianity is something of a folk religion. It is a part of our culture.

Most people think they know what Christianity is. People can spend a lifetime in or around Christianity and never know that Jesus died for them. They might know that Jesus died on a cross, but they don't know that Jesus died for *them*.

People who don't know that Jesus died for them most often don't really care that Jesus was crucified. This isn't because they are cruel or uncaring: they just don't understand how it applies to them.

Those who believe know the frustration they can feel at another's inability to see how Christ's death relates to them. But we must remember it takes God to turn on the light. No amount of badgering is really going to help. Love, prayer, and an honest confession of our own sin and forgiveness is the best witness going.

From *At Calvary* by William Newell

Hearing Is Believing

By God's Word at last my sin I learned,
Then I trembled at the law I'd spurned,
Till my guilty soul imploring turned
To Calvary.

I really didn't know I was a sinner until I heard the Word. Not everyone who hears the Word understands it. But you can't understand it without hearing it. "Faith comes from hearing the message," said Paul, "and the message is heard through the word of Christ" (Romans 10:17).

And when you hear the Word—if you understand it—it sets you trembling. Salvation always works this way. In order to be saved, you first have to know you're in trouble, and you don't know you're in trouble until you hear the Word. We call this *conviction of sin*. It always accompanies the preaching of the gospel for those who are in the process of being saved. They hear the truth and they tremble.

True conviction of sin brings *real* guilt. Deep inside my heart, I know I have violated the holiness and righteousness of God, and I can do nothing about it. Conviction brings me a sense of complete and utter helplessness that puts me at the mercy of God. When I receive that mercy from Him, it is as real as the guilt. That echo of mercy is reflected in this hymn's great refrain:

Mercy there was great, and grace was free;
Pardon there was multiplied to me;
There my burdened soul found liberty,
At Calvary.

From *See the Conqueror Mount in Triumph*
by Christopher Wordsworth

A Good Idea

He has raised our human nature
On the clouds to God's right hand.

Something of earth is now in heaven. "In my flesh shall I see God," cried Job (Job 19:26), raising the possibility that flesh will indeed be able to finally face God and enjoy Him forever.

We are so down on human nature. We keep trying to blame our humanness for all our problems, forgetting that Jesus elevated human nature to the right hand of God.

Jesus did not cry out, "Help! I'm trapped inside a human body!" Yet His was a human body. He greeted the disciples in that body, ate and walked with them in it, and ascended into heaven in it.

Humanity was a great idea. Through Christ, God redeemed that idea and took it to heaven.

In heaven, you and I will be perpetuating the idea that human nature was originally a good thing. We will be raised in bodies like these—bodies of which these are the seed. We will not give up being human. In fact, I would guess that everything we love about being human will go right along with us into eternity.

Think about that the next time you enjoy one of life's simple pleasures.

From *Dear Lord and Father of Mankind* by John G. Whittier

Confession

Dear Lord and Father of mankind,
Forgive our foolish ways...

Confession is a necessary part of a believer's daily walk. It keeps us humble, truthful, and compassionate. Without regular confession of sins, there will undoubtedly be pride and self-righteousness present in unmanageable quantities.

Confession keeps the log out of my eye and the pain of its removal current. This log, of course, turns everyone else's sins into a speck by comparison.

Confession is telling the truth. It keeps me from straying too far from the truth about myself, and it makes me seek as friends those who can accept me for who I am.

Confession makes me less defensive. It makes me open to criticism, since I am already familiar with putting myself on trial.

Confession keeps me eternally grateful because I am always reminded of my forgiveness and the heavy cost of Jesus' blood, which purchased it.

It's hard to imagine a spirituality that does not include and incorporate a regular pattern of confession in the dialogue of the Spirit. There is something to a regular time of self-evaluation. Sometimes our sins do not present themselves until we stop to reflect on them and ask God, like David did, to search our hearts and try our thoughts. Otherwise, when they do show themselves, it may be after great damage has been done to ourselves and those around us.

Would that we found our sins sooner, before they find us.

From *Dear Lord and Father of Mankind* by John G. Whittier

Simple Obedience

In simple trust like theirs who heard,
Beside the Syrian Sea,
The gracious calling of the Lord,
Let us, like them, without a word,
Rise up and follow Thee.

There is nothing more simple than obedience. Doing what God says is probably the most uncomplicated choice we can make with our lives.

When I complain that I wish God would clearly tell me what I am supposed to do, then I am in trouble. My Bible is full of directives, and I have in my heart a Holy Spirit who can illuminate God's Word and whisper His truth to my inner life. And yet I complain about not getting a clear signal? Something is wrong, and it is not my hearing. It is my will.

Oh, I have *heard*, all right. That is not the problem. I just don't want to *do*. And at that point it becomes much easier to say that I am not sure what God is telling me, that I am muddled or confused, or that God's will is too complicated.

If you're not sure what God is saying to you today, stop right now and ask yourself, what *are* you sure about? What *is* clear about His message? What *is* He asking you to do that is right in front of you? There is probably something looming so large that you are about to run right into it—if you haven't already. What is that thing? Start there, and you should find an opening in the clouds.

From *Dear Lord and Father of Mankind* by John G. Whittier

Do You Want to Get Well?

Reclothe us in our rightful mind;
In purer lives Thy service find,
In deeper reverence, praise.

"When they came to Jesus, they saw the man who had been possessed by the legion of demons, sitting there, *dressed and in his right mind*; and they were afraid" (Mark 5:15, italics mine).

It is a frightening thing to be well. To be rid of the demons that haunted us and to be free of the sins that mastered us is an awesome thing. It means we can serve and revere God with a clear and right mind. It means all our excuses are gone. It means that, since we are no longer identified with our problem, we are now expected to act on behalf of others and the Lord.

We should think twice before we seek the Lord. He might just make us well, then expect something of us. He asked the cripple by the pool the most challenging question of all: "Do you want to get well?" The man could not answer it straight-away. The thought of instantly changing the patterns of thirty-seven years of ingrained sickness was too overwhelming for him. He could not answer with a simple "Yes" because he was too afraid of not being sick anymore.

A man or woman dressed and in a right mind, serving God with a pure life and worshiping Him in deep reverence, is a holy and terrible thing. Do *you* want to get well, or would you rather stay sick for just one more day?

From *Come, Thou Fount of Every Blessing* by Robert Robinson

Tune Up

Come, Thou fount of every blessing,
Tune my heart to sing Thy grace...

I have played the guitar for more than thirty years. For at least twenty of those years, I had to tune all six strings by ear. Then someone came up with electronic tuners, which virtually eliminate the margin of error. With the touch of a button and the read of a dial, I can tune my guitar perfectly every time, string by string. So I'm more dependent upon technology now, but also painfully aware that until this machine came along, the accuracy of the tuning of my guitar strings was always in question.

There's something akin to this in the hymn writer's phrase, "Tune me up to sing thy praise." This is a part of God's graciousness.

All of us are out-of-tune praise-givers. God must cringe when we take a big breath. But somewhere between the note and His ear, He is able to straighten out the tone and make it suitable for Him.

The Spirit interceding for us in "groans that words cannot express" (Romans 8:26) is a little like this, too. Knowing there is an interpreter of our own uneven notes makes it easier for us to try.

Our hearts are not perfect. We are in the process of being sanctified, but tune-ups are being given every time we lift our voices in praise.

From *Come, Thou Fount of Every Blessing* by Robert Robinson

Wanderlust

Prone to wander, Lord I feel it,
Prone to leave the God I love...

Oh, but we are impatient little sheep, aren't we? We have this wanderlust. We keep thinking there is something else out there, that the Shepherd is keeping us from something better.

My daughter has a Siberian husky that has lived up to the one negative trait in that particular breed that trainers warned us about. They said Siberian huskies tend to be escape artists, and our Kita is no exception. We have not yet found a yard that can contain her. So we confine her to the garage and house, taking her for daily "walks" (more like pulling matches) on a leash.

Despite our precautions, Kita sometimes escapes our control, and her boundless energy can take her anywhere—often across crowded boulevards filled with fast-moving cars. We have all prepared ourselves for the distinct possibility that she could meet her end under the wheel of a car before she dies of old age.

There is a truth for all of us here: Wandering has consequences. We should keep that in mind before we consider breaking away from our loving Father. Maybe where He has us is not so bad after all.

From *Come, Thou Fount of Every Blessing* by Robert Robinson

The Good Shepherd

Jesus sought me when a stranger
Wandering from the fold of God...

He is the seeker, the Good Shepherd with the keen eye who knows His sheep. He is the one who has pursued us into the dangerous places we have fallen—steep ledges, crevices in the rocks, icy holes. He has risked His life to find us. And, yes, He has even lost His life so that He might win it—and us—back again.

We did not know His voice when He first came. We were strangers to Him, and mostly He to us. For many of us, He was not even welcomed in the beginning. *Who are you, and what business do you have with me?* we might have thought. Silly thing to think when you're stuck in a hole with no one else around. But He was—and is—patient with us.

At the time, we did not even know that we belonged anywhere or that there had ever been a fold from which we had wandered. We might not have seen ourselves as wanderers at all! We mostly fancied ourselves as more than that, probably thinking that *we* were the searchers. We saw ourselves as the ones who were going to set out and find our destiny, our pot of gold, our proverbial rainbow.

And He found us here, stuck in some sinkhole, some miry place with walls too high and too slippery to climb. (We might not have described it this way, but that's what it was.) And He had us in His sights all along. He knew exactly what was going on. And He never took His eye off us, not even once.

He does know His sheep, doesn't He?

From *All Your Anxiety* by Edward Henry Joy

Best Friend

No other friend so keen to help you,
No other friend so quick to hear;
No other place to leave your burden,
No other one to hear your prayer.

Friends can be a source of great comfort to us. They provide an ear for our problems, a touch in our loneliness, and a sounding board for the thoughts that fly about unrestrained in our minds. But even our best friends disappoint us at times. No human friend is capable of meeting all our needs. No one could be that selfless. We all have our own problems. We all know what it is like to turn to a trusted friend, only to find them needy as well—too needy to be of any help to us right then. And so we both stare at the darkness and feel helpless.

This is why we all need the friendship of Christ. He is the only friend that we cannot wear out, and the only friend with the resources to always be ready and available for us. He is the only friend who is totally selfless. He does not have His own interests to consider, and *His* interests are always in *our* best interest.

For this reason, He hears our requests and gives us what is best. (It may not be what we asked for, but it is ultimately what we want.) He is a friend who can be totally trusted.

"Cast all your anxiety on Him because He cares for you" (1 Peter 5:7). No other friend can do all this.

From *All the Way My Saviour Leads Me* by Fanny J. Crosby

All the Way Home

All the way my Saviour leads me;
What have I to ask beside?

Take heart. Whatever is happening, Jesus is leading you all the way. What He starts He always finishes (see Philippians 1:6). He never abandons anyone in mid-stream, even though you may feel like He has.

Jesus is responsible for completing our sanctification, and you can be sure that He will do this. He's made a major investment in us, and He's not about to walk away from what His own blood has bought.

And all along the way, He leads us. We may not always be aware of this leading, but it is there like an invisible hand, shaping and reshaping us by our circumstances. This happens in the good times and in the bad. This happens when we are conscious of God in our lives and when we are not. And should we come to our senses after a spell of forgetting Him or even running away from Him, when we turn around to start back, He is suddenly there to meet us. We may think we are running away from Him, but He never leaves. We are the ones who lose track, but He never will.

"If we are faithless, He will remain faithful, for He cannot disown Himself" (2 Timothy 2:13).

What more could we ask for?

From *Break Thou the Bread of Life* by Mary A. Lathbury

The Point of the Page

Beyond the sacred page
I seek Thee, Lord,
My spirit pants for Thee,
O living Word!

Don't stop at the sacred page. The page is not what we seek, and neither are the words on it.

We like the sacred page. We can study it, learn it, teach it, debate it, answer questions with it, prove things with it, write manuals based on it, quote it, create new versions of it, and sell it. We can hold it in our hands, carry it in our purses, and swear on it in court. The Bible offers hard, physical evidence of God. This is why we love it so much.

We love it because it has led us to Him, and it continues to bring Him to us through its words and messages. But it is not the page we seek. (If it is, we have not yet found the whole point of the page.) We seek what lies beyond the page. We seek Him, and His word brings Him to us, and us to Him.

The page is vital and necessary to our faith. But don't stop with the page. You cannot have Him without the page (except in places and circumstances where it is not available), but you can have the page and not have Him. This is usually dangerous.

Those whose faith is based only on the page tend to be haughty, brittle, and exacting. Those whose faith is based on *Him,* who lies beyond the page, are wise, kind, and humble. It is the page that shows you who God is.

From *Crown Him with Many Crowns* by Matthew Bridges

Keeping It All Together

Crown Him the Lord of years,
The Potentate of time,
Creator of the rolling spheres,
Ineffably sublime.

From the vast spaces of a universe populated by billions upon billions of rolling spheres that are somehow locked into their proper places every night, down to the tiniest known atomic particles, spinning similarly around their own nuclei, there is the great question: What holds it all together? What keeps all the flying bodies from flying apart?

The answer to such a question can still only be speculated upon by scientists, even though it was announced years ago by the apostle Paul: "For by Him [Christ] all things were created: things in heaven and on earth, visible and invisible... and in Him all things hold together" (Colossians 1:16-17).

Jesus Christ is holding together the molecules of the table I'm writing on, as well as the matter in this room, in my skin and bones, and on out into the heavens.

And I wonder if I can trust Him with my life...

From *A Mighty Fortress Is Our God* by Martin Luther

Striving and Losing

Did we in our own strength confide,
Our striving would be losing...

This is not to say that "our striving would be losing," if we were confiding in God's strength instead of our own. In such a case, our striving would be worth something.

We tend to think that the opposite of fleshly activity is no activity at all. But rendering all human effort as suspect and waiting on God to move us can be nothing more than laziness in the guise of a supposed spiritual maturity. I know, because I have used this little trick to skirt responsibility before.

The other side of striving in our own strength is striving in *His* strength. To tell you the truth, I'm not sure we are always capable of spotting the subtle difference—not in our own lives and especially not in anyone else's. But in any case, we strive. We strive and trust in God to be in our efforts, that they may bring eternal results. We strive to bring ourselves in line with His purposes and His will in the world. We strive to love and believe and honor God with our lives and our commitments. We strive according to His power that works in us.

"Work out your salvation with fear and trembling, for it is God who works in you to will and to act according to his good purpose" (Philippians 2:12-13). Strive, in other words, with a holy expectation that God is in your work.

From *A Mighty Fortress Is Our God* by Martin Luther

Wondering Where the Lions Are

For still our ancient foe
Doth seek to work us woe.

We often forget we have an enemy. James 1:14 says that "each one is tempted when, by his own evil desire, he is dragged away and enticed." And Paul reminds us that we cannot mock God by getting out of reaping what we sow (see Galatians 6:7-8).

But still, not all of our problems are our own creations. The Bible tells us that a roaring lion—the devil—walks around seeking someone to turn into his next lunch. This indicates that the more effective we become for Christ and His kingdom, the more targetable we are as prey.

We can never explain all the happenstances in our lives by merely what we see. There are other worlds and other dimensions caught up in our own. We do not deal only with flesh and blood—what we can see and touch and measure—but also with unfathomable, unseen realities, such as powers and principalities and rulers of darkness in heavenly places.

Therefore, we had best pray a lot. Pray through even the calmest day. What we see and touch is not the whole story. Be on guard. Don't get caught napping. It might be a nice day out, but don't forget there's a lion loose.

From *A Mighty Fortress Is Our God* by Martin Luther

Having Faith and Keeping All Your Stuff, Too

Let goods and kindred go,
This mortal life also;
The body they may kill:
God's truth abideth still...

Statements such as these by the courageous Martin Luther still challenge the church because of their stark confrontation with culture. When he wrote this, Martin Luther was experiencing the loss of all his worldly goods, the rejection of his family and friends, even the potential loss of his life.

None of us would necessarily wish for a similar situation. Yet under such duress, our eyes of faith would have to be more lucid and our choices fewer and more obvious than they appear to be today.

What if it were possible to have your faith and keep all you have, too? What if your faith brought you more friends rather than fewer? What if your faith enhanced your life rather than threatened it? Wouldn't that create an entirely different set of problems? This is, in fact, the cultural milieu facing the believer today. When religion actually advances one's position in society, we must ask ourselves: Why is everyone suddenly becoming a Christian?

In such a time, the responsibility to ferret out a true faith falls on each one of us. It's much harder to have an honest faith when culture is offering you something if you believe, than if it were taking something away.

From *Jesus Saves!* by Priscilla J. Owens

Jesus Saves

We have heard the joyful sound:
Jesus Saves! Jesus Saves!
Spread the tidings all around:
Jesus Saves! Jesus Saves!

Yes, Jesus saves. That much we know. But the big question is this: *Whom* does Jesus save? I grew up thinking Jesus saves other people—bad people. People who *needed* to be saved. I thought this as if I didn't need to be saved myself! Well, actually I didn't. You see, I was already saved. I was in. So, to me, "Jesus saves" always had to do with those who needed to be saved.

There used to be a *Jesus Saves* sign over a downtown rescue mission in Los Angeles. I remember seeing it from the freeway overpass as I traveled from our safe home in the suburbs to ball games at Dodger Stadium. There were always guys hanging out on the street under the sign who obviously needed to be saved: alcoholics, derelicts, freeloaders.

As a high school senior, I went to that same rescue mission to play my guitar and sing. To this day, I can remember not knowing what to say. I couldn't tell them Jesus saved me because I had forgotten what He saved me from.

Our message needs to be Jesus *saves* me just like He *saves* all who come to Him. Our experience of the saving life of Christ needs to be closer to the experience of those who come to faith for the first time. Jesus not only saved us when we first became Christians, He also saves us *now* from our sin. We need this salvation like anyone else needs it. In this way our salvation stays fresh and current.

Maybe those guys standing outside the rescue mission know "Jesus saves" better than anyone. When we all get to heaven, I bet they'll be standing outside the gate with white robes on and a big sign that reads: "Jesus Saves."

From *"Are Ye Able?" Said the Master* by Charles Wesley

Two Roads Converge

"Are ye able," to remember,
When a thief lifts up his eyes,
That his pardoned soul is worthy
Of a place in paradise

Two lives at the focal point of history—dying upon a cross alongside the Son of God. How could you hang there and not know it—that this one hanging next to you was the reason for the darkness and the shaking earth? Perhaps these men were too preoccupied with their own agony, and that would certainly be understandable. Dying makes most people rather self-centered, which makes the change of heart in the one thief even more remarkable: As he died, he was thinking about the innocence of the man next to him.

Clearly, similar lives don't necessarily lead to similar ends. One of these lives took a drastic turn at its end.

This story illustrates why we can never judge anyone or assume that someone didn't know Christ at death. People can make a decision to follow Christ just seconds before they draw their last breath. We are not privy to heavenly transactions that might go on at bedside, battlefield, or street corner. No one knows whether a dying man might in his last second find himself next to a wounded Christ and an invitation to paradise.

Our responsibility is to provide enough information through our lives and love so that others will have something to respond to in those last seconds.

At Calvary, two men made their individual choices before they died. We know about one. Do we really know about the other?

From *There Is a Green Hill Far Away* by Cecil Francis Alexander

Why Be Good?

He died that we might be forgiven,
He died to make us good...

God had a couple of things in mind when He sent Jesus to hang upon a cross. One was to forgive us, and the other was to make us into someone He could use in the world. Jesus died to make us good. The forgiveness we receive; the good we participate in.

We cooperate with both of these purposes. We must bring ourselves to the cross and repent of our sins in order to be forgiven. Even though forgiveness is supplied, it is not automatically applied to everyone. We have to appropriate it by faith, just as we must appropriate good works by faith. He died to make us good. God wants good people representing Him and carrying on His presence in the world.

How appreciative are you of your salvation? Are you after a free ride, or do you want to get yourself in on His program to bring His kingdom on earth as it is in heaven? Make your salvation count in the world for God today. Give Him yourself for what He wants to accomplish in and through your life. Let's give God a run on His investment. How about it?

From *There Is a Fountain* by William Cowper

Immanuel's Plunge

There is a fountain filled with blood
Drawn from Immanuel's veins;
And sinners plunged beneath that flood,
Lose all their guilty stains.

Welcome to the Christ Memorial Blood Bath and Theme Park, where sinners can find just what they need to cleanse themselves of their sin. Here is where the crimson flow is constantly available for every sinner's needs. Here, you also will find a variety of thrilling attractions to suit the individual tastes of the discriminating sinner.

We have the Sprinkling Spray Waterfall for those who need just an occasional light shower to wash off a sin or two. This attraction is most popular among those who are able to keep their noses clean most of the time.

Then there's the Little Tot's Wading Pool. It's for light sinners who are able to keep most of their actions and thoughts clean, and only need to get their feet wet in the blood of Jesus from time to time.

For the heavy-duty sinners, there is Immanuel's Plunge. This is for folks who need to be completely immersed and abandoned in the blood of Jesus, because they know who they are. This is for guys like Peter, who started with a foot-washing and ended up requesting a bath. And it's for those like Paul, who called himself "the chief of sinners."

For those who find their every word and deed tainted with sin and selfishness, who are unable to find within themselves enough righteousness to out-holy the next guy, we recommend Immanuel's Plunge. It's total cleansing for the totally sinful. This bath is for those who don't want to take chances with their own good intentions, who prefer to meet God immersed in the blood of Jesus because they can put no confidence in any other.

From *There Is a Fountain* by William Cowper

Log Jam

The dying thief rejoiced to see
That fountain in his day;
And there may I, though vile as he,
Wash all my sins away.

Jesus once suggested that people who felt they had a legitimate concern about someone else's moral character should probably first consider doing something about their own. He then put this into proper perspective by alluding to the "log" in one's own eye versus the corresponding "speck" in the other person's.

Now, how can He know that? Is it necessarily always the case that my sin is that much greater than someone else's? Isn't Jesus making a gross assumption here?

No, He's not. Jesus is merely saying that my sin is—and will always be—much more important to me than anybody else's sin. It all has to do with perspective. The speck in another person's eye is, in like manner, a log unto him.

Of course, we like to think of this the other way around. We see other people's sin as looming large in the face of our corresponding "errors in judgment" or occasional "lapses in discretion." We simply have slipups that necessitate a minor moral adjustment from time to time—a bit of spiritual tune-up, shall we say.

Instead, imagine the worst sinner you can think of, doing the most detestable things. And then say with the hymn writer, "and there may I, *though vile as he,* wash all my sins away." Then you will have this perspective problem straightened out.

From *There Is a Fountain* by William Cowper

The Last Sin

Dear dying Lamb, Thy precious blood
Shall never lose its power,
Till all the ransomed Church of God
Be saved, to sin no more.

We're somewhere in the middle here: saved, but still needing to rely on the power of the blood to wash away our sins. Though He died for our sins once and for all, we need His blood to wash us clean in the time and space of our own experience. The hymn writer referred to this continual cleansing as a flow from the cross that is always available to wash away our sins. It is greatly important to us that this blood still flows, that the fountain runs continually, and that the power of Jesus' blood to forgive sins never diminishes.

We are in the middle: saved by the blood, but still in need of its cleansing power on a daily basis. When I was a child, my parents made me take a bath every Saturday night, whether I thought I needed one or not. Now, I take a shower every morning. I wouldn't think of facing a day without one. Spiritual cleansing needs to take place with similar regularity.

There will come a time when the power of this blood will simply no longer be necessary—when the last sin has been drowned in its crimson tide and the end has finally come. Then we shall rise again, like Christ, with new bodies, and sin will be no more than a distant memory. Then we will shine like the stars and do God's will without a second thought. Then we will sing endless praises to Him for who He is and what He has done.

But I bet—and this is just a hunch—that we'll remember just enough of what sin was like to never forget that He saved us.

From *There Is a Fountain* by William Cowper

Theme Song

Redeeming love has been my theme,
And shall be till I die.

There are many kinds of love. There is need love, controlling love, tough love, erotic love, foolish love, blind love, puppy love. But there is no love greater than redeeming love. Redeeming love is the only love worthy of being adopted as a lifelong theme.

Redeeming love caused God to take on the form of His creation. It caused Him to be born of a woman, grow up as a child, serve as a man, suffer as a criminal, and die as a third-rate citizen at the hands of the very people He came to redeem. He did this to buy us back, even though we were His in the first place.

I guess you could say we are twice His. We are His by birth in the likes of His image, and His by rebirth into His Spirit. He went to a lot of trouble to do this. Seems sort of roundabout, when you think of it this way. It seems like the world is nothing more than a cosmic false start. Ever wonder why God didn't make us the way He wanted us to be in the first place? Why did He go to all this trouble?

Of course, we are in no position to answer for God. But it is something to note that we would never have known, at least first-hand, how far His love was willing to go for us without our sinning in the first place. We might not have known anything of redeeming love, and the universe might never have heard the grateful strains of our theme song that will fill up all eternity.

From *There Is a Fountain* by William Cowper

From a Lisping Tongue

When this poor lisping, stammering tongue
Lies silent in the grave,
Then in a nobler, sweeter song
I'll sing Thy power to save.

When the author of these lyrics referred to his "lisping, stammering tongue," he was not, as I had always thought, making a metaphor for a general human finiteness. He was speaking quite literally of his own physical disability. William Cowper had a speech impediment. His impediment, in fact, was only part of a deeply troubled life that led him in and out of insane asylums. Three times he tried to take his own life. Even today, his writings are widely studied by psychologists and psychiatrists as historical evidence of a classic case of severe mental depression.

Mr. Cowper's happiest moments in life were times when he was invited to stay in the home of another great hymn writer, John Newton, the author of *Amazing Grace*. It was during one of these visits that he wrote this great poem while meditating in Newton's garden.

What a dark context to some of the greatest lyrics ever written on the love of God! What an insight into the depth of His mercy! What a reminder of the stark reality of life and the fact that God doesn't always fix everything for us the way we would like.

And what a joke God and Mr. Cowper have pulled on us, to have us standing in pressed collars in staid congregations, singing one of our most revered hymns, the lyric of which was captured in a sane moment by the pen of someone regarded in his day as a madman.

From *Tell Me the Old, Old Story* by A. Catherine Hankey

The Cold Stone Rolling

Tell me the story slowly,
That I may take it in—
That wonderful redemption,
God's remedy for sin.

Take your time. Don't hurry through this. Drink in every word. Hear all seven of them from the cross. Sit with each one long enough for it to sink in through your brain, through the loud pounding of life all around you.

Imagine every picture. Imagine the Last Supper when Jesus reclined at the table. Imagine the glances of the eyes. Imagine the agony in the garden and the silent confrontation with a nervous Pilate. Imagine the walk up Calvary and the view from the cross. Imagine the limp, bloody body being rolled in cloth. Imagine the blurry view of a gardener through Mary's tear-filled eyes.

Imagine with all your senses.

Feel the wood on His back and the body trying to pull away from the nails. Feel the cold, damp ledge of an empty tomb.

Taste the wine and the vinegar.

Hear every sound. Hear the gravel being crushed under His feet and the whip cracking over His back. Hear the nails ignoring flesh as they are pounded into wood. Hear the conversation with the thieves, then the hell-bound shriek as He gives up His Spirit. Hear the grief of those around the cross and the cold stone rolling.

Take your time with this. A year wouldn't be too long to sit with each one of these images.

From *Tell Me the Old, Old Story* by A. Catherine Hankey

The Gospel Never Gets Old

Tell me the story often,
For I forget so soon,
The "early dew" of morning
Has passed away at noon.

Doesn't the gospel get old at some point? Don't we graduate from it eventually and move on to other things? Isn't the gospel story the thing that gets me started down this road? Isn't the gospel story kind of elementary—like the flannel graph phase of Sunday school or child evangelism? I mean, how many times are we supposed to go over Christ dying and resurrecting?

I can remember thinking like this. I can actually remember being bored by the gospel. God forbid, but it's true. What changed all this? What made the old story new? It was my sin that did it. Not that I went out and started sinning; I was doing a fine job of sinning all along, but I just never saw it that way. The gospel only makes sense to sinners, and I simply didn't appreciate it until I saw myself as one.

The cross doesn't mean anything to me until I see it as *my* sin that put Christ there. Forgiveness doesn't mean anything until I need to be forgiven. Resurrection life doesn't mean anything until I have no will to live. Being saved is simply not compelling to one who is not lost.

This is the way it goes with the gospel. It's new and fresh to the extent that I need it. And every time I do, it deepens in my heart.

From *Tell Me the Old, Old Story* by A. Catherine Hankey

Who Caused the Cross?

Remember! I'm the sinner
Whom Jesus came to save.

OK, here are the facts: I'm the one who caused the cross. You might think it was someone else, but it was I. You guys got saved in the process, but I'm the one who messed up.

Yeah, I know. They say it was Adam who caused all our problems. But hey, I don't even know the guy. I just know me, and I know I'm the sinner Jesus came to save. If you think any differently, you'll just have to take it up with Him.

You see, I don't really know anything about anyone else's sin. I can't tell you how bad life is for them. Nor do I know about you. I really don't know about anybody for sure, except myself. And I know I'm good enough at sinning to warrant going to the cross.

So, as far as I'm concerned, I'm the sinner Jesus came to save. You can think the same way about yourself if you want, but I'll know better.

From *Tell Me the Old, Old Story* by A. Catherine Hankey

A True and Lasting Peace

Tell me the story always,
If you would really be,
In any time of trouble,
A comforter to me.

Keep telling me the story of the gospel—what Christ has done for me on the cross—especially when things are not going well for me. Whatever you do, don't stop telling me the gospel. Other answers will not bring me any comfort. I may act as if they do. But right now, in a saner, more secure moment, I know that only the gospel will give me peace in the midst of trouble. And I want to give you permission now to remind me, should I forget under pressure.

Real comfort comes only from the gospel. God worked a miracle on the cross and did what I cannot do for myself. The gospel takes into account the truth about me. The gospel reminds me there is hope, not in what I can do for myself, but in what Jesus Christ has already done.

This is not to say I can't help myself to a certain degree or receive help from other sources. But ultimately, only the gospel will give me any lasting comfort. The gospel is primarily God loving me without conditions and doing for me what I could not do for myself. Whatever else I do depends on this.

So if I seem to forget, please tell me again!

From *Tell Me the Old, Old Story* by A. Catherine Hankey

Fair Warning

Tell me the same old story,
When you have cause to fear
That this world's empty glory
Is costing me too dear.

In order to maintain a life of faith, we need to have someone to whom we can be accountable. This world's glory, empty as it is, is still a mighty strong pull. The world comes to us complete with its own desires: "The cravings of sinful man, the lust of the eyes and the boasting of what he has and does" (1 John 2:16). When this attraction and this boasting game gets a good hold on someone, it is almost impossible for that person to see it.

We say "love is blind" to explain how a person in love is unable to see the faults of his or her partner. The love of the world is also blind. And when we are blind to something, it takes someone else who can see to point it out to us. Even then we may not listen.

The world's glory costs us dearly. The god of this world always exacts a price for everything he gives. He tried to get Jesus to pay it in the desert when he offered Him all the kingdoms of the world. But Jesus would not bow down.

We are not as smart or as strong as Jesus. We need help from each other to spot when we have been caught in a compromise. And then it will be the same old story that will get us out.

From *Tell Me the Old, Old Story* by A. Catherine Hankey

Tired of the Gospel

Tell me the old, old story
Of unseen things above,
Of Jesus and His glory,
Of Jesus and His love.

If someone is bored with the gospel, it is probably because that person is not saved. This is likely someone who is not saved every day. That person might have been saved a number of years ago, but by now that salvation is just an old, old story. It meant something then, but it has lost its appeal now that it is no longer necessary.

- You would get tired of hearing the gospel if you were always thinking it was for someone else.
- You would get tired of hearing the gospel if the sins it saved you from were old ones—so far back in your past that you forgot exactly what they were.
- You would get tired of hearing the gospel if you weren't aware of being a sinner.
- You would get tired of hearing the gospel if your place in heaven was assured by any other basis than its story.
- And, yes, you would get tired of hearing the gospel if you weren't saved.

But if you are saved—saved every day from the sins you find out about *and* the ones you didn't—then you are never, ever tired of this glorious message of Jesus on the cross and His love for you. You want somebody to tell it to you all over again. You would go out of your way to hear it. It doesn't even matter who is telling you or if they are getting it exactly right. You only sit and listen in amazement, like a little child. And it seems to you as if each time you hear it, you are hearing that old, old story for the first time.

From *The Days That Were, The Days That Are* by Hywel Elfed Lewis

Never Too Late

We tarry, Lord, Thy leisure still,
Thy best is yet to be;
Nought ever comes too late for us
that is in time for Thee.

The only time God could ever be late is when we measure Him according to our time. Frustration over God's timing comes from seeing things only from our perspective. But God is always right on time. He does not delay; He does not forget; He does not waver. Thus, our judgments on His timing are entirely inappropriate. He knows what He is doing, and we don't. He sees the whole picture, while we only see a few feet in front of us.

When I was a young student of the Bible, one of my teachers would lay out on the table a three-dimensional time line of Bible history with figures to represent various biblical characters along the way. One of his favorite illustrations was to set Moses at his place in history, turn the figure so it looked down the path toward all who would come after him, then block Moses' view to the future with a pane of tinted glass. My teacher did this while quoting 1 Corinthians 13:12 (KJV): "For now we see through a glass, darkly..."

Since we were looking at four thousand years spanned in the distance of a few feet, it gave us a more God-like view of things. The Moses figure saw what we are used to seeing: down to the feet and no further. It was a lesson I never forgot.

Sooner or later we must decide that "on time" for God is going to be "on time" for us. Nothing comes too late for us if it's on time for Him.

From *Come, Holy Spirit, Heavenly Dove* by Isaac Watts

In Love with God

Dear Lord, and shall we ever live
At this poor, dying rate?
Our love so faint, so cold, to Thee,
And Thine to us so great?

Can we believe in God without any passion for Him in our lives? Probably. But what's the point? Why have a faith if it isn't compelling?

A relationship with God is something that gets hold of you. You pick up a devotional book because you want to be reminded of God in the midst of a regular day, by someone who might offer you a new angle on truth. You go to church because you want to feed your soul on songs of worship and your mind on insights from the Word of God. You want to be with others who believe so that you can be encouraged by their faith. Attending church isn't some commitment you begrudgingly carry out. This is important to you, so you get there. You're in love, and church is a date with God.

Why else would you want to pay attention to your spiritual life? To make improvements in yourself? To make someone else happy? Because you want God to be important to your kids, even though He's not important to you? You can probably pull this off for a while. But sooner or later your faint, cold heart shows through.

If you're going to do this Christianity thing, you might as well be madly in love with God. That's the only way anything about faith will make sense to you, anyway.

From *Come, Holy Spirit, Heavenly Dove* by Isaac Watts

Catching Fire

Come, Holy Spirit, heavenly Dove,
With all Thy quickening powers;
Come, shed abroad a Saviour's love;
And that shall kindle ours.

Fire can spread by flying sparks or bits of burning debris. The fire season in California is particularly dangerous, and not only because of the dry heat. There are also hot winds that fuel existing fires with blasts of oxygen *and* carry along embers that spread the inferno to new areas. Houses with wooden shake roofs are as vulnerable as kindling waiting to be lit.

Of course, a wooden roof is not a particularly safe idea for a house. But it is an excellent idea for a heart in a high-fire area where the love of God is burning.

We want to be aflame with the love of God. We want to catch fire. We want to be in the path of the wind of God, where we might capture a burning ember or two on the dry roofs we use to protect our tender hearts.

How does this happen? What looses the Spirit of God on a people or time? I'm not sure we can know that, but we can pray for it, and we can keep from fireproofing our hearts.

And it probably wouldn't hurt to get ourselves in the path of the wind.

From *Christ, of All My Hopes the Ground* by Ralph Wardlaw

The Ground and the Spring

Christ, of all my hopes the ground,
Christ, the spring of all my joy...

Christ grounds my hope. He gives my hope substance. The hope of my present and future salvation is rooted in the historical Jesus who lived and died on this planet. It is grounded in what He accomplished while He was here. My hope is in a cross that was dropped with the Son of God on it into a hole in the earth somewhere in the Middle East.

And out of that hole flows a spring of joy. The resurrected, living Christ is what makes my heart dance and my eyes shine. He is the source of the effervescent fountain of living water that bubbles up from inside me.

Because I am linked to the heart of God, I have access to a rippling, never-ending flow of life and joy. This is a well from which I can drink continually. It is a well that will never run dry.

From *O God of Earth and Altar* by G.K. Chesterton

Wise Up!

From all that terror teaches, from lies of pen and tongue;
From all the easy speeches that satisfy the throng;
From sale and profanation of honor and the sword;
From sleep and from damnation, deliver us, good Lord!

No wonder Jesus referred to Himself as the Good Shepherd. Sheep are notoriously gullible, and historically we sheep have repeatedly fallen for lies and easy speeches that satisfy our egos. We have sold our honor down the river for nothing more than a privileged seat in the congregation, a name on a plaque, or a carnation and the right to usher someone down the aisle. Ironically, we have not realized that we were the ministers all along—the gifted ones, the wise and the knowledgeable, the prophetic and the inspired.

The hymn writer pleads for deliverance from "sleep and damnation." We know by faith that we will be delivered from damnation. But laziness is another story. From this we have not been delivered, often because we don't want to be.

We can't blame the false teachers; we've been warned about them from day one. We've even been told by Christ Himself that His kingdom on earth was going to include some bad apples—some leaven in the loaf.

It's time to wake up and wise up, so we won't be caught following the wrong shepherd. Sheep may seem dumb, but I think they are more lazy than stupid. They are surely smart enough to follow the right Shepherd.

From *O God of Earth and Altar* by G.K. Chesterton

Acts of God

Take not Thy thunder from us,
but take away our pride.

I live in southern California, an area that is famous for its natural and social disasters. Earthquakes, fires, floods, and mud slides have taken lives and caused millions of dollars in damage.

Most of these calamities are what we commonly call "acts of God." But to saddle God with the responsibility for such devastation tells us something about our God concept. I believe what this really says is that we have no other way of explaining these things. Undoubtedly, something deep in the psychology of even the unbelieving human mind connects God with thunder and lightning, rain that swells creek beds into rushing rivers, tornadoes, hurricanes, hot winds that whip fires into raging infernos, and most of all, the shaking earth.

These events remind us just how weak and small we really are—how dependent we are on God's mercy. They strip us of our pride and self-importance, and the sense of power that deludes us into thinking we are in control. These things that we call "Acts of God" put us in our place.

People often talk about wanting God to come in His power. But we want God to show us His power without being stripped of our pride. That isn't going to happen. You can be sure that as long as human beings continue to exert pride and the worship of self, there will be Acts of God to remind us of who we really are. If He took away His thunder, we might never see our pride.

From *O God of Earth and Altar* by G.K. Chesterton

Get Used to It

Bind all our lives together,
Smite us and save us all...

Does God actually do this? Does He punish us to save us? This does not sit well with modern theories of child rearing.

"My son, do not make light of the Lord's discipline, and do not lose heart when He rebukes you, because the Lord disciplines those He loves, and He punishes everyone He accepts as a son" (Proverbs 3:11-12 and quoted later in Hebrews 12:5-6).

This seems hard to swallow until you read Hebrews 12:7: "Endure hardship as discipline; God is treating you as sons."

Hardship (difficult circumstances, afflictions, temptations, perplexities) *is* our discipline. We must learn to expect these things and accept them.

We must get over the idea that everything is going to brighten up just around the next corner. In this life, we will have hardship. We would not be loved if we were not disciplined. "No discipline seems pleasant at the time, but painful. Later on, however, it produces a harvest of righteousness and peace for those who have been trained by it" (Hebrews 12:11).

Everything has a purpose, and even the most difficult things that happen to us can have a positive conclusion. So, the next time you're in the middle of a difficulty, remember God's purpose. He'll give you the courage to hold on.

From *O for a Closer Walk with God* by William Cowper

Throw It Down

The dearest idol I have known,
Whate'er that idol be,
Help me to tear it from Thy throne
And worship only Thee.

We have a tendency these days to think that we are too sophisticated for idols in that we don't bow down to wood and stone. And yet we bow down regularly to money, TV, jobs, food, status, position, material possessions, sex, power, and glory. Indeed, as we have become more sophisticated, so have our idols.

The first two commandments—and most of the Old Testament—have to do with idol worship. If dealing with idols was important enough to God back then to require that much attention, it must still be important now. Idols don't disappear, they just go incognito. This makes them harder to find and harder to get rid of once we find them.

It's much easier to smash a clay image than to rout the power of money out of your life. Most of our modern idols are things we can't just get rid of. They are things that will still be part of our lives in some form, even after we throw them down. This means that the temptation to worship them will remain.

The way to avoid idol worship then is to make sure we worship only Him. When we put Him on the throne of our lives, idols must be dethroned. He will not share His seat of honor.

Is there anything or anyone more important in your life than God? Does your happiness and security come from some other place? Then rout it out and throw it down! And worship only Him!

From *Near the Cross* by Fanny J. Crosby

By the Healing Stream

Jesus keep me near the cross,
There a precious fountain
Free to all—a healing stream
Flows from Calvary's mountain.

We need to stay near the cross, lest we get too casual about our sin or too forgetful about our need for forgiveness. I would stay distant from the cross if I didn't believe I needed it. I would stay distant from the cross if I knew my sin but didn't want to face it. What would keep me away from the cross is what keeps me from facing my need.

I can embrace my sin at the cross. At the cross I realize it was for *me* He died, and not just "the whole world." It is a place of ownership—a place where I claim responsibility for what I have done and yet know that I do not have to face it alone.

Jesus, keep me near the cross lest I forget about all of this. Keep me sensitive toward everything that has brought you to me and open me up to others. For it is here, beside this healing stream, that I realize both my oneness with humanity and my oneness with you.

From *Arise, My Soul! With Rapture Rise!* by Samuel J. Smith

A Day on Lend

The awful Sovereign of the skies,
Whose mercy lends me one day more...

Our days come at the mercy of God, who gives us "life and breath and everything else.... For in Him we live and move and have our being" (Acts 17:25, 28). These are basic realities common to our existence. The apostle Paul was not speaking only of Christians when he pointed out these things. He was also addressing Greek philosophers with a common truth that was echoed even by their own secular poets.

But how conscious are we of this, we who supposedly know this God personally? How prone we are to map out our days as if they are ours to control and live, one at a time. We do this without thinking that any one of them could be cut short in an instant.

Our days come at the mercy of God. We need to learn to live each day with a sense of deep gratitude and holy fear. Fear that is the beginning of wisdom and that respects the right of God to rule over His creation and the right of humankind to worship Him and walk carefully and circumspectly. For it is God who has said, "If I were hungry I would not tell you, for the world is mine, and all that is in it" (Psalm 50:12).

Your days come at the mercy of God. Live each one as if it were one more day that you don't deserve—a day on loan!

From *I Saw One Hanging on a Tree* by John Newton

Both Sides Now

Thus, while His death my sin displays
In all its blackest hue,
Such is the mystery of grace,
It seals my pardon too.

We're never quite sure what to do with the cross. It is like a hologram that changes depending on the angle from which we observe it.

The cross pardons us from the penalty of sin. It symbolizes our release from having to pay any wages for the sinful things we have done. But it also shows our sin for what it is. We can no longer rationalize it. It displays our sin in a place where we have to look at it and be reminded of what it cost the Savior. And it also puts our sin where others can see it.

This is often why people don't want to become Christians. Becoming a Christian means joining a group of people who know their sin and have confessed it to God, to others, and to themselves. The cross blows our cover. To follow Christ, you have to get used to having your sins on display.

But that's just the point. In knowing our sin, we also come to know our Savior and join a grateful group of folks who know what it is like to be forgiven.

From *Where Cross the Crowded Ways of Life* by Frank M. North

Above the Noise and Strife

Where cross the crowded ways of life,
Where sound the cries of race and clan,
Above the noise of selfish strife,
We hear Thy voice, O Son of man!

Virtually all of the major conflicts that go on in the world—all of the wars—can be traced to the cries of race and clan. These wars are full of hateful crimes, fueled by memories of injustice—atrocities one generation remembers and retaliates for by inflicting upon the next. The cycle goes on and on.

More "civilized" folks read the newspaper and wonder how people can be so ruthless in Bosnia, Ireland, Rwanda, or the urban centers of the world. Are they not all the cries of race and clan? Were they not the cries of Hitler and Mussolini?

And what would the Son of Man be saying if we could hear His voice above the noise of strife? He would be saying that we are all one. There are no divisions, no races or clans. There is only one race: human. And there is only one clan: the family of men and women He died for.

In a Croatian hospital, a Muslim and a Croatian girl lie side by side, healing from the wounds of war. They become fast friends. They represent two warring clans, yet they have heard the voice of Jesus above the noise and the strife. They are proof that there is a better way. Yet they will go home to opposite sides of the river. Will someone listen to the children?

From *Jesus, I Would Faithful Be* by J.O. Hillyer

Be Still and Keep Walking

In Thy footsteps place my feet,
As Thou dost will, as Thou dost will;
And if thorns my pathway meet,
Bid me be still, be still.

These lyrics conjure up images of a group of travelers making their way through difficult terrain, each placing their own steps carefully and directly in the steps of their leader. Those in front must endure the constant bickering of a few in the back who might be unhappy about the path that has been chosen.

Much about life can make us complain. Much about following Christ can tax our patience—and His. In Christ, we have chosen the harder way. Someone might have told us in the beginning that Christianity was the easiest trail to happiness and success. When we discover that it is not necessarily that way, we may feel discouraged. But that is only because someone lied.

The Savior made no such promises. On the contrary, He gave us fair warning. He talked about hating father and mother to follow Him, about carrying a cross, about letting the dead bury the dead. He said the world would not be favorably disposed to those who would join Him. He couldn't have spelled things out any clearer. Once, even while He was here, all the disciples except the twelve fell back because the way was too difficult for them.

Yes, there are certainly joys in this trip along the way, but probably not the ones we were thinking about when we first decided to follow Him. So when we are tempted to complain, it's best to just be still and keep walking.

From *When I Survey the Wondrous Cross* by Isaac Watts

Living with a Crucified Pride

When I survey the wondrous cross
On which the Prince of Glory died,
My richest gain I count but loss,
And pour contempt on all my pride.

How we hate our prideful self when we stand near the cross. The closer we get to the cross, the more awful our pride looks. We need to remember this and learn to see our sin this way all the time. It would save us a lot of grief if we could do this.

When we seem far away from Him, we need to remember what our pride looks like next to the crucified Christ. Our pride doesn't always look so ugly to us. Sometimes we are in the midst of temptation, and the enemy is pulling out all the stops to make his evil, deadly notions look bright and attractive to our "superior, wise minds." (He's been doing this trick ever since he first tempted Eve.) This would be a good time to remember the cross.

Learning to live near the cross is learning to live with a crucified pride. We keep our pride in check by standing where we can survey the cross on a regular basis.

From *When I Survey the Wondrous Cross* by Isaac Watts

The Way It Was

See, from His head, His hands, His feet,
Sorrow and love flow mingled down:
Did e'er such love and sorrow meet,
Or thorns compose so rich a crown?

Someone present at the crucifixion of Christ would have seen blood flowing from His head, His hands, and His feet. Two thousand years later, we remember the event as a strange and wonderful mingling of sorrow and love.

The sorrow was over the damage sin had wrought in His creation. He must have felt it the whole time He was here on earth. Everywhere He looked, He would have seen the devastation of sin. No one else would have fully understood this sorrow, because no one knew—as Jesus knew—what human life *could have been*. We might imagine it or dream about it, but Jesus knew. What He created life to be was not what He witnessed first-hand for thirty years. No wonder they called Him a Man of Sorrows (see Isaiah 53:3).

But love was mingled with His sorrow. Love made Him come and die. Love for the way it *could be* made Him die for *the way it was*. He knew it was the only way to redeem His creation and turn it back into what He had in mind in the first place.

No king ever wore a richer crown than the crown of thorns he wore when He died, for this blood purchased a people for eternity.

From *When I Survey the Wondrous Cross* by Isaac Watts

Sin Boulevard

All the vain things that charm me most,
I sacrifice them to His blood.

Are we willing to do this? Following Him gets difficult here. We can let go of some of our vanities, but we often have a few that have charmed us the most. And of course these are the ones that He wants the most.

I just spent a half hour chasing down my daughter's dog. Just before the dog bolts, there's a moment when she is looking right at me, hearing me calling her. Her head cocks as she ponders the situation for a couple seconds. Then she turns and races full-speed away from me, charmed by the call of freedom and her own boundless energy. Of course, this could lead her into the busy street near our house and almost certain death.

But a neighbor just told me how I can cure the dog of her waywardness. Twice a day, tie her to a post with twenty-five-foot cord, then let her bolt. "Be clever," my neighbor instructed me. "Let her think you don't know she's free." The next step is to cry out "No" right before she wrenches her neck on the end of the cord while running at full speed. My neighbor guarantees that within three days of this training, our dog will stop without the cord when she hears "No."

Would that God trained me like that. But I am not a dog, and I can't be trained out of the bad things that charm me. I must learn to voluntarily give them up. There is no other way and no one to help me do this.

I must believe that God charms me more than the charms of sin. It probably wouldn't hurt imagining myself as a stupid dog, bounding out onto a very busy Sin Boulevard, either.

From *Jesus, Rose of Sharon* by Ida A. Guirey

What Was That Fragrance?

That wherever I go my life may shed abroad
Fragrance of the knowledge of the love of God.

This lyric is taken from 2 Corinthians 2:14, which reads: "But thanks be to God, who always leads us in triumphal procession in Christ and through us spreads everywhere the fragrance of the knowledge of Him."

This verse implies that believers have an almost unconscious effect in the world. Christians, especially in America, are message-conscious and word-conscious. We have been told that there is no witness without proclamation. Though we don't all proclaim our faith all the time, we share at least the common distinction of feeling plenty of guilt for *not* sharing it. But we don't realize that we have an effect on people, simply because we know Christ.

The key element here is not knowledge but fragrance. It's the fragrance *of* the knowledge of Christ that is doing the business here. Like the scent of perfume left behind by a beautiful woman, this fragrance is the afterthought of our relationship with God. It is what comes off us because we have been with, and *are* with, Him all the time. It is something we cannot create or get rid of. It is a by-product of being in love with God. As such, it is the best witness possible.

From *My Jesus, I Love Thee* by William R. Featherstone

"My Jesus"

My Jesus, I love Thee,
I know Thou art mine...

How is it that we should get to claim ownership of the only begotten Son of God? What does He think of this? How does He take to being called the personal possession of a congregation of stumbling, ordinary people? To call someone your possession is to be beholden to them in some way.

And yet this is what He has done, isn't it? He has given Himself to us on the cross. He lowered Himself and became a servant, obedient unto death, that we might become the righteousness of God in Him. That I might want to call Him mine is one thing. That He would make Himself vulnerable to me is another.

Can you imagine somebody going around claiming to be your friend just because he or she wanted to? Wouldn't you want to have control over this? What if the people who wanted to be your friends in the worst way were people you didn't want to be associated with? Jesus is willing to belong to us in this way, to have His name used this freely and to have a whole congregation of fools sing "*My* Jesus..."

A socially sensitive political cartoon I saw recently featured a man pointing his finger at a small boy in the inner city and saying, "If you had any sense of family values you'd go get yourself a father!" This occurs to me—in its very audacity—to be pretty much what happens when we come to God through Jesus Christ, His Son. Orphans that we are, we just got ourselves a Father!

From *My Jesus, I Love Thee* by William R. Featherstone

The Follies of Sin

For Thee all the follies of sin I resign...

What a way to think about sin: folly and foolishness. This is truly what it is. I give sin more credit than it is due. When I call sin "temptation" it sounds appealing. But folly is the perfect word for it. Sheer foolishness.

It is folly to worship the creature when you know the Creator. It is folly to think you know what is best for you when it contradicts what God has in mind. It is folly to talk yourself into believing a lie when you know darned well that it is a lie. It is folly to play dumb when you know better. It is folly to make provision for sin when you are still hoping not to commit it. It is folly to play with fire. It is folly to love God and still try and hold onto something or someone else. It is folly to think you can get away with folly.

Sin, when it first appears, may look desirable and attractive, but its foolishness is always hidden somewhere behind a false front.

There is one way around the folly of sin: To love Jesus. In the love of Jesus, the foolishness is made known. In the love of Jesus, you can look at that relationship and say "no" to the foolishness. People who try to rid themselves of sin by only saying "no" to it are in for a losing struggle. You rid yourself of sin by saying "yes" to a love relationship with Jesus Christ. In His light, everything else pales, especially the folly of sin.

From *My Jesus, I Love Thee* by William R. Featherstone

Love Is Now

If ever I loved Thee, my Jesus, 'tis now.

Love is now, and this hymn has played a major role in many of my significant "nows." It has been sung most often to the blackness of night as I lay on my bed. Tears come to mind as common companions to the immediacy of its lyric.

If ever I loved Thee, my Jesus, 'tis now. Sing it now, then sing it again in a few minutes. It will be new and current the second time. Go ahead, sing it a third time. It's still true because "now" is and will always be the time when we know His love the most.

Take all of life's experiences past, present, and future. Take the lonely times and the good times, the times of great pain and hardship, and the times of carefree joy. Take the confusions and the doubts—even the times God felt far away and the times He felt close. Take childhood, when we knew so much about God, and adulthood, when it seems at times like we hardly know anything at all. Take all these memories—enter them and exit them at will—and then take the future and all its unknowns, then ask yourself when you loved Him—or when *will* you love Him—the most, and the answer will always be the same...

Now.

From *My Jesus, I Love Thee* by William R. Featherstone

First-Love

I love Thee because Thou hast first loved me...

We love because we have been loved. This is where it all begins. We cannot love out of a vacuum. We love out of God's love. We pour back what He has poured into us. He gives and we keep giving back again, because He is the source of all things.

Those of us who have not been first-loved by human parents or guardians may have a harder time with this than those who have. It is hard to imagine a God who loves you when you have been reared by those who don't. If that is the case, we need to look not at the examples in our lives, but at the longing in our own souls. Who put it there? Why do we know what we had isn't right? Why do we hope for something better? Is it not because He loved us enough to make us want Him, to make us want Him badly enough to fight through all the bad examples we have endured to find the good example? The best? The one to whom all lovers will be compared?

His love started this. He made us first, died for us first, and then He makes us long for Him before we even try. Out of His first-love we can find reason and room to love back. Because He gives love to us to give back to Him, we can even find something there to love back with when we reach in our hearts.

What kind of God is this who even gives what He receives?

From *My Jesus, I Love Thee* by William R. Featherstone

Value Check

And say when the death-dew lies cold on my brow;
If ever I loved Thee, My Jesus, 'tis now.

Death. What a time for love. Who has ever thought of this moment as a time to praise? And yet, is it not the greatest time of all?

I have always loved funerals. They force an encounter with the inevitable, and the inevitable usually has a better chance of leading us to our hope than an average day does. Average days only lead us to escape, distraction, exhaustion, or sleep. Average days lead to the vain repetition of what is supposed to be life. Death always calls the point into question.

Death is the ultimate test of one's values. What we lived for is known sometimes more in our deaths than in our lives. It shouldn't be this way. But often it is, because true values disguise themselves. Material things seem real in life—their tangible goals are so compelling. But death strips off the disguise. In death, earthly values burn up and eternal ones take substance and become solid. Intangibles such as faith, hope, and love become gold, silver, and precious stones at the door of death as they pass through the fire.

What better time for love than when the odds are against it. Death is so convincing, so final. And love, triumphing at the final door, is the greatest act of victory known to humankind.

From *My Jesus, I Love Thee* by William R. Featherstone

Friend or Pest?

And praise Thee as long as Thou lendest me breath...

"For in Him we live and move and have our being" (Acts 17:28).

How is it possible that God can be as near to each of us as our next breath? He watches the sparrows fall. He knows the number of hairs on our head, and He is intimately involved with the next breath we take. We live and move inside of His ever-present consciousness, while largely unconscious of this ourselves. What kind of intelligence is this? What kind of presence? We cannot understand it.

In choosing to become conscious of Him, we are simply choosing to be aware—for a few moments—of what God is aware of all the time. We are coming to see things the way they are. When we worship Him and become conscious of Him, we are simply acknowledging what is and has been true all along.

If you had someone following on your heels constantly, but you rarely acknowledged his or her presence, that person would assume you were trying to shake them off. That person would feel like a drag on you—a pest. But if you were constantly relating to this person, he or she would be taken as your best friend and confidant.

If God is as intimate as my next breath, how intimate am I going to be with Him?

From *Tell Me the Story of Jesus* by Fanny J. Crosby

The Story of a Lifetime

Tell me the story of Jesus,
Write on my heart every word...

The story of Jesus is known in the heart. It is an intimate story that touches me in my innermost being. It is not just a story that happened in history that I need to learn about and give mental assent to. This is a story in which I am a player. It is His story, and it is mine as well. That's why this story is written on my heart... I am in it.

You see, when God created the world, I was there—in His mind. Earlier than that, actually. I was chosen before the foundation of the world, the apostle Paul said (see Ephesians 1:4). And when the first man and woman sinned, I was there too, receiving through Adam's seed a nature that is bent away from God and a heart that is deceitful. And when Jesus Christ died on the cross, I was *definitely* there, since it was my sin and rebellion that was laid on Him when He died. And I was there when He rose up from the grave, and joy leaps inside me when I hear that part of the story.

But, you see, it's not just a story. It's reality. I'm living it right now. The choices I make today will be a part of the story tomorrow. There are even some pieces of the story that I know in advance, and I know that I will be there when they come true.

This is why this is not just an ordinary story to entertain or delight or frighten, as most stories do. It is the story of history, the story of Christ, the story of me, and the story of you.

From *Tell Me the Story of Jesus* by Fanny J. Crosby

You Whisper; I'll Cry

Stay, let me weep while you whisper,
Love paid the ransom for me.

Please, tell me the story again one more time. Yes, I know it so well, but something happens inside me when I hear it again—something I can't do for myself. I can read the gospel. I can tell it to myself, but it's not the same as someone speaking it to me. The story itself ministers to me as if it had its own power to touch my heart, remind me of His love, and give me peace.

I come to church to hear the story again. I need to hear it proclaimed. Merely knowing it is not enough. I know that I am saved forever by His blood on the cross, but something in me, something of my daily pilgrimage and struggle with sin, is saved each time I hear it. Each time I hear the story, peace and love flood my soul, like a rush of mighty cleansing waters.

I also want to be around those who love this story and who know they need to hear it every day. Having a friend share the story with me is as important as hearing it proclaimed from some platform. Both touch me. So whisper it to me one more time. You whisper, I'll cry. Tell me again and again: *Love paid the ransom for me.*

From *Not All the Blood of Beasts* by Isaac Watts

The Final Payment

Not all the blood of beasts
On Jewish altars slain
Could give the guilty conscience peace,
Or wash away the stain.

All the blood from all the animals ever slain for all the sins of all people could never salve the guilty conscience of any one of us for even a day. Nor could all that blood and all that effort do anything to remove the real stain that remains on our permanent record with God.

Still, it must have felt good in Old Testament times to have something to *do* about sin. Taking an animal to the priest transferred the guilt somewhere else. Animal sacrifice was a tangible act that drove home the seriousness of sin. The Jews had to pay for their sin by giving up an animal, which was no small thing for people in an agrarian society.

But it was presumptuous for the Jews to think that this practice itself had actually absolved them of sin, just as it is presumptuous for us to think that God's forgiveness means we can now be casual about our transgressions. Grace is not a pocketful of get-out-of-jail-free cards.

The carnage of lambs, rams, bulls, goats, and doves constantly reminded the Jews that someone was ultimately going to have to pay for their sin—and pay big.

We need to remind ourselves daily that someone already did.

From *We Plow the Fields and Scatter* by M. Claudius

Simple Gifts

Accept the gifts we offer, for all Thy love imparts,
And what Thou most desirest, our humble, thankful hearts.

Our gifts must look like kindergarten craft projects to God. I wonder if He receives them with the kind of mimicked joy an earthly father shows. Of course, an earthly father takes into account the age and ability of the giver and receives the intent of the gift as much as anything. I believe God acts in a similar way with us.

God cares most about the intent of our gifts. The humble, thankful heart brings Him the most joy. Humble yourself before Him. Set your heart to thanking Him whenever you think of Him. Set aside bickering and judging, impatience and dissatisfaction. These things rob Him of praise and us of joy.

His love is a given. It is true at all times. It has snatched us from hell, and it will usher us into heaven. These things are true at all times, regardless of what we are feeling. One thing we can always have, no matter what, is a humble, thankful heart.

Go ahead and bring Him your gift. Don't be embarrassed. He'll love it!

From *May Jesus Christ Be Praised*
(A German hymn translated by Edward Caswell)

Silent Weapon

The powers of darkness fear,
When this sweet chant they hear,
May Jesus Christ be praised!

Praise is a valuable weapon against the enemy. War cries, frontal assaults, or special words of exorcism can't drive back the forces of evil. Neither can the brandishing of the sword or the charge of the brigade. What keeps the powers of darkness at bay is the simple and true praise of the Savior from a heart set free.

Christians are engaged in a battle, but going on the warpath usually isn't the best way to win the fight. The best way is to go about a life of faith with Christ on our minds and praise for Him on our lips.

We do this unconsciously, all the time. We sing a little song of praise as we go about our tasks, and unseen demons scurry for cover. Though spiritual battles are constantly being fought on every side, we need not be conscious of them. We do not require sentries on the watch every hour, fearing an attack. We do not have to check behind every door. We need only be in the presence and the praise of Jesus. The enemy flees at the mere sound of His name.

From *May Jesus Christ Be Praised*
(A German hymn translated by Edward Caswell)

Battle Plan

The powers of darkness fear
When this sweet chant they hear:
May Jesus Christ be praised!

We are better off knowing less about spiritual warfare. The New Testament tells us that we are involved in a battle, but it never tells us to fight. It never outlines attack strategies or search-and-destroy missions. It contains no briefing and debriefing sessions. When it comes to dealing with the enemy, we're simply told to stand our ground, to pray, to watch, and to be on the alert.

Why? After all, our enemy has already lost. At the cross, he lost all hope of winning this war over human lives. Sin and death have been conquered. In Christ, we are already on the winning side. Our job is simply to stay with Jesus.

We don't need to live as if we are in daily hand-to-hand combat, searching for demons around every corner and explaining every setback as a loss to the other side. This gives Satan far more credit than he deserves or could ever account for.

On the contrary, we need to enjoy the Lord and see Him in everything we do. We need to turn our daily life into a running dialogue of praise. Our defense is praise.

Yes, there *is* a war going on. But it is out of our realm. We are not to fight this war. If anything, we are to steer clear of it. Stick with Jesus. Make praise a habit. Stand firm in Him. All Satan can do is distract us and get our minds off Jesus. Remember, the battle is already won!

From *May Jesus Christ Be Praised*
(A German hymn translated by Edward Caswell)

Why?

Does sadness fill my mind?
A solace here I find:
May Jesus Christ be praised!

Praising God comforts us in sadness. It does not always remove our tears or their cause, but it brings our sadness company, because the Holy Spirit comes to us.

We keep thinking and hoping that God will remove our problems or remove us from them. But instead He comes alongside us. He gives us comfort in our sorrows and He collects all our tears in a bottle (see Psalm 56:8). (Notice He does not wipe them away. That part comes later.)

He sits with us, groans with us, comforts us, understands us, and gives us strength to go on. Praise welling up next to our sorrow, even when we don't feel like praising, is evidence that His Spirit is there and working. That in itself is a certain solace.

God in us is a source of strength, not something we fabricate. And I believe He sometimes allows sorrow in our lives just so we can find this out. And then He can get next to us.

From *Ivory Palaces* by Henry Barraclough

Under No Obligation

Out of the Ivory Palaces,
Into a world of woe,
Only His great, eternal love
Made my Savior go.

What would make Him leave heaven? What could possibly be so compelling or demanding? Was it us? Was there some intrinsic value to our cumulative personhoods that pulled Him away from His place with the Father and the Holy Spirit? Were we worth the trip? Was it the disaster of a creation gone bad that made Him come and rescue it from its own destruction?

As Paul asked, "Does not the potter have the right to make out of the same lump of clay some pottery for noble purposes and some for common use?" (Romans 9:21). Take Paul's question one step further. Does not the potter have the right to discard the whole lump? Smash all the pots? Is he under some artistic obligation to save his own creation? Is there a law higher than God?

God was under no obligation to save His creation, not from us or from the universe, and not from some higher law or court. Not even from Himself. He came for only one reason: His love. He wanted to come. He chose to express Himself this way. He wanted to show us what love was and how far it could go.

And believe me, it came a long way when it found me.

From *And Can It Be?* by Charles Wesley

The Question of Grace

And can it be that I should gain
An interest in the Savior's blood?

How can I earn interest on an investment into which I paid nothing? How can I be the beneficiary of a transaction like this? How am I even in this picture, a picture that has the Creator and Sustainer of the universe thinking of me as He dies? How can His loss be my gain?

It is appropriate to put these great truths in the form of questions, because mere statements could never hold the wonder of the truth they call for. It is appropriate to leave them as questions, for we will never know the full answer. To answer them would be to take the truth for granted. To ever be anything other than awed by God's grace is to make ourselves deserving of what we cannot possibly deserve. No one can be around the gospel without feeling a sense of profound wonderment. To approach the gospel in any other way would be an affront to grace.

Oh, we can discuss the gospel intellectually and do word studies on *grace*. We can put doctrine in a book and spend our lives devoted to understanding it and explaining it to others. But when it gets personal—when it comes down to considering me and my own personal sin—then even the greatest quotable statements ever made have to give way to questions.

And can it be?

From *And Can It Be?* by Charles Wesley

The Reduction Principle

...emptied Himself of all but love,
And bled for Adam's helpless race!

God made Himself of no reputation when He came to earth to die. He set aside all of His rights. He walked around earth in the presence of common human beings. And the people did not stop what they were doing and immediately fall on their faces and worship Him, which would have been the politically and spiritually correct thing to do. After all, it was He who created them and gave them life and breath and every good thing.

This is not only a statement of His love for us, but an example for us as well. Love cannot hold onto itself. Love has no rights to begin with. This is the pain of love. Love does not plan on getting anything back. Love does not expect to be noticed. Love possesses nothing. Love has given up everything. If it doesn't do these things, it would not be love.

Love is not even conscious of what it is giving up. Love sacrifices without noticing—or getting anyone else to notice—what it is sacrificing. Love gives everybody else attention.

God gave all of us His attention when He hung His Son on the cross. Imagine what He gave up to get there, and you have a picture of the reduction principle of love.

Paul tells us in Philippians 2:5-8 that our attitude should be the same as Christ's when He did all this for us. That's a tall order, indeed.

Oh, Lord, reduce me to love.

From *And Can It Be?* by Charles Wesley

The Immensity of God's Mercy

'Tis mercy all, immense and free,
For, O my God, it found out me.

If you've ever wondered how far God would go to show His love, look in the mirror and wonder no more. We need not look any further than ourselves to find the most shocking and amazing displays of God's grace. If we think otherwise, it is only because we have not seen ourselves as we truly are.

It has been said and sung many times, "There but for the grace of God go I." At first this sounds grateful, but such sentiment masks a dangerous pride. It is missing any real statement of grace, and sounds more in line with "Lord, I thank thee that I am not like that poor man over there." That is the Pharisee's prayer, which Jesus condemned. The more appropriate perception, I think, would be: "Here, because of the grace of God, and for no other reason, am I."

"Lord, have mercy on me, a sinner," was the poor man's prayer, and Jesus was quick to point out that this prayer was the one that sent heaven scurrying.

The immensity of God's mercy is not displayed in what He did for the world, or for someone else. Nor is it discovered through some theological understanding of the many nuances of His grace. The immensity of God's mercy is revealed finally—and only—in the incredible realization that, lo and behold, it found out the worst of the lot. It looked from heaven and found out *me*!

From *And Can It Be?* by Charles Wesley

The Audacity of Our Faith

Bold I approach the eternal throne,
And claim the crown, through Christ my own.

How is it that on one hand, we stand amazed and overwhelmed at the good fortune of our salvation, and yet on the other hand, we stand poised boldly to claim a crown that is rightfully ours? Don't these two images seem to contradict each other? Yes, they do! But like other paradoxes in the Scriptures, they are both true in the heavenly economy of God.

Amazing grace will always be amazing to us; there is no place for taking our salvation for granted. Yet at the same time, God does not want us standing around heaven or earth with our mouths hanging open, waiting for what might happen next. He did not merely save us *from* our sin, but He saved us *to* a holy life to which He invites and expects our cooperation.

For all the Scriptures indicating the undeserved nature of His grace, there are also plenty that call us to meet our responsibility. "I press on," said Paul in Philippians 3:12, "to take hold of that for which Christ Jesus took hold of me." This is faith grabbing back. Grace, properly received, does not leave me dumbfounded. It moves me into an active relationship with God.

God brought us into His kingdom. He gives us a host of promises in His Scriptures and expects us to lay hold of them. He accepts—and responds to equally—the wonder of our worship and the audacity of our claims to faith.

Such is the nature of God.

From *The Way of the Cross Leads Home* by Jessie Brown Pounds

Seeking After the True Light

I shall ne'er get sight of the Gates of Light,
If the way of the cross I miss.

People are constantly looking for light, because light symbolizes revelation, illumination, and knowledge. Almost all religions, including New Age philosophies, see light in this way.

Many people seek light. Some go to great lengths and distant lands to talk to gurus, shamans, philosophers, and spiritualists who claim to offer illumination. But sooner or later, if one is truly searching, that search will lead to Jesus. How can anyone possibly ignore a historical figure who said "I am the light of the world" (John 8:12)?

The problem is, you can't just take a little light from Jesus. You can't make Him part of a search that takes a little bit of truth from here and a little bit from there. Jesus' own words preclude this possibility. He did not say He had *some* truth and light to add to everybody else's. He said *He* was *the* truth, *the* life, and *the* way. And this way leads to a cross.

That narrows the search considerably. The search for light leads to a cross, and yet on the other side of that cross is a blinding light so bright you cannot look at it without falling to your face. It is a light that illuminates your present reality and lights up all eternity, too.

It is impossible to find light and miss the cross. Those who say they have are not speaking of the true light.

From *O Comforter, Gentle and Tender* by Albert B. Simpson

In the Fire and the Flood

Oh, come as the heart-searching fire,
Oh, come as the sin-cleansing flood;
Consume us with holy desire
And fill with the fullness of God.

Fire... flood... He can come to me in any way He wants to. I need His presence and I'll take it any way He chooses to bring it to me. But I do need to know where to look.

Often He comes in hardship and in pain. Take Job for example: At the end of all his sufferings, he received a visit from God. By the time God came to him, Job was ready to know God in a way he could never have known Him had he still possessed his health, his wealth, and his family.

God comes to us in various forms. But we are often so busy looking for Him at the end of the rainbow that we miss Him in the rain. We are often asking Him to deliver us from the fire and the flood, when in actuality He *is* the fire and the flood.

Next time we ask for deliverance, we should probably also ask to have the eyes to recognize Him and what He is teaching us at the time. It could involve the very thing we are trying to escape.

From *And Can I Yet Delay* by Charles Wesley

Heavyweights

Settle and fix my wavering soul
With all Thy weight of love.

Without God's love, we are all lightweights. We can be swayed and blown about so easily. Even our spiritual activities are weightless without His love. But love gives substance to all we do. It connects us to God and to others whom He loves. To operate out of love is to be settled and fixed in our soul about the right thing to do. It means thinking the way God thinks—to be driven not by what is best for us, but by what is best for those we love.

Love gives us character. Without love, we are tossed about by winds of doctrine or feelings or whatever happens to be the prevailing issue. Love gives substance to our doctrine, our movements, and our revivals. If we claim to have God moving among us, but do not have love as our identifying mark, we are lying.

Love gives meaning to commitment. It takes a relationship with God and makes it mean something to someone else's life. If our spiritual life affects no one but ourselves, we are only lightweight Christians—harmless and ineffective in our faith. Those around us should know if we have God's love. They bear either the marks of our love or the absence of it.

March 22

From *Lord, Speak to Me, That I May Speak* by Frances R. Havergal

White-Winged Dove

O teach me, Lord, that I may teach
The precious things Thou dost impart;
And wing my words, That I may reach
The hidden depths of many a heart.

The Word of God runs deep into a heart. It goes places mere human words cannot go. It can be spoken with confidence because it is carried home by the wings of the Spirit.

Understanding the Word of God is not merely a product of human intellect. It uses human intellect as a doorway into the depths of the soul. No one knows how far in that goes, but the Word of God can go there. It can go there on its own, to unknown places.

This is why we must speak not only our words but God's Word as well. God's Word can always go farther in than ours can. This is because the Spirit not only carries the Word, but also receives it in the heart. Not everyone has the Spirit, and to those without Him, even God's Word will fall short of the mark. However, we must remember that we are not speaking to everybody. We are speaking as Jesus spoke, only to those who have ears to hear.

So when you use God's Word, you can be confident that, though you may not speak to everyone, you will speak deeply to someone. And His Word never returns to Him empty. The dove always flies back with something in its mouth.

From *Love Divine* by Charles Wesley

Beginning at the End

End of faith as its beginning...

Ends, then beginnings: This is the order of truth. We always start at the beginning and finish at the end. God apparently gets bored with such predictability. He likes to finish everything off and then end with the exciting possibility of something new.

It's always been this way. The end of our righteousness is the beginning of His. The end of our resources is the beginning of His power. The end of our sin is the beginning of His forgiveness. But I don't want to spoil it for you because you have an assignment today. Fill in some blanks below. I suggest you leave a few open for the coming years, because our perspective is always changing. That's one of the beginnings right there!

THE END OF_____________IS THE BEGINNING OF_________________

THE END OF_____________IS THE BEGINNING OF_________________

THE END OF_____________IS THE BEGINNING OF_________________

THE END OF_____________IS THE BEGINNING OF_________________

THE END OF_____________IS THE BEGINNING OF_________________

THE END OF_____________IS THE BEGINNING OF_________________

THE END OF_____________IS THE BEGINNING OF_________________

THE END OF_____________IS THE BEGINNING OF_________________

THE END OF_____________IS THE BEGINNING OF_________________

THE END OF_____________IS THE BEGINNING OF_________________

THE END OF_____________IS THE BEGINNING OF_________________

March 24

From *Love Divine* by Charles Wesley

Entirely Other

Love divine, all loves excelling,
Joy of heaven, to earth come down....

God's love is like nothing we know of from any human source. It came down from heaven, so it has no earthly counterpart. All our attempts at love are mere shadows of His. It's almost as if we need another language if we are going to talk about God's love.

We have loves that fill up our days with familiar things: friends, pets, food we like, and things we like to do. And if we are fortunate, we have loves that fill up our nights with human companionship, maybe even sexual love. And then there are loves we long for. For those who have no one to warm their nights or brighten their days, as well as for those who do, we all have aches that go unexpressed or unheeded.

God's love does not seek to fill any of these holes or warm and brighten us in these ways. That is why Christians are sometimes confused when they have God, yet still experience loneliness. God's love is entirely other than this. It is creating love and redeeming love. It is forgiving love and, most of all, dying love: "God commended his love for us in that while we were yet sinners, Christ died for us."

This kind of love will not instantly warm your nights, brighten your days, or fulfill all your dreams. But it will reserve you a place in heaven. And eventually it will change the way you look at your life down here.

From *Love Divine* by Charles Wesley

Humble Dwellings

Fix in us Thy humble dwelling...

That divine love can dwell in these walking human tabernacles is a mystery first entered into through the incarnation of Christ and then carried on in us. In Christ, Paul said, dwells all the fullness of God, bodily (Colossians 1:19).

If one of us (and Christ is one of us) could contain all the fullness of God, then this would reveal a great deal about us as bearers of the image of God. You could not put all of God in a cat, a dog, a mountain lion, or a porpoise. But you could put all of God in the form of a woman or a man and have the essence of Him, because that's exactly what God did.

This should make us feel both great and small. Great that we could contain Him, that we are that much like Him. Small that He would humble Himself and become intimately involved with the workings of our inner beings.

The end result of all this is the incomprehensible fact that God dwells in us now by faith. He not only humbled Himself by coming to earth as the Son of Man, but He also keeps coming as He takes up residence in us through His Spirit. And if it were a humble dwelling He took on that first time, how much more humble is this dwelling He now "fixes" in me?

Makes you feel special and humble all at the same time.

From *Love Divine* by Charles Wesley

The Trembling Heart

Enter every trembling heart...

I wonder what the hymn writer means by this? Enter every human heart because all hearts tremble? Enter only those hearts that are trembling because some don't? (They may beat, but they don't tremble.)

Maybe a trembling heart would be the opposite of a hard heart. Even God's Spirit would have a difficult time entering a hard heart, not because He couldn't get in, but because He would not be welcome.

A trembling heart is weak, vulnerable and too afraid to hide its fear. It has probably been broken a number of times and is afraid of being broken again. And yet, in the face of God's love it is willing to venture out.

This is the proper fear of God—not of His meanness, but of His magnitude. The trembling heart has finally gotten it straight. It's been afraid of the wrong things all along: afraid of being hurt, afraid of being alone, afraid of being rejected, afraid of getting caught. Now it wants only to tremble before God and do what He wants. This heart has decided that if it is going to be afraid of anything, it might as well be afraid of the *right* thing for a change.

Have you ever held a pet bird in your hand and felt its tiny heart clicking in its chest so loudly, that you thought it would burst? Trembling hearts must feel a little like this in the kind hand of God.

From *Love Divine* by Charles Wesley

Which Way Are You Bent?

Take away our bent to sinning...

The direction we are bent is sometimes contrary to our actions. I can imagine a person sinning a lot, though not being bent to sinning. Such a person would indeed be miserable, but it happens (for instance, Paul in Romans 7). I can also imagine a person bent to sinning, though living an outwardly religious life. Such a person would most likely not be miserable, only clever (the Pharisees, for example).

The way we are bent is the thing we are true to. No Christian is going to be sinless, nor are all unbelievers living purposefully sinful lives. But our bent is the way we are inclined to go. Our bent is going to win out in the end, no matter how much we fight against it along the way.

Our bent is the way we really are inside. A person without Christ is bent to sinning, regardless of how much good he or she may accomplish. Conversely, entering into a relationship with God through Christ takes away our bent to sinning, regardless of how much appeal sin may still have to us. Our bent tells us whether we have been changed.

It is simply good to be true to yourself, to live life according to the way you are inside. This is why Jesus would have us either hot or cold. He can work with us either way. The lukewarm people are the ones who are bent one way and living another, and that is the worst place of all to be.

From *Love Divine* by Charles Wesley

Lay It Down

Till we cast our crowns before Thee,
Lost in wonder, love and praise!

"You can't take it with you," is a popular phrase that implies that when we die, we leave everything behind. It assumes we will be walking into heaven empty-handed. This is not true. According to Paul in 1 Corinthians 3, the quality of our faith will be tested by fire on our way in, and that fire will determine whether we will be bringing anything along with us.

Paul says we are building now upon a foundation of faith, using various materials: gold, silver, costly stones, wood, hay, and straw. Now, it doesn't take a genius to figure out that not all of these are going to make it through fire. The wood, hay, and straw parts of our efforts on earth are obviously destined for a brief object lesson in combustion. But gold, silver, and costly stones will turn into our reward on the other side.

And yet there are other biblical pictures that show us laying down our rewards at the feet of Jesus. We will realize that whatever made it through the awards ceremony came from Him in the first place. We will be so lost in wonder, love, and praise that we will not want to keep anything for ourselves.

So a crown is worth working for. (We don't want to enter heaven empty-handed.) But once we get into heaven, we will have done our work of faith only so that we will not be left standing around with nothing to offer Him.

From *Just As I Am, without One Plea* by Charlotte Elliott

I Come

Just as I am, though tossed about
With many a conflict, many a doubt,
Fightings and fears within, without,
O Lamb of God, I come, I come.

When God pulls you to Himself, you can do nothing but come. You get up and you come to Him. It happened to me at the age of eight at a Billy Graham film in my church. Yes, *a film*—not even a real crusade! The invitation and the choir on the screen was all it took for me. I was a basket case. I can remember it to this day; and though it's not necessary, I would go forward again. I would follow Billy Graham around and go forward every night because I am a dead ringer for salvation.

It wasn't an intellectual decision. After all, how intellectual can an eight-year-old be? I was drawn to God, and I had no choice. I was grabbed by the heart and pulled. Jesus said no one could come to the Father unless the Father drew Him. What He didn't say was that no one can sit there and refuse to come if they *are* being drawn. No one.

It doesn't matter what's going through your head at the time—conflicts and fightings and fears and doubts. It doesn't matter what is happening inside or outside your life. When He calls you, you come. You come because you can't stand to be without Him.

From *Just As I Am, without One Plea* by Charlotte Elliott

I Am Yours

Just as I am, Thy love unknown
Hath broken every barrier down...

OK, God. You win! You have been hammering away at me for some time now, and I give up. I can no longer resist your love. How can I say "No" to your grace? How can I refuse a gift of such infinite value at no cost to me? My defenses are shattered. Your eyes have bored their way into my soul. I can no longer hide. You know everything about me. I have tried to run away from you, but each time I thought I had lost you, you were there, waiting for me at the next place when I arrived.

It is impossible to escape your love. Even when bad things happen to me, you are disciplining me to help make me strong. This too is love.

I am helpless. You have won me. Take all that I have; I commit myself to your grace. I rest in the security of your arms. I am weary of trying to prove that I am worthy of being loved. I am ready to accept your love, which is already proven to me. I am yours.

From *I Know Whom I Have Believed* by Daniel W. Whittle

What *Do* You Know?

I know not why God's wondrous grace to me He hath made known,
Nor why—unworthy—Christ in love redeemed me for His own.

I know not how this saving faith to me He did impart,
Nor how believing in His Word wrought peace within my heart.

I know not how the Spirit moves, convincing men of sin,
Revealing Jesus through His Word, creating faith in Him.

I know not what of good or ill may be reserved for me,
Of weary ways or golden days, before His face I see.

I know not when my Lord may come, at night or noon-day fair,
Nor if I'll walk the vale with Him, or meet Him in the air.

Well, for heaven's sake, what *do* you know? How ignorant can you be? Don't you think you should be a little more knowledgeable about your own faith than this? How are you going to be able to sell this to anyone with half a brain if you don't have any answers?

And what's your point anyway? Just what are you trying to get at? I mean, if you were going somewhere with this, that would be one thing. But for crying out loud!...

What's that? Oh, I didn't let you finish? OK, go ahead.

But "I know whom I have believed,
and am persuaded that He is able
To keep that which I've committed
unto Him against that day."

Oh well. Never mind.

From *Jesus Loves Even Me* by Phillip P. Bliss

Screwtape Revisited

This shall my song in eternity be:
"Oh what a wonder that Jesus loves me."

My dear Gall:

I want to compliment you on how well your self-image campaign is going. Getting our subjects to embrace the need for self-esteem was brilliant enough, but making it the reason for the untimely death of God's Son is nothing short of a stroke of genius. Your cousin Wormwood would be proud! You've actually got some of them thinking that His death proves how worthy they are!

But be careful. As you well know, there are a great number of those detestable hymns that slipped through our spy network a few centuries ago. You know, the ones that talk about the Enemy's kindness toward undeserving sinners and all that. Get them to write new songs, Gall—songs that have nothing to do with how bad they are.

Make them think they deserve to be saved. This will diminish their love for the Enemy and get their eyes back on themselves. Then we can move in with countless self-help programs and keep them busy focusing on themselves, like the others. The more they think they can improve themselves, the less they will need the Enemy. Let them even think they're doing it *with His help*. We'll know better.

Soon, we should be able to pull them away entirely.

Yours affectionately,
Screwtape Jr.

From *Gracious Spirit, Holy Ghost* by Christopher Wordsworth

The Greatest of These

Gracious Spirit, Holy Ghost,
Taught by Thee, we covet most
Of Thy gifts at Pentecost,
Holy, heavenly love.

What is it that God wants us to desire over any spiritual gift or power or knowledge? That's not hard to figure out. It's love. The famous Love Chapter of 1 Corinthians begins with "And now I will show you the most excellent way" (1 Corinthians 12:31), and ends with the three great spiritual virtues of faith, hope and love. "But the greatest of these is love" (13:13).

Solomon did a good thing when he chose to receive wisdom from the hand of God to rule his people. But he would have chosen even more wisely had he chosen love. Love would have put him in touch with the very heart of God, something that Solomon ended up missing in all his wisdom. In the end, we find that all of Solomon's great wisdom only led him to futility (Ecclesiastes 1-6).

Ask for love in a troubling situation and you will undoubtedly be praying according to the will of God. Ask for love and you will gladden the heart of God. Ask for love and you will never go wrong. Nor will your request ever be rejected, for God is love.

From *Over the Way* by Flora E. Breck

Go

Close to your door there is illness and strife;
Go in God's name with the water of life.

Go? Today "Go" means walk out your front door. Illness, strife, hunger, and homelessness are no longer a missionary's slide-show away. They are now between your front door and your driveway. They are on the way to the supermarket. They are on the way to church (depending on which route you take, of course).

The world has never been smaller, and life has never been more dangerous. Six people were shot one day recently in Los Angeles, and three of them were in the hospital in critical condition. How did the victims put themselves in harm's way? By watching a ball game in a neighborhood park.

Children are at risk in war zones around the world. Long-standing hatreds fuel territorial battles, and children are often the first casualties.

And in the cities, people are moving farther and farther away from urban areas to avoid the problems of hunger and homelessness. But the problems of the big city accompany them there, sometimes through their own children.

The world is at our doorstep. Just open the door and walk outside. All of us are missionaries to an alien culture. Walk out your door with a cup of cold water and the Water of Life. Go down the street to the supermarket in the name of Jesus. For Jesus, the marketplace was teeming with needs on every hand. And it is much the same today.

From *Himself* by Albert B. Simpson

Our All-in-All

Once it was the blessing, Now it is the Lord;
Once it was the feeling, Now it is His Word;
Once His gift I wanted, Now the Giver own;
Once I sought for healing, Now Himself alone.

Sooner or later, everything else falls away. God gets our attention first on the basis of our need for lesser things, then He starts the weaning process. Blessings, feelings, gifts and healings—they dominate our early years as Christians. We clamor for those things like a baby clamors for food and attention.

There's nothing wrong with gifts and blessings. They are all good things. But that's the point: They are only *things*. In time, we find out that it was *Him* that we were longing for all along.

This is not to say that we lose these other things in finding Him. Quite the contrary! We find out that in Him, the blessings, the feelings, the gifts, and the healings come in their completeness. We were not seeking these things after all. They were just other names we put on Him for a while, until we could see clearly enough to recognize Him as our all-in-all.

It is in this way that growing up simplifies our lives. Once we were frustrated and confused. There were so many options, so many needs. Now there is only one: Our need and love for Him.

April 5

From *Himself* by Albert B. Simpson

Spiritual Workout

Once I tried to use Him,
Now He uses me...

It is always more satisfying to be emptied than to be filled, to love than to be loved, to give than to receive. But there is a process to these things, a proper order. Before we can be emptied, we must be filled; before we can love, we must be loved; before we give, we must receive. And so we all begin at the elementary level of filling and receiving.

This is truly a glorious place to begin, because we are all so needy and empty. We bask in our good fortune when we first come into a relationship with God. But soon we become dissatisfied with only taking in. This is the first sign of real growth: a distaste for spiritual obesity and a desire to get into the trenches and work some of this bulk off. Suddenly, we find ourselves aware that other people have needs, too, and that maybe we can help. In fact, this could be one explanation of the way works fit into a life of faith. They become a spiritual workout, where we enjoy keeping in shape. It may be a little hard starting, but a thrill once we get going.

For it is in serving that we discover that those things that fed our needy souls turn even sweeter and richer and fuller on their way to feeding someone else's.

From *The Head That Once Was Crowned with Thorns*
by Thomas Kelly

So You Want to Be a King?

The head that once was crowned with thorns
Is crowned with glory now...

It was mockery—pure mockery. Someone had heard that Jesus was a king, or at least thought He was or wanted to be. We don't know who had Him mocked as a king with the robe and the crown of thorns. I imagine the soldiers were talking, spreading rumors, and things got carried away. They must have made a habit of playing havoc with the righteous ideologies of zealous Jews.

Pilate had a notice prepared and affixed to the cross in three languages: Aramaic, Latin, and Greek. It read: JESUS OF NAZARETH, THE KING OF THE JEWS. A number of Jewish leaders protested to Pilate that it should be correctly stated that this man only *claimed* to be king of the Jews. But Pilate replied, "What I have written, I have written" (John 19:22). That could have meant that he simply didn't want to be bothered with this matter any further. Or maybe Pilate was having second thoughts.

Ironically, regardless of Pilate's motives, Jesus had the last word. He died properly identified. There will undoubtedly be a lot of second thoughts when we all see Him in His new crown.

From *The Head That Once Was Crowned with Thorns*
by Thomas Kelley

Now and Later

The joy of all who dwell above,
The joy of all below.

Christ as "the joy of all who dwell above" I can understand. But "the joy of all below" doesn't quite make sense to me unless the hymn writer is thinking about some kind of millennial experience. Asking average unbelievers if Christ is their joy would probably result in quizzical looks at best.

But in some ways, Christ is the joy of all below, even those who do not believe in Him. Whenever there is joy, He is there. In Him we were created and in Him we live and move and have our being. This is not just true for Christians; it is true for everybody.

Unbelievers live on borrowed breath. Simple pleasures of everyday life come from His hand. If people weren't so prejudiced against God, they would actually like Him. Unfortunately, they are predisposed *not* to like Him, even though He is sustaining the very life they enjoy.

Maybe this is what it means that every knee shall bow. When the veil is removed, all will know. Our joy now is the preview of the coming Christ. Would that everyone knew Him now!

From *More Love to Thee* by Elizabeth P. Prentiss

Building a Choir

Let sorrow do its work, Send grief and pain;
Sweet are Thy messengers, Sweet their refrain,
When they can sing with me:
More love, O Christ, to Thee.

All that comes into my life, be it good or bad, merely adds more voices to the same song—the one that tells of my love for Him. Grief? Sorrow? Join in. There's plenty of room in this chorus for all of you!

An abiding relationship with God is indomitable. Sorrows only dredge the soul, making more room for Him to fill. And each dredge removes more of self and makes the song more real. The worst brings out the best. When sorrow makes its way into our lives, instead of resisting it, we can eventually turn it into joy. God meets us in our sorrow and turns it into song. It's all in how we receive it.

We can fight with our sorrow and pain, but that only slows down this process. We can think they are our enemies and close ourselves off to spiritual growth. We can be hard and bitter and miss what they are here to teach us. We can blame ourselves and those around us and we can compare our lives to others. We can turn away the singers and sit alone in the silence.

Or we can open ourselves to what He sends and welcome the singers. We can give them their parts and arrange the music to glorify the one we love. Let sorrow join in. The more the merrier! The more to sing about His love. All right pain, come along with me, if you can lend one more refrain to the song. In the end, all these voices add up to more love for Christ. That is what we want anyway.

From *Holy God, We Praise Thy Name* by Ignace Franz

New Math

Holy Father, Holy Son,
Holy Spirit—Three we name Thee;
Though in essence only one,
Undivided God we claim Thee.

We cannot fathom the Trinity. God expresses Himself in three unique personalities with three distinct areas of responsibilities, and yet each one acts not as a part of Himself but as all of Him.

We imagine Christ acting in the world from the stories told by His disciples and know that it is God doing and speaking. We wait for the filling of the Holy Spirit and know that it is God Himself who comes to us—not just a messenger from God. We worship God the Father, not as some far-off being in the heavens, but as all three. We try unsuccessfully to understand this, but like other paradoxes about the truth, we simply believe this to be true. We act on this truth as if it could be divided up into parts even though it is all one truth and can't be separated. Our minds can't contain this, but since when did God ever expect to be contained?

For those who are having trouble with this, here's a suggestion. Call it new math: 1+1+1=1. This shouldn't be too hard. After all, if He's God, He can do anything He wants. And we can worship Him for all of this that is beyond our comprehension.

From *Holy God, We Praise Thy Name* by Ignace Franz

Real Men; Real Women

Lo, the apostolic train
Joins Thy sacred name to hallow;
Prophets swell the glad refrain,
And the white-robed martyrs follow...

By faith, we are connected to an impressive group: apostles, prophets, and martyrs.

The apostles built the church. These men went out on a limb for something totally new and daring. The new church broke all their traditions, yet these people had nerve to do what they did. They were part of a revolution.

And the Old Testament prophets were no less bold. They ran against the current tide of opinion during their watch on earth. They heard the voice of God on a different wavelength than anyone else. They spoke to the people like madmen—speaking the truth and calling the people to repentance.

And not to be forgotten are the martyrs. They were mocked, beaten, burned, and sawn in two. They were tortured to death and fed to lions. But they were proud to identify with the sufferings of Christ.

Talk about *real* men and *real* women! These people devoted their lives to God and His purposes in the world.

Now what was that compromise you were thinking about entertaining today? And with *these* witnesses looking on?

From *I Sing the Mighty Power of God* by Isaac Watts

Look Up!

I sing the mighty power of God
That made the mountains rise,
That spread the flowing seas abroad
And built the lofty skies.

Every once in a while, we need to walk outside and look up. God recommended something like this to Job after he had exhausted himself trying to understand his afflictions and justify himself before his four "friends."

God finally showed up to Job and asked him questions that initially must have seemed irrelevant, questions about whether he was able to make mountains rise up out of the ground, command the borders of the sea, or fling stars in the sky. Surprisingly full of sarcasm, these questions served to put Job in his place. But they also gave him a fresh encounter with God. "My ears have heard of you," he said, "but now my eyes have seen you" (Job 42:5).

And then Job repented. He repented of speaking too soon. He repented of thinking he could understand and figure out what was only God's prerogative to know.

Sometimes we need to walk outside, look up into the heavens, and say, "Hey, am I able to make mountains rise up out of the ground, command the borders of the sea, or fling stars in the sky?" Well then, until further notice, it is probably best to worship the one who is, and reserve comment on my situation for a time in the future when we will be able to see what He sees and understand all.

From *I Sing the Mighty Power of God* by Isaac Watts

Yes!

I sing the goodness of the Lord
That filled the earth with food;
He formed the creatures with His word
And then pronounced them good.

"For everything God created is good, and nothing is to be rejected if it is received with thanksgiving, because it is consecrated by the word of God and prayer" (1 Timothy 4:4-5). This is nothing less than a great big "YES" marked out across the borders of the universe. This is God's way of saying that all this belongs to Him, no matter what anyone else says. This is God, stretching out His hands over all that He has made and virtually laughing His way through this invitation: "ENJOY!"

This was the same God who after creating something new each day had stepped back and proclaimed it "good." This was the same God who after making us commanded us to be fruitful and multiply. This means that to obey Him, we must engage in the giving and receiving of sexual love.

It's no wonder, then, that while Jesus was here, He equated His visit as a sort of honeymoon—a limited time to enjoy His company. "How can the guests of the bridegroom mourn while He is with them?" (Matthew 9:15).

Indeed, how can we mourn very long when He is with us in our hearts through His Spirit, helping us to see the world—and each other—as He intended?

From *I Sing the Mighty Power of God* by Isaac Watts

Seeing God

There's not a plant or flower below
But makes Thy glories known...

A flower can be looked at in a variety of ways. A scientist might study its cellular structure and reproductive system. A farmer might want to know its economic value. An artist might wonder how best to capture its beauty. A doctor might see it as either a possible source of natural medicine or a nemesis to those with allergies. A wife might see it as an expression of the love and thoughtfulness of the absent husband who sent it to her. But all of them, whether or not they realize it, are staring the glory of God right in the face when they look at its glorious petals.

Some people can stare for the longest time and never see Him. Others see God everywhere. Finding God and things about Him is not a factor of a spiritual environment, Christian surroundings, or sacred mementos and reminders. It is more accurately a factor of one's eyesight. Put simply, you see what you are looking for.

Proverbs 25:2 says that it is the glory of God to conceal a matter and the glory of kings to search it out. That means that if you are interested in finding God, you will be searching for His hidden nature everywhere. You have to look for it, though it is never very far away.

From *I Sing the Mighty Power of God* by Isaac Watts

In the Boat

And clouds arise and tempests blow
By order from Thy throne...

All things come from the hand of God, including clouds and tempests. Otherwise, they would have not obeyed Jesus when He hushed them from a small boat in the middle of the sea of Galilee (see Luke 8:22-25).

It's always hard to imagine bad things coming from the hand of God. But it is better to have Him in control of these things than not. If He weren't in charge, then one of these tempests could rise up and surprise even Him. Imagine the Son of God standing helplessly by as clouds build up on the horizon. I wouldn't want to be in the boat with *that* Jesus.

And yet it becomes very difficult when we experience—first or second hand—the devastation wrought in people's lives by sickness, evil, accident, or natural disaster. How can these things exist on the same earth with a God who is omnipotent and could at any time—if He wanted to—do something about the dreadful courses this world takes? How can you have a God who even gives demons permission to act in His world?

We will probably never answer this question with the limited capacity of our present minds. But one thing's for sure: If I had a choice (and, of course, I don't), I would choose the God in control, even of an incomprehensible world. He may not stop the storm every time, but I wouldn't want to be in the boat with Him, wondering if He could.

From *I Sing the Mighty Power of God* by Isaac Watts

The Borrowed Life

While all that borrows life from Thee
Is ever in Thy care...

Life is on loan to us. Every living thing gets its breath from God "because he himself gives all men life and breath and everything else" (Acts 17:25). This is a far-reaching fact, but not entirely incomprehensible when you consider the wonder and complexity of life and personality. What's really incomprehensible is how so many people can go on living and not know that this is true, or even wonder about it.

For those who believe, seeing God as the source and giver of all life makes the world look a little less hostile. It may even open the possibility of finding God in places that He would not usually be thought of as inhabiting. For if this fact is true, then *everyone* lives the borrowed life, and not just those who decide to take one out on loan.

If pagans borrow their lives from God, then anyone's life can be something we appreciate and acknowledge God for, even if that person doesn't. Whether they are aware of it or not, artists, thinkers, politicians, ballplayers, lawyers, scientists—you name it—have all received life and talent from the Father of Lights. That means you and I can receive from them what we recognize as truth and thank God for it.

I can worship God over the scientific discovery of an atheist. I can worship God through the music of someone who claims to be a Bahai devotee. I can worship God through the theater of a nominally Jewish playwright. I can worship God through the unbelievable catch of a hedonistic professional baseball player. I can worship God wherever I find people. And I can know that even the very breath to curse God with comes from God, making such an activity quite ironic, indeed.

From *I Sing the Mighty Power of God* by Isaac Watts

He's Staying

And everywhere that man can be,
Thou, God, art present there.

"Where can I flee from your presence?" cries David. "If I go up to the heavens, you are there; if I make my bed in the depths, you are there. If I rise on the wings of the dawn, if I settle on the far side of the sea, even there your hand will guide me, your right hand will hold me fast" (Psalm 139:7-10).

A fellow Christian whom I respect a great deal told me a story of how he unwittingly found himself in a nightclub of questionable repute as a guest of a business associate. A punk band was screaming its variety of "music" on a small stage as crowds of young Generation Xers were "moshing" up and down to the thumping rhythms and thrashing guitars. My friend told me how uncomfortable he was in this scene and how much he wanted to leave. But just when he was going to excuse himself, he distinctly heard a message from God: "You can leave if you want, but I'm staying."

I'm not one to hear from God in this way. But neither am I in a position to doubt the words of a trusted friend who often does. Besides, this sounds like something Jesus might say. After all, He was a friend of sinners. He forgave those who were crucifying Him even as they were carrying it out. And He seemed to enjoy loud parties and wedding receptions. Wherever there are people, it's a sure bet that God is somewhere near. It is we who sometimes can't handle the company and have to ask to leave. Never mind... He's staying.

From *Jesus, and Shall It Ever Be* by Joseph Grigg

As It Is in Heaven

Till then nor is my boasting vain—
Till then I boast a Saviour slain.
And, oh, may this my glory be,
That Christ is not ashamed of me.

Now is the time to decide that we are not going to be ashamed of Christ in the company of people. Otherwise, He will be ashamed of us in the company of our Father and His angels in heaven (see Luke 9:26). I would not want to go through that experience.

We need to lock into a heavenly perspective on a regular basis, and this outlook should become second nature. Perhaps this is what He meant by His kingdom coming and His will being done "on earth as it is in heaven" (Matthew 6:10). This means seeing things on earth with a mind toward heaven.

We can't do this without contemplation. A heavenly perspective doesn't just drop out of the sky, so to speak. We must cultivate it by meditating on the Word of God and spiritual truths. We must set our minds on things above, not things on the earth. Unless driven back, the weeds of current issues and demands will always choke out the good seed.

We need a well-maintained garden where we can meet God and focus on our heavenly destination. Otherwise, everything we do will constantly be weighed on its earthly merit. We need to do these things now. If we wait until we are standing before God, it will be too late. By then, everything will have been said and done and lived. Second chances will be no more.

From *Jesus, and Shall It Ever Be* by Joseph Grigg

Reason to be Ashamed

Ashamed of Jesus! yes I may,
When I've no guilt to wash away;
No tear to wipe, no good to crave,
No fears to quell, no soul to save.

Why would a person be ashamed of Jesus? According to Mr. Grigg, a person would be ashamed of Jesus if he or she had no guilt to forgive, no desire to be more righteous, no sorrow over sin, no fear of God, and no soul in need of salvation.

What Mr. Grigg didn't know when he wrote this in 1765 was that he was describing with shocking accuracy the spiritual condition of Christianity 230 years later.

The cross where the Son of God died only has power when sin and guilt are real, when the justice of God has been violated and men and women are shaking in their boots with fear. It has power only when people are overcome with genuine remorse for the sin in their lives, and when the soul is desperate and lost without Christ. In the face of these sensitivities, the gospel of Jesus Christ is good news, and any personal shame associated with it is gladly borne by the forgiven sinner.

But when we turn sin into psychological disorder and poor self-esteem, when we explain away guilt as being just bad feelings from childhood, when we remove the concept of the wrath of God because it makes too many people uncomfortable in church and scares away the seekers, and when we cheapen grace to where it comes without repentance, then we, of all people, have every reason to be ashamed of Jesus.

From *Rock of Ages* by Augustus M. Toplady

It Wouldn't Be Enough

Could my tears forever flow,
Could my zeal no respite know,
This for sin could not atone—
Thou must save, and Thou alone.

I could cry eternal rivers of tears and it would not be enough to wash my sins away. My tears would roll right off my sin like water off a permanent stain. I could be forever sorry—I could heap sad remorse on myself and God—and it would do nothing to alter my guilty status. The deeds are done, and being sorry does not change anything about my actions. I am still guilty.

I could attempt to pay for my sin by doing service for the Lord. I could try to make up for my transgressions against God by giving Him my every waking moment. I could start new organizations that spread the gospel. I could serve on committees and give to Christian organizations, or I could volunteer at my church. I could burn with zeal until I burn out in the night sky like a shooting star, and it wouldn't be enough. No amount of good I could do would change my guilty status.

I cannot save myself. I cannot improve my status with God one iota. Only He can save me. I am at His mercy.

From *I Know That My Redeemer Lives* by Charles Wesley

Hang In There

Jesus, I hang upon Thy Word;
I steadfastly believe...

As Christians, we hang on the Word of God for everything we believe. The gospel hangs there, dangling on the authority of Scripture.

In his letters to young churches, Paul points out how our faith hangs on the resurrection of Christ. "If Christ has not been raised, your faith is futile" (1 Corinthians 15:17). Our future also hangs in the balance of the Word of God. Many of God's promises will be fulfilled in the future—the resurrection of our bodies, our completed sanctification, our full knowledge of God, and our glorification, just to name a few. Christianity does not include instant delivery on all our promises, though we try to make it so, pressured as we are by the insatiable demands of our society.

The Word of God challenges this mentality. "If only for this life we have hope in Christ," writes Paul, "we are to be pitied more than all men" (1 Corinthians 15:19). In other words, much of what we hope for we don't get in this life. This seems logical. If we got it all right away, we wouldn't need hope anymore, would we?

From *Showers of Blessing* by El Nathan

Water, Water, Everywhere...

Mercy drops 'round us are falling,
But for the showers we plead.

It's the little drops that are the problem—the little drops all around us that we take for rain. We get a little wet and we think we've got the blessing. There's Christianity all around us, but so little of Christ.

Our coins tell us we trust in God, but we trust in the coin instead. Our pledge tells us we're under God, but if we ever were, we slipped out a long time ago. Churches dot the villages and towns of our countryside, yet factions tear them apart. Empty cathedrals grace our cities as guns go off at the doorstep.

Christianity has permeated all areas of popular culture, from talk shows to rap videos. But our kids display the same values as the secular songs they tried to sanctify. Christians wield power in Washington, D.C., and Washington, D.C. wields power over them. Christians broadcast on television as the lure of fame casts its spell on them.

Christianity is everywhere in our culture, and yet Christ is so hard to find. We have an institutional Christ, a political Christ, a social Christ, a popular Christ and a cultural Christ. Where is the *Lord Jesus* Christ?

Lord, it's sprinkling everywhere. But PLEASE send the showers.

From *Spirit of God, Descend upon My Heart* by George Croly

Men As Trees Walking

I ask no dream, no prophet ecstasies,
No sudden rending of the veil of clay,
No angel visitant, no opening skies;
But take the dimness of my soul away.

"I see people; they look like trees walking around" (Mark 8:24).

Jesus once performed a two-step healing of a blind man: He spat in the man's eyes and asked him if he saw anything. The man wasn't sure. Yes, he could see better than he had seen before. But he could not see clearly. The man saw a blurry world that he couldn't quite make out—were those men or trees walking? Then Jesus touched his eyes again and the man's sight was fully restored (see Mark 8:22-26).

I wonder if God gave us this story because He wanted us to know that sometimes He does this with us too. He doesn't always let us see all at once. Sometimes He only gives us half-sight. In other words, there is a process to coming to see things as God sees them. There might be periods of dimness in our lives when we can't quite make out what God is doing.

And when He finally lets us see, it's just a clear view of the way things are: Men walk and trees stay rooted. But something else very wonderful happens. Jesus put His hands on the blind man's eyes a second time, and when the man opened them, what was the first thing he saw? The glorious face of Jesus Christ at arm's length.

When *we* finally see, it is always Jesus that we see first.

From *Spirit of God, Descend upon My Heart* by George Croly

Sacrifice Fly Rule

My heart an altar, and Thy love the flame.

sacrifice—*n. 1. a) the act of giving up something valued for the sake of something else more important or worthy.*

Outside of the sacrifice fly rule in baseball, we don't hear this word much in our current culture. This is not only because the word is out of vogue, but also because the concept is gone from our society. Ours is a grabbing, getting, deserving age. You deserve a break, a promotion, a new car. And if you don't get it through the front door, then go around back and sue for it.

Into this culture, Jesus' words about giving up and sacrifice, about losing one's life, about taking the rap for someone else, and about turning the other cheek fall to the floor with a loud thud. They clank on the fortresses of self-esteem that we have labored so hard on. Turn the other cheek? Ha! We would never let anyone hit us in the first place.

What is it you treasure—idolize? What is the one thing you value above everything else? Put it on the altar of your heart, and His love will come and consume it. But catch that again: *His love* consumes it! What could be more valuable than that? Let it burn! When it's all gone, the fire of His love will still be burning, ready to turn all our efforts in the right direction.

From *With Christ and All His Shining Train* by Thomas Prince

Serve Now; Serve Later

There glorious services we'll do;
And He'll unveil His wondrous ways,
His love and glories ever show;
And filled with joy, we'll ever praise.

Heaven is going to be a busy place. But to hear some people talk in traditional terms about heaven is almost enough to make me cancel my reservation. All that stuff about sitting on clouds and playing harps bores me.

If God has challenged our hearts, minds, souls, and our wills here on earth, why wouldn't He keep challenging us in at least the same way—if not new ways—in heaven? Are we not in His image? Isn't this image *for* something? Is He not preparing us here to rule with Him and serve Him and worship Him in heaven?

Why do we have a tendency to think of heaven as a place where we will be doing nothing—a celestial retirement home? Are we really that tired? It may indicate we do not see the significance of our lives and our service now. Anyone who is busy and fulfilled in serving the Lord naturally will want to keep on doing the same thing in heaven. God didn't give us these desires just to burn ourselves out on earth. Serving Him is part of the equipment of faith that makes us fit for heaven.

From *Great God, How Frail a Thing Is Man* by Mather Byles

Is This All There Is?

Great God, how frail a thing is man,
How swift his minutes pass;
His age contracts within a span,
He blooms and dies like grass.

Thoughts about our frailty start creeping into our consciousness sometime during middle age. Oh, we had them before. But it was different then. These thoughts were intellectually known long before they are ever experienced. *Thinking* about time passing and *watching* it pass are two different things. At middle age, the reality of the shortness of our lives hits home.

Suddenly, the words about saving for our retirement make sense, but a little too late. We wish we had listened to advice and started saving money earlier, back in those days when we believed we were going to live forever.

Now our children have started checking out colleges, and we're wondering whether to attend our twenty-fifth class reunion. We welcome the added time we have now that we no longer have to cart our kids from place to place. But we didn't realize how much we would miss those conversations we had with our children when we were driving them around in the car. Now they are driving for themselves, living their own lives.

We are beginning to feel a lifetime pull on us from the other end. And when it does, we suddenly realize that it is all true. Our forefather and foremother *did* die when they ate of the fruit. And our "life" here is not all it was purported to be by those who think this is all there is.

Good thing it isn't.

From *Beneath the Cross of Jesus* by Elizabeth C. Clephane

No Shortcut to Glory

Content to let the world go by,
To know no gain nor loss,
My sinful self my only shame,
My glory all the cross.

My sinful self is also my glory. I must embrace one to know the other. I have tried to glory in the cross without embracing my sinful self and found that it cannot be done. The cross has no meaning to me apart from my sinful self.

Being a good Christian sometimes makes you think that you can take a shortcut to the glory of the cross and bypass your sinful self. You start to think of the cross as something in your distant past—a magic wand that sprinkles forgiveness dust over your life so that you don't have to think about sin.

After a while, you realize you are trying to manufacture pity for Jesus around the communion table. You wonder why the joy seems to have gone out of your salvation, or why some new convert seems to be more in love with Jesus than you are. Suddenly, like the elder son at the prodigal son's party, you feel put out at the attention your little brother is getting. And then, out of His mercy, God shows you your own sin in a way you have never seen it before. You melt in a heap of tears at the ugliness of it all, and right then and there, the cross becomes your glory, too.

From *Beneath the Cross of Jesus* by Elizabeth C. Clephane

Two Wonders

And from my stricken heart with tears
Two wonders I confess:
The wonders of His glorious love
And my unworthiness.

Here is one wonder: God's love. Love that is unconditional, undeserved, unending, and unearned. Love from which nothing can separate us. Love that sought us out while we were still sinners and hostile to God. Love that cost the sacrifice of His only begotten Son. Love that is working with us now and perfecting His will in our lives so that everything that happens to us will somehow be made good. Love that follows us on into eternity and will be our joy forever.

We have no knowledge of love like this. When we think of love, we see the loved one as being lovely, as eliciting love. When we say we don't love someone anymore, we don't mean we don't have love for them. Rather, we mean that we no longer find them lovely.

Here is another wonder: Our unworthiness. Nothing in any one of us can make us lovable to God.

This second wonder is more glorious than the first. How could we ever think that we are lovely to God? How could we presume that in our sin He would somehow be compelled to come and die for us? Our only value is the value He places on us. If there is anything good in us, it is only through His redemption.

These are two wonders. And together, they are all too wonderful.

From *Nearer, My God, to Thee* by Sarah Flower Adams

Raised by the Cross

Nearer, My God, to Thee,
Nearer to Thee!
E'en though it be a cross
That raiseth me...

When a cross raises me, nothing can keep me down. When a cross raises me, only resurrection life lies ahead.

The cross may have put Jesus in the tomb, but it raises me. The cross raises me to walk in newness of life, a life outside of myself, where others are more important than I am. It raises me to live astonished that I am still alive after the death of me.

"I am crucified with Christ; nevertheless I live" (Galatians 2:20). What a bizarre thing for Paul to say! What did he mean? If I am dead, it is the true me—united with Christ, loved by Him and living by faith in Him—who lives.

The cross killed the other guy, the guy I thought I was—the one who had to prove and lie and defend himself to try and save his own hide. Well, that guy's out of the way. The cross saw to that. The cross took care of him, and then it raised me.

From *When Quiet in My House I Sit* by Charles Wesley

Alone With the Book

When quiet in my house I sit,
Thy Book be my companion still,
My joy Thy sayings to repeat,
Talk o'er the records of Thy will,
And search the oracles divine
Till every heartfelt word is mine.

The Bible is more than a book. Over time it begins to have a voice of its own in my heart. I sense it breathing over me the way the Spirit first brooded over the waters before God spoke and light shined.

This book is alive. The words smile at me when Zaccheus climbs a tree. They glare when Nathan points his bony finger at David. They comfort me through the assurances of Paul. They challenge me through the Sermon on the Mount. They blow away the best science fiction in the visions of Ezekiel and the revelations to John.

Going through this book is like moving around a big house: It has so many rooms that I'm never quite sure I've been in them all. I double back and walk into the rooms I've been in before, but they look strangely new the second time, as they will the third. Every room is a place I'd like to stay in for a while and investigate. When I'm there, I talk to Him and ask and seek and ask some more.

I love it most of all when I find something in a room that seems as if it was put there just for me.

From *O Thou in Whose Presence* by Joseph Swain

The Look

He looks! and ten thousands of angels rejoice,
And myriads wait for His word;
He speaks! and eternity, filled with His voice,
Re-echoes the praise of the Lord.

What heavenly drama... based on nothing but a look and a voice! This is probably going on all the time up there. God looks, and a host of angelic beings hold their breath. He speaks, and the universe echoes His praise.

I imagine this happened a few times when Jesus was here on earth. Consider these examples:

- Simeon had been told by the Holy Spirit that he would not die without seeing the Messiah. The look of the infant Jesus in the temple told the old man that he was seeing God's promise fulfilled.
- The children saw the look on Jesus' face. They knew. That is why they had their own parade in His honor.
- Jesus looked at a fig tree once and it withered.
- He looked at Mary in the garden after His resurrection, and by His look, she knew who He was. Also after His resurrection, the two men on the road to Emmaus saw the look. Suddenly their eyes were opened and they realized who they had been with. "Were not our hearts burning within us while He talked with us on the road?" (Luke 24:32) they echoed.
- Jesus looked at Peter once, and he went off and wept bitterly.

He's looking at us today, and heaven and angels wait for our response.

From *O Thou in Whose Presence* by Joseph Swain

Welcome Back

Restore, my dear Saviour, the light of Thy face;
Thy soul-cheering comfort impart;
And let the sweet tokens of pardoning grace
Bring joy to my desolate heart.

The writer of this verse knew what it was like to come back to the Lord after being away for a time. Every Christian knows what this is like. No one can boast of a perfect record. We all have our moments. Yet when we come back, we can't believe how easy it is, how wonderful it is to again experience His grace. Because in our sin, we forgot the most important part of our relationship with God: that He forgives sin. God is down by the edge of the property straining His neck to see if we're coming home. The welcoming party has been standing by for days because He heard someone say we were on our way back.

Why do we stay away so long when we stray? Mostly because we believed Satan's second lie. His first lie was to get us to sin—to believe that God didn't really have our best interests in mind. His second lie was against the very character of God—that God doesn't want us back, that He's disinterested at best. And at worst, if He *is* looking for us, it's only because He is going to let us have it when He sees us. When we believe this lie, the last thing we will do is go back to Him.

But when we do go back and are met by His grace, we want to kick ourselves for ever having left in the first place. We would do well to think about all of this *before* we buy the first lie again. It would save us all a lot of grief.

From *O Thou in Whose Presence* by Joseph Swain

Skin Deep

O Thou in whose presence my soul takes delight...

We live in an age of titillating emptiness. We are a hollow humanity, hooked up and quivering to virtual reality. We are connoisseurs of pleasure with starving souls—experts on sex without any deep or lasting relationships. "When it comes to illusion," reads a current ad for cosmetics, "we're the realists."

"What else does this craving... proclaim," wrote Pascal in his *Pensées*, "but that there was once in man a true happiness, of which all that now remains is the empty print and trace? This he tries in vain to fill with everything around him—*and never have there been more of these things to choose from*—seeking in things that are not there the help he cannot find in those that are, though none can help, since this infinite abyss can be filled only with an infinite and immutable object—in other words, by God Himself," (italics mine).

Our culture can make us happy. It can give us pleasures, entertain us and make us laugh. But these joys only run skin deep. Only God can satisfy the deepest longings of the heart, and there is no pleasure equal to the delight of the soul in His presence.

From *And Now, O Father, Mindful of the Love* by William Bright

Satan's Finest Hour

For lo! between our sins and their reward,
We set the passion of Thy Son, our Lord.

Passion: the sufferings of Jesus on the cross. It was the last dark period before the end. From the last drop of wine in the upper room to the last drop from His side, it was the agony stretched out over the world, over the universe, and over all time.

As the earth shook, the sky went black and demons danced in His face, evil unleashed its fury on the Son of Man. But He did not fight back. It was Satan's finest hour. It was also Satan's *only* hour, and he knew it. So he would make this time as hideous as he possibly could. And when the soldiers came to break His legs, the God-man was already dead.

Set this passion in front of your sins today and forget it not. Take the wine and the bread, and remember His death as He taught us. Do it around your own dinner table, if need be.

Before your sin whispers its lies one more time, remember that its power is gone. The ransom has been paid. Satan already had his hour. His time is up. Don't give him another minute of yours.

From *Must Jesus Bear the Cross Alone* by Thomas Shepherd

Looking for the Next Hill (To Die On)

Must Jesus bear the cross alone
And all the world go free?
No, there's a cross for everyone,
And there's a cross for me.

Every believer has two crosses: the one Christ died on, which forever set us free, and the one we pick up and take along with us. We pick up our own cross voluntarily, though Jesus said we couldn't follow Him without carrying one.

I've always assumed this cross I'm to carry represented my death. But I wonder. Literally, the cross would not be my death, but the *instrument* of my impending death. This is the cross Jesus carried.

For me, this means I am always on the way to my death. I am always looking for a place to sacrifice myself. I am ready to lay myself down. I am looking for a hill to die on. Not that I don't die, but having died, I am always ready to die again. That is what this cross must mean. It is an attitude of service, an attitude of sacrifice.

It's easy to explain away spiritual death as a vague abstraction. It's so hard to understand it in the first place. But "carrying my cross," as in *looking for the next place to die*, is much easier to understand. Then it becomes an attitude—a way of thinking about myself in situations that demand something of me as a follower of Christ. And even in dying to myself, I would be picking up my cross again and looking for the next hill.

From *To God Be the Glory* by Fanny J. Crosby

Loving the World

So loved He the world that He gave us His Son...

God's love for the world is not a contradiction of John's call to do the opposite. "Do not love the world," John tells us, "or anything in the world" (1 John 2:15). John's admonition refers to the *ideas and philosophies* of the world. It refers, most likely, to the *appeal* of the world, which he describes as the lust of the eyes, the lust of the flesh, and the pride of life. Advertisers exploit these lusts when they announce that the car, house, stereo, or backyard barbecue we currently possess is obsolete. We now need a new one.

But God loved the world. This is not to say that God is talking about loving people and that John is talking about hating everything else. When God loves the world, He also loves the whole idea of the world. He created it, this material world, and He gave us the ability to make even material things for our use and enjoyment. Materialism is not necessarily inherent in the possession of things. Materialism is found in the lust for things and the perpetual discontent they produce when we try to fill our emptiness with them.

God likes the idea of the world populated with people using their minds to create and enjoy life. One day He's going to make such a world possible. He will even showcase it—the way it was supposed to be—for a thousand years. So He's not against the world as much as we think. He just knows that apart from Him we will fall prey to our own lusts and to the perversion of all the good things He gave us. He didn't die to save us from the world. He died to save us from our sin, and to show us how to put the world in proper perspective.

From *To God Be the Glory* by Fanny J. Crosby

Instant Pardon

The vilest offender who truly believes,
That moment from Jesus a pardon receives.

Finally, something about God that the modern world can appreciate! In an age of fax machines, cellular phones, ATM checking, and fast food, God long ago introduced instant pardons for the repentant sinner. No waiting necessary. No standing in lines. No credit checks. Just your name, your sin and your statement of faith, and *voilà*!... instant pardon. That's all there is to it.

This is welcome news for busy sinners like you and me. We can pick up our pardons any time—even on the run. We don't even have to gather up a huge pile of guilt to take with us to church or to confession—or worse yet, to lay on some hapless friend. Instant pardon means we can operate with clear consciences concerning the things we are aware of in our lives.

The next time you realize you have sinned in some way, don't dwell on it or beat yourself up over it. Don't try to feel bad for a while, as if you could pay for it with your sorrow. Just take it to God through any one of His convenient branch offices and receive your instant pardon, free of charge!

And remember to tell Him Jesus sent you.

From *To God Be the Glory* by Fanny J. Crosby

Who's the Vilest Offender?

The vilest offender who truly believes,
That moment from Jesus a pardon receives.

Pardon is something we are much more apt to receive than we are to give. This reminds me of the story Jesus told of the worker who complained about putting in a whole day's work and getting paid a day's wages, while others who didn't start working until noon received the same amount he did. When he questioned the master about this, the worker was reminded that he had been paid as agreed, and it was the master's prerogative to pay the others as he chose.

Jesus was telling us that what God does with His abundance of grace is none of our business. We are not the dispenser of grace in this world, and we do not decide who qualifies and who doesn't. We are not the judge, or even the jury. We are the convicted, and it is only His grace that has released us from the sentence for our sin. We don't have anything to say about anybody else.

All we know is, we have offended God and yet received His mercy. It should not matter to us who else receives it. If He let us in, He can let anybody in.

From *I Am His, and He Is Mine* by George W. Robinson

In Every Hue

Heaven above is softer blue,
Earth around is sweeter green—
Something lives in every hue,
Christless eyes have never seen.

Properly experienced, Jesus enriches life. Just think of the beginning of His ministry in the Gospel of John alone: Jesus performs His first miracle at a wedding reception, and just a few days later He clears the temple of money-changers and sacrifice-sellers. (That brought some color to His face, I'm sure.)

Then Jesus meets Nicodemus by night, and He talks of being born again as if He were talking in code. Later we find Him by Jacob's well, engaged in a private conversation with a Samaritan woman, telling her all about her many husbands. (That must have brought the color to *her* face!) He reveals more of His identity to her than He had to anyone up to that point. Then after a couple of remarkable healings, Jesus throws an outdoor picnic for five thousand guests.

Too often we forget who Jesus was and how He lived. We believe our own stilted caricatures of Him, rather than the Christ we encounter through the writings of those who knew Him. We make Him harmless, so that we can live safe, harmless, conforming lives and raise safe, harmless, conforming kids.

Faith is a colorful adventure. Christ is bound to bring some life into the drab color schemes of our everyday routines. If we let Him, that is!

From *May God Depend on You?* by W. C. Martin

God Believes in You

God requires the brave and true;
May the Lord depend on you?

Did you know that God has faith in you? That almost sounds sacrilegious doesn't it? We are the ones who are supposed to have faith in Him. We seldom hear any talk about God having faith in us, but He does. He wouldn't have chosen us to be His if He didn't. God wouldn't have picked me if He didn't believe in me.

He wouldn't have picked Abraham to be the father of many nations if Abram didn't have the courage to go to a land he knew nothing about. He wouldn't have chosen Moses to set His people free if He wasn't counting on him to go before Pharaoh—even if he *was* scared and stuttering. He wouldn't have crowned David as His favorite king (He named His Son after him—"Son of David") if He didn't believe that David's heart was after pleasing Him, even when he sinned. Down through history, God has worked with people He could count on.

God is depending on us. Let's not let Him down.

From *May God Depend on You?* by W. C. Martin

Gardening for Jesus

See, they come on sable pinions, come in strong Satanic might—
Powers come and dark dominions from the regions of the night.
God requires the brave and true;
May the Lord depend on you?

How about this picture to start off a seemingly normal, insignificant day? This is the stuff of science fiction thrillers, the stuff that sells thousands of books. This is little ol' you and me going up against the forces of the dark underworld. This is you going out to trim your hedges, while overhead legions of angels go hand-to-hand with Düreresque ghouls,* spearing and bleeding and shrieking in the quiet blue sky. Christian writers can retire painting pictures like this. Dürer already has.

And it's true—a battle *is* going on. We don't know exactly how it is happening or what it looks like. But a conflict is taking place, even as you read this. Someone would rather you not read this, and someone would rather I hadn't written it. Someone would rather you drag yourself miserably through this day, debilitated by so many mental anguishes that you are rendered inoperative for the kingdom of God.

But wait. God is depending on you. He called you to march in His army. He meant for you to share in this conflict. He doesn't need you waving a sword; He just needs you awake and alert, your eyes and your heart wide open to His will. It's His battle, and He's fighting it. But He's counting on you to show up for duty.

So get up and get out there, for heaven's sake... and trim those hedges!

**Abrecht Dürer was the sixteenth century German artist who was famous for etchings of angelic battles over peaceful landscapes.*

From *"Whosoever" Means Me* by J. G. Badger

Open Invitation

Whosoever cometh may the promise claim,
Precious blood of Jesus cleanseth every stain;
God so loved the sinner, oh! how could it be?
"Whosoever," said the Savior—that means me.

Remember raising your hand and waving it in the teacher's face? Remember jumping out of your chair because you wanted to be picked for a team or to be first in line for a field trip? This is how I picture our response to God's invitation to cleanse us from sin. Our hearts are eager to respond to God, and our awareness of our need for Him is what makes us eager.

This awareness removes any sense of what is the socially cool or "right" thing to do. We no longer care about our image. When we follow God, we must give up propriety. Responding to His grace includes a stripping away of pride. When we see our sin *and* God's invitation, we see the *only* thing to do. Intellectualism falls away, as does station and prestige in life. When we see the log in our own eye, we clamor to receive the gift God offers. We abandon ourselves to the grace of God.

"Whosoever," said the Savior. That leaves it wide open for anybody, doesn't it? *Whosoever*! There are no conditions to this invitation. Anybody who wants salvation; anybody who believes.... Hey, wait a minute! *That means me*!

From *Sing Praise to God Who Reigns Above* by Johann J. Schütz

A Very Thorough God

What God's almighty power hath made
His gracious mercy keepeth...

God makes and He keeps. And He also keeps what He makes. This is God's creating power and His sustaining mercy. His power made the world and all that is in it; His mercy keeps Him interacting in the world and ultimately redeeming it, in spite of the damage done by evil.

His creative power made man and woman in His image, and His mercy sent Christ to the cross to redeem us. His creative power has caused His Spirit to be born in us, and His mercy sustains us and keeps us day by day.

We would be saved by His death but lost to daily temptations were it not for His gracious mercy that keeps us. He is intimately involved in ushering His creation through the sanctification process until He presents us to Himself as a spotless bride. His mercy makes good on His promises, and His promises are true and "Amen."

He creates and He sustains. We can count on Him being there and following through. He is, all in all, a very thorough God.

May 13

From *Launch Out* by Albert B. Simpson

Getting Your Sea Legs

Launch out, launch out in the ocean divine,
Out where the full tides flow.

Nothing ventured, nothing gained. So goes the popular proverb. It is true of many things, and it is certainly true of God's mercy. We have to venture out into His mercy in order to know it.

Many of us talk about the mercy of God. We may even teach about it. But we are like coastline dwellers who admire the seascape and watch the sun set over the water every afternoon, but never go sailing.

When I launch into the depths of God's mercy, I no longer get to blame others—or myself—for my problems. When I launch into the depths of God's mercy, I lose my excuses, and I actually start going somewhere—somewhere I've never been before. A world of uncharted waters for my venturing soul opens up before me. I leave behind the small calculations of my shoreline existence and am buoyed by the ocean of His grace. New possibilities exist for me out in the ocean—new ways of seeing myself and those around me and new ports of call.

It's hard to allow yourself to receive something for nothing. It's hard to not measure yourself or compare yourself to others. It's hard casting rules and judgments overboard. It's hard to be thrown about in an uncontrollable sea of God's overwhelming love and mercy. But that's OK. In a little while, you'll get your sea legs.

From *Launch Out* by Albert B. Simpson

Out of Control

The mercy of God is an ocean divine,
A boundless and fathomless flood;
Launch out in the deep, cut away the shoreline,
And be lost in the mercy of God.

The hardest part of launching out is cutting away the shoreline. The idea of getting lost in the boundless ocean depths threatens us. We like knowing we are tethered. That way, we can experience the thrill of the ocean swells without the danger of getting lost in them. That way, we can also be on the boat without losing track of the shoreline. We always know where we are, and we can measure things better.

We feel the same about God's mercy. Sure, we want to experience His mercy. But we also want to control it. Many Christians—even those who talk a lot about the mercy of God—don't experience its fullness because they are unwilling to cut away the shoreline. Being lost in the mercy of God means to be just that: lost and out of control.

Being lost in His mercy means I can no longer control spirituality. I can no longer measure it for myself, so I lose the standard of comparison by which I can separate myself from other people. If I take this mercy as being all I need, then I am going to have to give it out in the same manner to anybody and everybody.

Most of us want it both ways. We want to be able to tether up to the Shoreline of Judgment while still getting a little roll in God's grace. It can't happen. We've got to launch out!

From *Let Me Come Closer to Thee, Jesus* by J.L. Lyne

Here and There

Thirsting and hungering for Thee, Jesus,
With blessed hunger here,
Longing for home on Zion's mountain—
No thirst, no hunger there.

Hunger here; no hunger there. Here, our lives are marked by hungers. We are hungry for much more than food. We are needy people, and we hunger for love. We hunger for attention and for something to satisfy the longings of our souls. Pascal said that God left us with an empty print and trace of Himself that we unsuccessfully try to match with anything but Him.

Sin here; no sin there. Here, we struggle, even though freed. We carry around a body of impulses trained to respond to all the wrong stimuli. We cannot retrain it; it is incorrigible. We must render it dead and carry it around, still twitching like a chicken without a head.

Crying here; no crying there. Much here makes us cry: pain, loss, war, disease, depression, abuse, rejection, lack of trust, addiction, wickedness. Tears come, and we cannot stop them. This is good.

Hope here; no hope there. Here is a switch. Hope is one good thing we have here that we will no longer need there. A heavenly possession we hold on earth that will vanish once we get to heaven.

Love here; love there. Notice there is no negative here. This is love—pure and true. We have it here; we will have it there, and it is the same in both places. Hunger, tears, sin, and hope will all pass away, but love will stay. This love is worth a heavy investment.

From *Let Saints on Earth in Concert Sing* by Charles Wesley

Shall We Gather At The River?

One army of the living God,
To His command we bow;
Part of His host hath crossed the flood,
And part is crossing now.

One big company of saints. One teeming horde of humanity fording the river between time and eternity. On the far side, the Savior pulls them into the waters. One by one, He steadies them, still wearing the soiled clothes of their earthly life. One by one, they enter: the old and feeble, the sick and maimed, the diseased and dying—now dead. One by one, they emerge on the other side, clothed in white raiment, shining like the sun, their faces young, bright, and alive.

It is an endless, slow, deliberate procession. Further back from the river are those who make their final approach escorted by angels. Further still are towns and cities of many who live as if the river weren't there. They acknowledge it only when one of their company has to leave, and then only reluctantly. Only the older ones long to gather at the river. The younger ones argue about whether it even exists.

But those who are a part of the company know—even the youngest. They know and they see with eyes of faith those who have gone before. They realize they are a part of a large host of believers, and they gain courage from the words, songs, and poetry of those who have gone on. A few have even started up the road, far enough to see the river and come back to affirm that it is all true. One day they will all gather on the other side.

From *Let There Be Light* by John Marriot

A Glimpse of Jesus

Health to the sick in mind,
Sight to the inly blind,
Oh, now to all mankind
Let there be light.

My New International Version has two renderings of John 1:9. The text reads: "The true light that gives light to every man was coming into the world." A footnote offers an alternative translation: "This was the true light that gives light to every man who comes into the world." Either way, it is clear that the light of Jesus Christ in some way and at some time touches everyone. This is hard to figure when you think of people born into cultures that have not yet heard the message of Christianity.

Taken literally (which is the way I like to take Scripture, unless the writing suggests it be taken figuratively, as in the poetic writing of David or Solomon), it would indicate that everybody born into the world—at some time or other—somehow encounters the light of Jesus Christ.

According to this verse, everybody knows *something* about the light of Jesus Christ. They may not know what it is—or was—but they have encountered it in some way.

So, rather than treat all unbelievers as blind to the light of Christ, we might try assuming Jesus is the light that everyone has seen somewhere, sometime. They just didn't know what or who it was. Everyone has had or will have a glimpse of Jesus. We might get further in sharing our faith if we attach what we know about Him to that glimpse, rather than treating others as if they know nothing at all.

From *Lo! What a Glorious Sight Appears* by Isaac Watts

When Death Dies

His own soft hand shall wipe the tears
From every weeping eye;
And pains and groans and griefs and fears,
And death itself shall die.

It's the final blow. The ultimate counterstroke. Ah, sweet twist of fate: when death dies—when that which has defeated man shall by its own hand be defeated.

We've seen it before in crime stories—how the bad guys turn on themselves in the end. The lesson in this is simple: You play with fire, you get burned. Live by the sword, die by the sword. It's the grand irony that after killing so many, death itself should die.

Death's days are numbered, and it knows it. Satan fell for the bait and took God's Son when the taking was good. This deed turned out to be Satan's ultimate undoing. I sometimes wonder if he was fooled at all by this—if he ever really thought he had Him. I figure the devil knew the plan all along, but he was just going to revel in as much glory and power for himself as he could, while he had the chance.

It is a comfort to know—especially on those occasions when we have to stare death in the face, for ourselves or for a loved one—that Jesus won the stare-down competition. He died and kept staring at death until He had risen again. Now death is doomed. Death is not the end. Never was. And soon, death too shall die.

From *Lo, Jesus Comes!* by Phoebe P. Knapp

Window of Opportunity

Sinners, come, while Christ is pleading,
Now for you He's interceding;
Haste, ere grace and time diminished
Shall proclaim the mystery finished.

The phrase *window of opportunity* is getting a lot of use these days. Dynamic economies and global markets in an ever-shrinking world mean that large sums of money can be made by the shrewd investor who is in a position to take advantage of financial windows of opportunity as they momentarily open and close. Brokers constantly have a "window" on this or a "window" on that.

In the much more serious economy of salvation, we are also in a window of opportunity. We are in the age of grace or the day of salvation. God is favorably disposed to His creation despite its waywardness and sin. Two thousand years ago, He sent His Son to pay the price for the sin of the human race, and because of this, He no longer counts transgressions against those who believe in Him (see 2 Corinthians 5:19). Fortunately for all of us, that window is still open and the offer of His Son still stands.

Some may think the window has been open for so long that it is hardly fit to think of it as a "window of opportunity." But in God's timetable, two thousand years is not even two days—or two seconds. That He has left the window open this long is a statement of His grace. Be warned: It is a window that could shut at any moment.

From *I've Found a Friend* by James G. Small

Love Comes First

I've found a Friend, oh, such a Friend!
He loved me ere I knew Him;
He drew me with the cords of love,
And thus He bound me to Him.

Love has bound me to Christ. No one can take me away from Him or Him away from me. His love, not mine, has sealed this relationship, and it is all I can do to love back. It may take effort to do the loving, responsible things that He asks of His children. But to love Him is effortless. His love inspires and energizes me to do His will.

Most of us learned something that is the opposite of this. We learned that love is based on performance. Love was withheld until we performed properly, and it was doled out as a reward. It was used as a way to manipulate our behavior. Love was misrepresented, and because of this we are suspicious of love *and* suspicious of God. But God is different than any earthly parent. Even those of us with genuinely loving parents have not known such pure love before.

Regardless of the kind of family we come from (some Christian families can be the most manipulative of all) we have to learn to be loved all over again. Everything starts here. Everything is different about this love. We have to learn to be loved first, as if we knew nothing at all. Only then can we learn to love as He loves.

From *Deeper and Deeper* by Oswald J. Smith

Into the Heart of Jesus

Into the heart of Jesus,
Deeper and deeper I go...

I read these words, and images abound. I see a space ship traveling at warp speed into a limitless universe. As stars and galaxies whiz by, the ship is trying to find the center of the universe but never reaches it. I also see a shepherd holding a lamb close to his heart as he makes his way through the rocky, thorny terrain from where the lost animal has just been rescued. And I picture the eyes of a man on a cross, eyes so deep that to look in them is to fall, down, down, down... never landing.

The most difficult image to describe is the one that captures the depth of His love, a picture that shows how far He was willing to go for all of us.

As a child, did you ever dream about falling and never landing? I can never remember actually landing. I would always wake up in the middle of a fall.

Falling into the heart of Jesus must be a little like this. We will never land. We will just wake some day and be in heaven, in the middle of His heart.

From *Holy, Holy, Holy* by Reginald Heber

No Greater Love

Holy, Holy, Holy!
Though the darkness hide Thee,
Though the eye of sinful man
Thy glory may not see...

We can't see Him in our sin, and He can't look upon us. He is pure in His thoughts, true in His heart, fair in His judgments, and consistent in word and deed. There is no darkness in Him at all—no charge anyone in the universe can bring against Him.

We, on the other hand, harbor dark thoughts. We conceal deceitful hearts and we justify biased judgments and inconsistent words and deeds. His presence lays us bare.

And yet His Son, who is the fullness of the Father, walked with our kind and talked with them. He ate with them and slept with them. They looked at Him and did not recognize Him. The one from whom they should have hidden their faces looked right back at them. Think of how much of Himself He concealed in order to walk among our kind and not be known.

And then think of how He was able to look upon us after all. How much did He see? How much did He know? How could He bear it? It must have been the knowledge that He would soon die to pay for what He saw that gave Him the courage to look—to look, and not cringe—and even to love.

So much glory was concealed in God's Son, so much love, forgiveness, patience, and tolerance. There has never been, nor ever will be, a greater love.

From *O Light That Knew No Dawn* by Gregory Nazianzen

Mind Overload

O Light that knew no dawn,
That shines to endless day...

Every light has a beginning. Even the sun was spoken into existence, and now each day has a dawn. But God is the light that always was and always will be.

We cannot fathom this because we are part of the created order. Everything created, including ourselves, had a beginning, a time when it was not, and then a time when it came to be.

We want to think of a time when God was not—some time when God started. That's how we see ourselves and everything around us. But God has no beginning. "In the beginning was God...." He was already there. Pre-existent. God is the eternal *I AM*. He mixes up tenses on us all the time. "Before Abraham was, I AM."

Now you can write this down on paper, and you can read it in your Bible. But try finding a spot in your brain to store such a thought. You'll discover there is no such place. Even thinking about these things as I write has thrown my mind into overload. We cannot think like God, nor can we imagine God—even the parts that He has revealed to us. Our thoughts carry us to a point beyond which we can only stop and worship. Make this one of those times.

From *Alas! And Did My Savior Bleed* by Isaac Watts

Disarmament

Thus might I hide my blushing face
While His dear cross appears;
Dissolve my heart in thankfulness,
And melt mine eyes to tears

It's almost a spontaneous reaction for sinners to fall apart when they get near the cross. They end up tongue-tied trying to explain the mixture of joy and shame they feel. This comes from finally being completely known and accepted.

Being known is what we all want. But we often have second thoughts once it actually happens. That is because being known necessitates full disclosure of who and what we are. Like a blooming flower that closes up when a dark cloud obscures the sun's light, we shrink back from the dark blot of our uncovered sin. But it must be this way if we are going to be fully known.

If it weren't for His love and acceptance, we would be stripped and humiliated by this process. But because of it, we are loved more deeply than we ever thought possible.

Most people love us for who we are trying to be. In other words, our performance shapes our relationships. But at the cross, we are loved for who we are. This is such a raw, unnerving experience that it totally disarms us.

From *Alas! And Did My Saviour Bleed?* by Isaac Watts

De-Worming the Hymnal

Alas! And did my Saviour bleed
And did my Sovereign die?
Would He devote that sacred head
For such a worm as I?

I found this particular version of this hymn in one of a stack of dusty Free Methodist hymnals stored in the gymnasium of a Christian camp outside Seattle. This is the original version, the one penned by Isaac Watts in the eighteenth century. Though I remember singing the hymn this way growing up, almost all the current hymnals have changed the last line to read: *For sinners such as I.* One now even reads: *For someone such as I.*

Cultural Christianity has de-wormed this hymn.

If Mr. Watts had wanted only to be a sinner in this hymn, he certainly had the ability to be able to state that. Instead, he called himself a worm. He was pointing out that Christ's death did not make rational sense. *Worm* was exactly the word Mr. Watts wanted.

The point of the song is this: Mr. Watts' own value could never justify the price paid by the suffering and death of Jesus, and neither could ours. Only love can explain it—a love given, not stimulated by any loveliness on our part.

Isaac Watts was purposely making a profound statement in this hymn: He was not worth saving, and neither are you or I. We find worth *in* our salvation, but our worth can never be the reason for our salvation. To say it is diminishes the magnitude and depth of God's love.

Personal amazement at the cross is the only appropriate human response to it. Anyone who is not amazed—who thinks they *are* worth saving—is not yet ready for the cross of Christ.

From *Breathe on Me, Breath of God* by Edwin Hatch

To Do, or Not to Do

Breathe on me, Breath of God,
Until my heart is pure,
Until with Thee I will one will
To do or to endure.

Most of the problems we face present at least two options· Change the circumstances or learn to live with them. Sometimes we have no choice in these matters, such as in times of sickness, injury, or loss of job, property, or a loved one. Other times we are living in difficult situations that we could do something about, but for one reason or another, we choose not to. In any case, there is no place in a believer's life for complaining or bickering, especially about what can be changed.

For several years now, I have been putting my family at risk economically by perpetuating a debt-producing, upside-down financial portfolio (that's a nice way to say that we spend more than we make). I can complain about this, but that wouldn't change a thing. I could live with it, but that wouldn't be endurance. At best, that would be stupidity. At worst, it would be sin. This is something I must treat as a bad habit and change. I don't get credit for suffering over what I can change.

What we know we must change, we call on the Spirit of God to help us change. What we can't change, we endure with His strength. With everything else, we ask for His breath on us that we might know the difference.

From *Breathe on Me, Breath of God* by Edwin Hatch

Holy Barbeque

Breathe on me, Breath of God,
Till I am wholly Thine,
Till all this earthly part of me
Glows with Thy fire divine.

Have you ever blown air on dying embers? I usually do it after we've had a barbecue and I want to resurrect the coals so the kids can roast marshmallows. Dead ash from previously burned charcoal flies away, revealing—if still alive—small glowing embers that brighten with each blast of air. There is a direct relationship between the brightness of the glow and the amount of air put upon the coals, be it from a fan or from bellows or from blowing by the mouth. (For a real shot of air, use the vacuum cleaner switched to the blowing end. This will produce a flame in no time.)

The breath of God on our souls does the same thing. First, it blows away the ash of former fires and reveals any life hiding under the quiet gray mounds of our spirits. Then it turns whatever life is glimmering into a bright glow that can at any minute burst into flame. God's breath can make even that which is earthly and temporal glow with His presence.

From *Breathe on Me, Breath of God* by Edwin Hatch

Breath of God

Breathe on me, Breath of God,
Fill me with life anew,
That I may love what Thou dost love,
And do what Thou wouldst do.

The Breath of God replaces the tired, overworked air of human excuses and rationalizations. With the Breath of God comes God's way of seeing things. It not only fills me with life, it also carries fresh blood to my brain and gets me thinking, feeling, and acting as God would.

Once there was a law—an old covenant—to get us to conform to the desires of God. Once there was a standard set from above that dictated to us what was important to God. We were required to keep the law whether or not we understood it. What was in our own hearts and minds was irrelevant to this task, as long as we obeyed.

Now we have a new covenant. Now He has put His law in our minds and written it on our hearts. Now He is our God and we are His people. No longer do we have to tell each other, "Know the Lord." In Christ, we all know Him, from the least of us to the greatest, for He has forgiven our wickedness and remembered our sins no more (see Jeremiah 31:31-34).

He has breathed in us His own breath that we might love what He loves and do what He would do. This law is not outside us to break our spiritual backs. It is inside, and it is here to lift up our backs and move us forward.

So put your shoulders back and breathe in more Breath of God. Go ahead, take a deep one. It's full of His heart, His mind, and His will for you today.

From *Marching with the Heroes* by William George Tarrant

The Overcomers

Marching with the heroes, comrades of the strong,
Lift we hearts and voices as we march along;
O the joyful music all in chorus raise!
Theirs the song of triumph, ours the song of praise.

Hebrews 11 is the famous hero chapter of the Bible—a Hall of Fame for believers. From Abel to the martyrs, it features the faith of ordinary people pitted against the unbelief and persecution from those around them.

Then in the next chapter of Hebrews, *we* enter the scene. We are encouraged to look at the sins and hindrances that so easily entangle us in light of these who have gone before. Those who conquered kingdoms, administered justice, gained what was promised, shut the mouths of lions, quenched the fury of the flames, and escaped the edge of the sword, while others who did not escape persecution considered their torture and imprisonment a road to a better resurrection.

I often read this account and think "Gee, and what did I do today? This isn't just faith. It's Indiana Jones and the Chapter of the Overcomers!" And then I remember that these are my heroes. These are the men and women who have gone before me and are in the choir singing around me right now. If I try, maybe I can hear them.

Theirs is a song of triumph, because they have already conquered. We are singing the same song. But from our side of eternity, it is a song of praise—a song to keep us going to the end. And with all these comrades cheering us on, how can we help but succeed?

From *Marching with the Heroes* by William George Tarrant

Heroes

So we sing the story of the brave and true,
Till among the heroes, we are heroes too.

Get ready to take your place among them—the heroes of faith, that is. We will be heroes some day. This momentary, light affliction is earning for us an eternal weight of glory far beyond comparison and a place in the heavenly choir.

You may not see yourself as a hero, but you are. We are all heroes in the making. The foes we are fighting are formidable, the temptations huge. The world, the flesh, and the devil are all lined up against us. Foes without and foes within. The lull of an affluent society wears a mask of deceit. The technology and materialism that surround us are addictive drugs. The self-deserving messages thrown at us daily are as potent as any idolatry. We fight a battle of believing that God and His Spirit and truth are actually there and are true. We fight to keep from falling over—or falling asleep.

Our foes are no less formidable than the martyrs' foes were. In some ways maybe even more so, since they are so hard to see. Sometimes, we stare them in the face and never see them. Simply believing is not simple at all. This is a life-and-death, heaven-and-hell struggle.

Be brave. This is your chance to join the real heroes.

From *O Word of God Incarnate* by William W. How

Leta's Bible Hour

O Word of God incarnate,
O Wisdom from on high,
O Truth unchanged, unchanging,
O Light of our dark sky.

At this writing, my mother is eighty-five years old. Throughout her life, she has had a passionate love for the Word of God. She has imparted this passion to me, and it is a most valuable gift for which I will be eternally grateful. Even when I fought with it, I still heard it—words that could be picked up later in life by the Spirit of God and infused with meaning.

My mother has memorized a lot of Scripture, and the words now flow from her mouth like honey. In my memory, I can still hear her quoting large amounts of Scripture over the telephone to people who had called her for prayer and counseling. She literally had a verse for every occasion. She also had a daily devotional time after breakfast every morning. My brother called it "Leta's Bible Hour." She would read four or five selections from various devotional books. It gives me great joy to know that she will soon be holding this book in her hand, reading for the first time what you are reading right now.

If you were to call her today, I can almost guarantee that this is the verse you would hear: "Thy words were found, and I did eat them; and Thy word was unto me the joy and rejoicing of mine heart: for I am called by Thy name, O Lord God of hosts" (Jeremiah 15:16, KJV).

Lord, give us a hunger for your Word that it might not be a duty to read or a drudge to remember, but a welcome feast for our hungry souls.

From *Be Thou My Vision*
(an Irish hymn translated by Mary E. Byrne)

"Thou" and "It"

Be Thou my vision,
O Lord of my heart.

Nowhere is the *good* more the enemy of the *best* than in the pursuit of God. One step short of God lay treasures gleaming with spiritual brilliance—all desirable to the spiritual seeker, and all good. Holiness, purity, godliness, moral character, goodness, humility, brotherly kindness, and, yes, even love itself can entice us away from what should be our focus.

Add to this the tangible marks of success and blessing that carry so much weight in our present society—things such as wealth and prestige, a good marriage and family, health, happiness, or even a place of importance in the church leadership—and our vision can get pretty cluttered.

Yet none of these things, holy and right as they may be, are meant to fill all our vision. None of them can be referred to as "Thou." Only One is big enough to fill all our vision and He is not an "It." When filling up our vision, "Thou" automatically guards against pride, prejudice, superiority, and self-righteousness—the straining of gnats and the swallowing of camels.

"Thou" fills up my sight and humbles my spirit. Be *Thou* my vision—*Thou* alone. Anything else is one step short.

From *Be Thou My Vision*
(an Irish hymn translated by Mary E. Byrne)

One

Thou in me dwelling,
and I with Thee one.

In the Gospel of John, Jesus is quoting a special prayer on behalf of his disciples and those who would believe through their message. (That would be us.) "Father," he said, "just as you are in me and I am in you. May they also be in us so that the world may believe that you have sent me" (John 17:21).

One with God. It seems so presumptuous, so audacious. How could I have the nerve to claim such a thing? I often find myself trying to explain it away. Maybe He didn't really mean this as a reality for today. Maybe it's something to look forward to in our completed state.

It's much safer for me to think of oneness with God as a future realization. Otherwise, I have to realize that God is around at times when I would rather not have Him around—such as when I'm contemplating a sin, enjoying a pity party, or immersing myself in self-indulgence. Not a happy thought. It's even worse to think of God being in me when I sin. His eyes see what my eyes see? His mind knows what my mind thinks? He does what I do?

If I *really* believed God is in me, it would change forever how I see, think, and act. If God is in me, what would He want to be doing today? Where does He want to go? What does He want to be thinking about? Are we in this thing together, or not?

From *Be Thou My Vision*
(an Irish hymn translated by Mary E. Byrne)

Just the Way You Are?

Naught be all else to me,
Save that Thou art.

Don't confuse this statement with the popular sentiment of our day: *Don't be anything but what you are*. Far be it from the hymn writer to be giving God the permission to be. Such a thing would border on blasphemy—as if God somehow needed permission from us to be Himself.

The hymn writer is simply saying that his soul, spirit, heart, and mind require nothing of God but to know Him. He is not asking God to fix his life or show him the way. He is not asking Him to make him well or take away his pain. He is not asking God to make him successful or improve his golf game. He's not asking for Him to save his marriage or make his kids honorable. He isn't asking Him to straighten out his thinking or get him a promotion. He isn't even requesting the strength to get through another day.

The great God of heaven and earth has invited us to ask anything of Him. Yet when we come into His presence, all we can do is ask to be filled up with the vision of God Himself. Suddenly, that is enough. In fact, it is more than we can contain. And should our vision indeed be filled up with God, we would know that we need nothing else beside.

From *Be Thou My Vision*
(an Irish hymn translated by Mary E. Byrne)

My Best Thought

Thou my best thought,
By day or by night...

My best thought yesterday was God.

I may have closed the deal or come up with an ingenious new way to filter coffee. Or maybe landed on the moon or written a book. I could have been elected to office, or perhaps I just made it through the last diaper change before I collapsed into bed....

But my best thought yesterday was God.

My best thought today will be God.

I'll get the garage cleaned up and my phone list called. I'll organize the storyboard so I can set out my work projects. I'll run my errands and I will spend some time with my children....

But my best thought today will be God.

I was just thinking, since it's likely that my best thought tomorrow will also be God, why not get started on *that* best thought right now?

From *O God, Our Help in Ages Past* by Isaac Watts

Reminders

O God, our Help in ages past,
Our Hope for years to come...

Our hope for the future is related to the help that we found in the past. If we have forgotten that help, the future may look hopeless. We must not forget all God has done for us.

The Israelites had their ways to address the problem of forgetfulness: Parents told their children stories of how God set His people free from Pharaoh's hand, how He led them across the Red Sea, drowning the pursuing armies behind them. They talked about how God fed and watered them in the wilderness and led them into the Promised Land. Some of those stories were made into songs to make them easier to remember.

God also had the Israelites erect memorial stones in places where He had met them in power and performed great miracles. The stones were put in place as reminders to them and to future generations of what God had done in the past. Those memorials gave them hope in their future.

Like the Israelites of old, we modern-day believers also need to erect reminders of God's goodness and power. Photographs, letters, journals, recordings, and family stories can all act as valuable reminders for you today. Tuck away some reminders for yourself of what God is doing for you now. Put them in a place where you might stumble upon them in the future.

I never know what's going to fall out of one of my books that I haven't opened in a while. Maybe I'll come across a memorial stone or a song. Or perhaps I'll find a picture of a God-given friend who was there at an important time in my life.

You never know how much you need such a reminder of God's goodness. You never know, that is, until you find it.

From *O God, Our Help in Ages Past* by Isaac Watts

God's Standard Time

A thousand ages in Thy sight
Are like an evening gone...

We should come up with a new time zone for God. We could call it *God's Standard Time*, or maybe *Heavenly Daylight Time*. Whatever we would call it, I'm sure it would have little to do with measuring out time as we know it here on this little green and blue spinning ball. The closest we could come to a comparison between *God's Time Zone* and our concept of time would be something like a thousand ages to a day.

This discrepancy between human timing and that of God's has a number of implications, and some of them are deadly. For example, it says something to those who mock God about His promise to return someday. We've all heard statements like, "Yeah, sure. It's been two thousand years since He left, and everything goes on as it always has." A person who says things like that needs to come to an understanding of *God's Time Zone*.

This discrepancy in the measurement of time should also say something to those who think they can continue to get away with evil without fear of punishment. God's reaction time may seem nonexistent to those who are unaware that He operates in a different time zone than we do. When someone forgets that God's timing is different than ours, that person can begin to believe judgment will never come and that he or she can do and say anything without fear of reprisal. *Those who think that way should look out!*

The difference between God's definition of time and ours also shows us something about how and when He responds to our prayers. We get impatient waiting for answers to prayer, thinking that God is just slow. But the Bible says that God is not slow as some of us count slowness. He's just in a different time zone. We might end up waiting a lifetime for what was for God a quick turn of the head.

From *O God, Our Help in Ages Past* by Isaac Watts

Under the Overpass

Under the shadow of Thy throne
Still may we dwell secure;
Sufficient is Thine arm alone,
And our defense is sure.

Somehow, the image of huddled humanity under the shadows of freeways popped into my mind as I read these lines. Homeless people in urban areas often camp under the overpasses of railroads, freeways, and major surface streets. There they find some protection from the weather, and at least one wall blocks the wind—but they are still vulnerable.

Some day we will stand next to God's throne in heaven. But right now, we are caught under it as if under an overpass of His glory. The hymn writer's words, *Still may we dwell secure*, seem to indicate a security that is at odds with the situation.

Believers have always been and will always be in some way spiritually homeless and vulnerable in this world. And as we huddle on earth under the shadow of His throne, the security of God may feel like nothing more than a cold night under a freeway.

We have no right to expect much more than this. God's security is not measured the way stocks, bonds, and certificates of deposit are. It is not even measured by the quality of one's life on earth. Security is measured by the faith He gives us to believe with, and by the reality of His arm, which is always sufficient protection from the cold.

From *O God, Our Help in Ages Past* by Isaac Watts

Around the Edges of the Mind of God

Before the hills in order stood
Or earth received her frame,
From everlasting Thou art God,
To endless years the same.

Imagine the earth receiving her frame. Imagine how God created the universe. An artist might have us picture God throwing mud from hand to hand until it was shaped into a ball, and then flinging it far into space. But a scientist might describe it another way, talking about bangs and explosions, heat and cold, and nuclear fission.

God is a God of order. He made His universe to be observable. The fact that the universe can be studied by the principles of scientific theory is proof that there is a pattern to all things. There's a frame around the universe. We live in a universe of order, not of chaos.

Some have reasoned that scientific theory eliminates God from the equation. But I think it just proves God is a good scientist. How could there be physical laws and order in the universe if there were not a designer behind it all?

I have been through enough late-night sessions preparing science projects with my children to know that the universe can be studied by hypothesis, experimentation, observation, and conclusion. And that comes out the same every time. The balls fall at the same rate, the calculation works each time, certain chemicals affect certain properties.... It all conforms to a grand order.

I always finish these sessions feeling like I have been dabbling on the edges of the mind of God. Science can be—and should be—a high form of worship.

From *O God, Our Help in Ages Past* by Isaac Watts

Presumed Insignificance

O God, our help in ages past,
Our hope for years to come....

Everybody's faith has a past and a future. This is a truth that brings hope to one's present state of affairs. It says that God has been involved with our lives long before we knew about it. It says that He has serious intentions for where He wants to take us in the future. Because He is God, those intentions are not empty promises.

Faith is a long-term project, and God is the producer and director of it. We have a past that shows that someone noticed us, and we have a future that includes an eternal retirement plan. Without the knowledge of God, these fundamental securities can't even be addressed. Otherwise, questions such as *Where did we come from?* or *Where are we going?* and *How long have we got?* leave gaping holes in the soul. These questions are the reasons many people distract themselves and avoid thinking very deeply. Without a presence in the past and a promise for the future, one is left with only a presumed insignificance in the present and an aching cry in the soul.

From *Jesus, Thy Blood and Righteousness* by Nicolaus L. Zinzendorf

Everyone and Anyone

Lord, I believe were sinners more
Than sands upon the ocean shore,
Thou hast for all a ransom paid,
For all a full atonement made.

Only one man died, but there was enough blood to cover everyone—so much blood that writers have referred to it as a fountain. They are saying that there is enough—enough blood for everyone.

Everyone and anyone is welcome. That is the theme of the cross. There is plenty of forgiveness to go around. No one is excluded. This is not a private club.

There are not some people in on this and some people left out. We talk sometimes as if this were the case, but we should not. In fact, we do not know for sure who is in and who is out. We cannot read the heart, and reading the heart is not our business if we could. All we know is there is enough forgiveness for everybody. There is enough blood for all the sin.

Everyone and anyone. God is no respecter of persons. Even as He died, He forgave His executioners. They did not even know who He was or what they were doing.

Get the word out. There is enough. The fountain is still flowing and the offer is good. We will never run out of blood to wash away sin. Don't leave anybody out.

From *We Have an Anchor* by Priscilla J. Owens

Connected at the Heart

And the cables, passed from His heart to mine,
Can defy the blast, through strength divine.

A cord connected through the heart is ten times stronger than any tie that binds. The new covenant we have through Christ is like this. It is a cable through the heart. "I will put my law in their minds," says the Lord, "and write it on their hearts. I will be their God and they will be my people" (Jeremiah 31:33). This is the strength of relationship. It is the new basis under which we come to God and do His will. We are connected at the heart. We no longer act out of law and fear, but out of love and response to Him—who He is and what He has done for us.

The law is like a thin cord wrapped around us a number of times. It is restricting and uncomfortable. It is also incapable of holding us for very long. It can be broken fairly easily, as the children of Israel did with the old covenant. "...they broke my covenant" (Jeremiah 31:32). You don't have to be a strong person to pop these little cords off your chest. They were never designed to hold anyway.

The cable through the heart is both stronger and freer. It is the way God wants to be with us—the way He planned it from the beginning. But He had to take care of the sin problem first before He could set us free to love Him.

From *We Give Thee but Thine Own* by George Matheson

The Power of Trust

All that we have is Thine alone,
A trust, O Lord, from Thee.

To enjoy anything, one must learn to hold it lightly. This is one of the hardest lessons to learn because it runs against human nature. From infancy, we learn to get what we need by crying for it. From our childhood, we learn to get by bullying, lying, and cheating. Older children learn to trick younger ones out of things. Second and third siblings learn to outsmart the older and bigger. We continue these patterns as adults, and we become more adept at concealing them.

If we're lucky, somewhere along the way we learn the power of trust. It might come through a relationship in which two people are so confident in their love for each other that they do not need to be "hooked" or "pinned" or "going steady." Nor do they need to be suspicious of other relationships. In this kind of relationship, one learns that trust is invisible strength. It is a cord connected through the heart that is ten times stronger than any tie that binds.

Not only is it strong to trust, but it is equally strong to be trusted. It brings out the best in us. "Love believes all things." It makes us rise to the occasion. It gives us respect. This is the way God deals with us. He has entrusted us with His creation, our lives, and the lives of those around us. When this is understood properly, it should bring out the best in us all.

From *The Strife Is O'er* by Francis Pott

Out of Business; Open for Business

He closed the yawning gates of hell;
The bars from heaven's high portals fell;
Let hymns of praise His triumphs tell.

What a crash! He closed up hell and broke open heaven on our behalf. He transacted eternal business when He did this. The Son of God descended into hell to satisfy the requirement of His Father's justice, and then He shut the gate forever for you and me. "He who descended is the very one who ascended higher than all the heavens, in order to fill the whole universe" (Ephesians 4:10). See, He fills the whole universe! No place is beyond the scope of His presence—no place He hasn't been before.

Hear the big gates slam shut below! Hell is closed! Out of business, I hear. It can no longer place any claim on one who is hidden with Christ. Hell has already extracted its worst from Jesus, and He promptly walked out and shut the gates behind Him. We will never know what He knows about this place—one piece of knowledge we are happy to be barred from knowing!

Hear the bars collapse from heaven and tumble down! Heaven is open! Open and waiting to receive us. He knows your voice, and the angels are familiar with your name. Reservations have been made, and there will be no confusion or mix-up at the entrance. They're waiting for you, and they have forgotten your sin. Jesus left it down below before He closed the gate.

From *The Strife Is O'er* by Francis Pott

To Live and Sing

Lord, by the stripes which wounded Thee,
From death's dread sting Thy servants free,
That we may live and sing to Thee.

To live and sing—that is what you are here to do. No need to wonder over purpose. *To live,* and that is enough. To live and not die. To live and not give up. To live, meaning to go through life no matter how hard it is. To live because He has a reason for your being alive and paid a high price to keep you that way. He knows what He wants accomplished in and through your life, and it can only happen with you alive. So live!

You may not see the point all the time. You may not see it right now. But your purpose is to live, to make it when so many aren't making it—when so many have no reason to. It is not that complicated. Live! Stay alive! He wants you alive for one reason: to live for Him.

Oh yes, and He wants one more thing: He wants you to sing. Can you do that? He wants you to live and He wants you to sing while you're living. It really is pretty simple when you get right down to it.

From *The Strife Is O'er* by Francis Pott

Holy Joy

The powers of death have done their worst,
But Christ their legions hath dispersed;
Let shouts of holy joy out-burst!
Alleluia!

Down with the joyless pietist! Away with the heavy-spirited religionists—tinkerers in the boring trade of gnat-straining! Banish the furrowed brow forever! Squelch the long "o" in "hoooooly" and let out the "Ho!" of holy joy! Let the saved sinner sing! Empty the streets and bring in the uninvited! Pick the poor publican up off his knees in the middle of his prayer and dance with him! Let the heavens ring with joyous laughter!

The Worst have done their worst, and it simply wasn't bad enough. Not bad enough to shut Him up. Not bad enough to hold Him down. Not bad enough to stop the music. The Worst have done their worst, but all that did was throw open the door to anyone who wants to come and enter into the joy... Holy joy!

From *Praise, My Soul, the King of Heaven* by Henry Francis

The Forgetfulness of God

Praise Him, still the same as ever,
Slow to chide and swift to bless...

BLESS BLESS BLESS BLESS BLESS CHIDE BLESS BLESS
BLESS BLESS BLESS CHIDE BLESS BLESS BLESS BLESS
BLESS CHIDE BLESS BLESS BLESS BLESS BLESS BLESS
BLESS BLESS CHIDE BLESS BLESS BLESS BLESS CHIDE
BLESS BLESS CHIDE BLESS BLESS BLESS CHIDE BLESS
BLESS BLESS BLESS BLESS BLESS BLESS BLESS CHIDE
BLESS BLESS BLESS CHIDE BLESS BLESS BLESS

If you papered your wall with a rendition of how God treats His children, it might look something like this. God has always treated His children this way.

Fortunately for us, God is always inequitable when it comes to blessing and chiding. God revealed this about His nature to the children of Israel as early as the second commandment, when He told them: "I, the Lord your God, am a jealous God, punishing the children for the sin of the fathers to the third and fourth generation of those who hate me, but showing love to a thousand generations of those who love me and keep my commandments" (Exodus 20:5-6).

God chooses to remember the things that bring Him joy longer than those that sadden Him. This is great news for us, and should be cause for thankful worship. With this kind of God, we have a chance.

From *Praise, My Soul, the King of Heaven* by Henry Francis

Grace and Mercy

Alleluia! Alleluia!
Widely yet His mercy flows!

Grace and *mercy* are two terms that are often used interchangeably in Christian circles, when in fact they are distinctly different concepts.

Grace is undeserved favor, God's free gift of salvation. It is also the common graces we all live under, whether or not we are believers. "He causes His sun to rise on the evil and the good, and sends rain on the righteous and the unrighteous" (Matthew 5:45).

Grace is receiving what we don't deserve. Mercy, on the other hand, is *not* receiving what we *do* deserve. Mercy gets us off the hook of judgment, while grace puts us in a relationship with God on a basis other than the law.

Mercy is the opposite of judgment. "Listen to my cry for mercy...." said David. "Do not bring your servant into judgment for no one living is righteous before you" (Psalm 143:1-2). In other words: *Don't think about that part of yourself that is holy and righteous and just. Instead, think about that merciful part of yourself, Lord, when you think about me.*

We must always remember to be as eager to give these wonderful gifts as we are to receive them. To have mercy shown to us and then turn around and wreak judgment on others is an offense to Jesus. We remind ourselves of this every time we pray the Lord's prayer: "...and forgive us... as we forgive." The church is a congregation of forgiven sinners—each as grateful as the next at the grace and mercy that has been shown to them.

From *Jesus, I Come* by W. T. Sleeper

The Opposite of Sin

Out of my sin and into Thyself,
Jesus I come to Thee.

The opposite of sin is not the absence of sin. It is not even righteousness or holiness or perfection. The opposite of sin cannot be described in terms of behavior, character, or conduct. The opposite of sin is much more exciting than any of this. Righteousness, holiness, and perfection are actually quite boring apart from a relationship with God. But being with Jesus, who is the opposite of sin, is never boring.

Turning from sin does not mean living a life of resistance. Stopping sin, like stopping smoking or drinking or drugs, is almost impossible to do. And once done, it has to be done over and over again. But we are not forgiven of our sin to live in a morally sterile vacuum. We leave our sin for something so much better: a relationship with God. If you somehow were able to stop sinning, but never got into a relationship with Christ, you would be the most miserable of all people.

Getting into Jesus is not the same as stopping sin. It is no longer *having* to sin. When you're into Jesus, you don't want to be into anything that He is not into. You want to be with Him, where He is. Since He is not where sin is, you are not there either. You want more than simply to resist sin; you want to be with Jesus, because Jesus is the opposite of sin.

From *Search Me, O God* by Albert B. Simpson

The Test

Oh, let my work abide the testing day
That shall consume the stubble and the hay...

"And the fire will test the quality of each man's work. If what he has built survives, he will receive his reward. If it is burned up, he will suffer loss; he himself will be saved, but only as one escaping through the flames" (1 Corinthians 3:12-15).

This describes a judgment of works, not of righteousness. This has nothing to do with whether we are pleasing to God—nothing to do with salvation. It has to do with what we built on earth and how we built it. The foundation—Jesus Christ—has already been laid. What's at issue here is what we build upon that foundation.

If the foundation is Jesus Christ, then what we build on it has to do with Him as well in order to last. It can't be our idea only.

A lot of what has been done "for God" will not last into eternity because it was not done "in Christ." God doesn't need anything done for Him. He is building His church on the foundation of Jesus Christ and His finished work on the cross. What is done "for God" usually has human ego attached. What is done "in Him" is the natural outgrowth of being a part of Him, like being a branch on a vine. What we do while attached to Him is what will survive the fire.

From *Joyful, Joyful, We Adore Thee* by Henry van Dyke

Time-Lapse Faith

Hearts unfold like flowers before Thee,
Opening to the sun above.

I have vivid memories from my childhood of time-lapse photography in the Moody Science Films that were shown on Sunday nights at my church.

To make these films, a stationary camera exposes one frame every few seconds over a period of time. Then the pictures are sped up and viewed as if they were movies. Thus, an entire day can pass over an Arizona desert in the span of a few minutes. Or a sports stadium can fill up with people and empty in a matter of seconds. But the pictures I remember most are those of flowers instantaneously opening, literally exploding from within with petals and pollen. Those images always come to mind when I hear this lyric.

There is nothing more delicate or more beautiful than a heart opening to God. Pretense falls away, fear and suspicion are banished, pride and self-consciousness vanish. Sensitive parts of the inner flower that have never seen the light of day are laid bare to the eye of the beholder.

In a flower, this is part of the course of nature. But in a heart, it is something only God can bring about. It is not natural for the human heart to open this way. It is more likely to protect itself, to close in on itself in a tightly formed bud.

This opening doesn't happen overnight. But I wonder what our lives would look like captured by the cameras of faith and sped up over time. It might encourage us to see that something *is* happening after all.

June 21

From *Joyful, Joyful, We Adore Thee* by Henry van Dyke

Openings

Hearts unfold like flowers before Thee,
Opening to the sun above.

We do not open our hearts easily. We are careful about this. We have opened our hearts and been hurt before. We have trusted in the wrong giver before and have been handed a stone.

But that doesn't deter God. He is like the sun. Day in and day out, He warms and softens and ensures that the delicate opening flower will be touched and rewarded with His presence. He is persistent. Each day, His warm, loving rays reach us again, even if the clouds hide some of His light. And we open a little bit more.

And suddenly—we can't even remember how it happened—there we are: arms out and all aghast, bashful in the glory of sunlight—beautiful and full, and bouncing with life on the winds of the Spirit.

From *Joyful, Joyful, We Adore Thee* by Henry van Dyke

A New Weather Report

Melt the clouds of sin and sadness;
Drive the dark of doubt away...

Some days it seems I have a personal cloud that follows me wherever I go. Usually I don't notice it until I've been under it for a while. Those who know me best say it wrinkles my forehead and curls my eyebrows.

Often, this dark cloud is not formed by my circumstances. It is not created by high and low pressure areas around me. Nor is it shaped by the wind. Rather, I forecast this bad weather report with my circumspection—the little circle of guilt and doubt that I draw around myself that determines how I look at life.

This does not have to be. Neither you or I have to live under a cloud of sin and doubt.

It's possible to put our hope and trust in God, step out from under our dark cloud, and laugh at ourselves a little in the process. We need to take our sin seriously but ourselves less seriously. I fear we are just the opposite about this: too casual with sin and too serious about ourselves.

If you're under a cloud today and it's your own doing, then you can do something about it. There is forgiveness and faith. There are promises in the Word. There is a Holy Spirit to give you strength. Step out from under that cloud, please, and get a new weather report!

From *Joyful, Joyful, We Adore Thee* by Henry van Dyke

Animation

Field and forest, vale and mountain,
Blossoming meadow, flashing sea,
Chanting bird and flowing fountain,
Call us to rejoice in Thee.

What an invitation! Who could refuse such a thing?

It is a recurring theme in Scripture and in the hymns that creation knows its Creator. The psalmist tells us that the mountains break forth into singing and all the trees clap their hands. Day to day the earth is chattering about the glory of God, and night to night reveals who He is. Jesus told the Pharisees that the rocks could be expected to cry out if the children were hindered in their praise of Him. Paul tells us that all creation is presently groaning under the weight of our fallen nature, since it has been subject to the consequences of our sin.

In other words, the Word of God animates creation. I have been in the presence of a grove of redwoods and felt wisdom bearing down on me. And I have been thrown around by the heavy surf and felt its punishment. And I have stood on a mountain top and felt the strong wind blow so hard I could lean into it and trust it to hold me. And though I was too far away to hear them, I did once see a hillside of golden aspen trees applauding something.

Doesn't all this commotion make you want to join in?

From *Joyful, Joyful, We Adore Thee* by Henry van Dyke

With the Best of 'Em

Mortals join the mighty chorus
Which the morning stars began...

"Excuse me, I think I'm in the Milky Way section. Yes, that's right... first bass—baritone, actually. I'm a little unfamiliar with this music. How do you read this? Am I holding it upside down or something? Pardon me, I hate to bother you again, but is that the director over there? Who are we supposed to watch? And do you think you could you move over a bit? You're shining on my music here and I can't see for the glare...."

We seem a little out of place in this company of stars. But do we ever have a grand significance in the big plan! The stars have their say. The angels have theirs, and the mountains and trees, too. But none quite like us. We are in God's image, you see. We are the apple of His eye. And though right now we know what it is like to fall and just how far down we can go, we will also know what it is like to get up, to soar, to take our place in the heavens and sing with the best of them.

And we will sing about the one who covered this great distance to save us. We will sing praises to the one who came from the heights of heaven and went lower than we will ever go, so that we would be rescued.

So move over, you blazing, blinking ball of fire. I believe I have a solo coming up!

From *Jesus, Plant and Root in Me* by Charles Wesley

A Quiet Mind

Jesus, plant and root in me
All the mind that was in Thee;
Settled peace I then shall find;
Jesus is a quiet mind.

A noisy mind is restless—unsure of itself and unsure of truth. A noisy mind is suspicious—unable to trust anyone because it can't be trusted itself. A noisy mind clatters with doubt and insecurity. It alters itself regularly to match or clash with the climate of belief or unbelief around it. A noisy mind always has to prove something.

A quiet mind is sure of itself and sure of the truth. It is strong and trustworthy. It is quiet because it has nothing to prove. A quiet mind knows the truth will defend itself, so it rests on the self-evident God.

A quiet mind doesn't have to explain itself or its actions. It does not have to speak for itself, so it speaks for someone else—for the truth and for God. When neither of these will serve the situation or be served respectfully by it, a quiet mind stays quiet. Jesus refused to participate in the noisy ramblings of mind games.

A quiet mind does not waste words. It does not try to be cute or clever, and neither is it simplistically obvious. It lets itself out in pieces and parables, so that noisy minds won't be able to ingest the truth until they quiet down long enough to figure out what it is.

Would that we had more quiet minds.

From *Lord, in the Morning Thou Shalt Hear* by Isaac Watts

"...And Will Look Up"

Lord, in the morning Thou shalt hear
My voice ascending high;
To Thee will I direct my prayer,
To Thee lift up mine eye.

"Give ear to my words, O Lord; consider my meditations. Harken unto the voice of my cry, my King and my God. For unto Thee will I pray. My voice shalt Thou hear in the morning. O Lord, in the morning, will I direct my prayer unto Thee and will look up" (Psalm 5:1-3 KJV).

Two things strike me about these verses: the bold statement of intent to pray and the waiting for a response. "My voice shalt Thou hear in the morning...." Before speaking so confidently to God, you'd have to be sure you could follow through on your words. How audacious. And yet the Lord seems to enjoy such audacity when we worship Him. Consider Jacob. He wouldn't let God go until he got the blessing he was after. And God let him hold on. We have no indication God was offended by Jacob's approach.

And this verse pictures expectation. I will direct my prayer to you and wait for a response, the psalmist says. I will direct my prayer to you and look up. In other words, if God doesn't answer right away, this man will still be looking up. Not a bad way to spend a day, actually. We should do the same. Why not direct our prayers to Him in the morning and then spend the rest of the day looking up? He might not answer us right away... just to keep us looking in the right direction.

From *Lead, Kindly Light* by John Newman

One Step Enough

Keep Thou my feet! I do not ask to see
The distant scene—one step enough for me.

"Thy word is a lamp unto my feet," says the psalmist in Psalm 119:105 (KJV). The hymn writer would add that this is as far as the light needs to go. We only need enough light to see the next step. No further.

There is wisdom in this. Suppose we could see the distant scene. Suppose we could see our lives mapped out before us. If they were full of hardship, suffering, and pain, we would wonder how we would be able to endure it. We would be overcome with the weight of what we would have to bear long before we would need to bear it. And if our paths were laden with gladness and success and joy, we would lose patience waiting to get there—and we would lose sight of the present.

The distant scene is most likely full of both hardship and joy. Knowing what's ahead will not help me live my life now. What I need is strength to endure the present troubles and sight to see the present joys.

All I need to know about the distant scene is that this light will still be with me when I get there.

From *Lead, Kindly Light* by John Newman

Disclaimer

I was not ever thus, nor prayed that Thou
Shouldst lead me on;
I loved to choose and see my path; but now
Lead Thou me on!

We all have plans for our lives, some bigger than others. Whether our plans are fulfilled doesn't really matter, because our plans make us feel as if we are in control. When we come to Christ, however, this changes. Suddenly we must consider not only what we want, but what He wants for us as well. Sometimes these wants are in conflict.

We resolve this conflict by starting to see things His way. In other words, we learn to want what He wants. This is not a simple adjustment. It usually involves time and struggle. It's not that He necessarily wins, either. But as we begin to think more like Him, the things He wants become the things we want, too. In the end, we both win.

There's no way we can always be certain about the paths we choose, no matter how close we are to God. He does not give us a blueprint for our lives. "In his heart a man plans his course, but the Lord determines his steps" (Proverbs 16:9). That means that the Lord may end up leading our steps somewhere that was not in our plans. (After all, we can only make our plans based on what we know at any given time.) That's why it's OK to make plans. We just need a disclaimer at the bottom of all of them: *These plans are temporary and subject to change at any moment by the Holy Spirit.*

From *In the Cross of Christ I Glory* by John Bowring

Collision Course at Golgotha

In the cross of Christ I glory,
Towering o'er the wrecks of time...

Time has seen many great wrecks—train wrecks, ship wrecks, auto wrecks, airplane wrecks, space shuttle wrecks. These are collisions of mass and metal that have cost many human lives. But one great collision towers over them all. At the cross, God and sin collided, and God prevailed.

Sin was transporting all of humanity on a highway to hell. Time rushed headlong to the Place of the Skull, where the awesome crash would take place. While God's Son, Jesus, had been walking the earth for three years teaching, healing, and performing miracles, He and sin had been on a crash course at Golgotha all along.

Other than the sky going black and the earth giving up its graves, what happened when God and sin collided at the cross? For days all lay in rubble. The human race was hanging in the balance. It was as if time stopped. But on the third day, a stone moved on its own, a blinding white light burned from the center of a tomb, and God walked out. When God and sin collided, only God walked away from the scene.

From *Holy Bible, Book Divine* by John Burton

Something from God I Can Hold

Holy Bible, book divine,
Precious treasure, thou art mine;
Mine to tell me whence I came;
Mine to teach me what I am.

The Bible is truly a precious treasure. It is something from God that I can hold. I don't attribute any mystical magic to it, but I see the Bible as a hand-held vehicle of revelation to me. The Holy Spirit can speak through these black and white pages.

Many practical sacrifices have brought this book into my hands—many have labored over its translation, prayed over its contents, refused to alter its words, and died to preserve its integrity. All of this is cherished when I open it.

The book itself will not do anything for me. Swearing on it will not make me tell the truth. Putting another book on top of it will not disgrace it. The Bible is not alive in the same way Christ is alive in me. But it came from God, and its words were inspired by the Holy Spirit. In this way, it is unlike any other book. To those without the Spirit of God, this book lies dormant. To those with the Spirit, it can burn a hole through their very being.

The Bible is something from God you can hold. Cherish it and learn from it.

From *Begin, My Tongue, Some Heavenly Theme* by Isaac Watts

Just a Whisper

O might I hear Thy heavenly tongue
But whisper, "Thou art mine!"

All who have come to know and love God must have, at one time or another, longed to hear His audible voice. No big lightning bolt for me, though. But a real whisper now and then would be nice—something I could not explain away as my imagination or my own construction. *Is it too much to ask, Lord, for just a whisper*? How often I have asked for such a thing, and it seems to me not an unreasonable request. Yet I have still to hear it.

I welcome these lines from the hymn writer as proof that I am not alone in this wish. On the other hand, I think of how solid my faith has become, even though my wish has never come true. I can remember wondering twenty years ago what it meant that faith was "the substance of things hoped for" (Hebrews 11:1, KJV). Today, I know confidently what that means, though I can no more explain it than I can hear my name called from heaven.

Yes, I know this "substance" as if I could touch it. I know what it means to consider the spiritual things of God as more certain than the things that I can see or hear or touch. I know what it means to be more sure of God than I am of my next breath.

But still, just once in a while, I think of how lovely it would be to hear God's whisper, to know He spoke to me in space and time. To know sound waves were displaced near my ear without any physical cause.

From *Begin, My Tongue, Some Heavenly Theme* by Isaac Watts

A Builder's Promise

His very word of grace is strong
As that which built the skies;
The voice that rolls the stars along
Speaks all the promises.

The same power and presence that are evidenced in the creating and the maintaining of the universe are made available to me by faith on a day-to-day basis.

That's a solid guarantee. If God delivers on the universe, then we can be confident He will deliver on His promises, such as "I will never leave you nor forsake you," or "I will come back and take you to be with me," or "He who believes in me will live, even though he dies," or "Whoever believes in me, streams of living water will flow from within him..." to name a few.

If God's voice is still rolling the stars around—maintaining the universe, that is—then it can still maintain its promises to me. The voice that spoke creation into being is the same voice that keeps it going, and is the same voice that speaks to me in promises I can rely on.

God never forgets. He never sleeps.

I have a friend who always tells me that I can go to bed at night and give my problems over to God because "He's going to be up all night anyway."

That's because His light never goes out.

From *Begin, My Tongue, Some Heavenly Theme* by Isaac Watts

Begin, and Never End

Begin, my tongue, some heavenly theme
And speak some boundless thing...

Go ahead, tongue, begin. Start anywhere and try to find the last word in the heavenly realms of God. Try to sound His praise until there is nothing more to be said. Still, you will never reach the end of it. Start anywhere and work any direction. You will never run out of reasons to praise.

Begin, my tongue, some heavenly theme. Try grace alone, and you will speak volumes of truth and sing from ten thousand songs. And when you are exhausted from this, though you will not have exhausted grace, go on to truth, just to hear another side of God's wisdom. And while there, take up wisdom as a theme in itself. How unsearchable and unfathomable His ways.

Then bounce around in His glory for an eon or two, or merely take the light of one small star—the very smallest in His twinkling universe—and begin to tell the glory of that.

Begin, my tongue, some heavenly theme of how the Son of God came down and became the Son of Man. And tell the stories of those redeemed, which number like the stars and the sands of the sea. Tell the story of each one and how all the stories intertwine, layer upon layer, in the details of their lives.

Begin, my tongue, some heavenly theme. Begin, and never end.

From *Love Lifted Me* by James Rowe

Somebody's Got to Do It

He your Saviour wants to be,
Be saved today.

Something about this strikes me in a new way today. Jesus *wants* to be my Savior. I guess I know this, but it still catches me off guard sometimes. When I consider realistically the pain and the sorrow Jesus went through to save me, it's easy to forget that He *wanted* to do this.

Jesus was not like Jonah, a reluctant prophet on an obligatory mission to salvage something out of the mess we got ourselves into. This is Jesus the Christ, who had this whole thing planned from the beginning.

Jesus *wants* to be my Savior. He wants to be your Savior, too. Love drove Him to this. The love and the joy and the pain are all mingled together in Him and cannot be unraveled. He *wanted* to walk in our shoes. He *wanted* to take our place. And He *wanted* to die for you and for me.

He wants to set us free. He wants to forgive us and have mercy on us. He wants to share His life with us, walk with us, and talk with us.

He was invested in this all the way to the cross. Nobody could have gone through all He went through without wanting to. And no one would choose to die if they didn't have to. No one, except Jesus.

From *A Glory Gilds the Sacred Page* by William Cowper

One-Way Light

A glory gilds the sacred page,
Majestic, like the sun;
It gives a light to every age;
It gives, but borrows none.

The Word of God shines with its own light. Through the Spirit of God, it illumines all that it touches. It casts its light upon all generations, and borrows nothing. It does not blend with any other supposed revelation. It is not the composite result of primal religious cults that worked their way into the nation of Israel. Rather, it is revelation handed down from the hand of God. If there are any similarities between this book and surrounding pagan religious origins, it is because of its influence on culture, not the other way around.

God's Word is not an evolving light. It does not give and take from its culture. It is not understood in one generation as one thing and something else in the next. It is not a relative light or a situational light. It can be studied and understood in any age as the unchanging truth.

Revelation pours out from this book, and it does not pour back in. God's Word does not mix with anything. It is itself: the Word of God—a strong beacon of light emanating from the sacred page—shining down through all generations and all cultures into our hearts and minds, turning on the light for us to see.

From *Praise the Savior* by Thomas Kelly

Desperate Straits or a Desperate Heart

Keep us, Lord, O keep us cleaving
To Thyself, and still believing...

Sometimes I wonder if God keeps us in suspense so we'll stay close to Him. I wonder if there are times when God chooses not to do what we ask, when He decides it's best *not* to fix the problem or solve whatever it was that made us call upon Him in the first place.

Why would God remove from us the thing that made us cling to Him in the first place—especially if we would not cling to Him without it? Wouldn't that be the worst thing He could do? To heal us only so we could walk away well? Or to fill us only so we could walk away full? To answer us so completely that we would not need to call Him again?

In other words, if hardship is the only thing that keeps us cleaving, then for Him to refuse to rush to our aid would be answering the deeper request of our hearts.

There is a better way, of course: We could grow up and cleave to Him out of sheer love and abandonment—having less to do with desperate straits than with a desperate heart. Then maybe we would be getting at what this relationship is all about. Until then, if we don't cling on our own free will, He may give us a little incentive. He loves us too much to let us go.

From *Praise the Savior* by Thomas Kelly

He Will Not Forget

Neither force nor guile can sever
Those He loves from Him.

Two babies with their umbilical cords still attached were recently discovered on two different days, washed up on the beaches of south Orange County, California. It is awful to think these infants had been abandoned by their mothers. But with no reports of accidents coming in, that is the most probable explanation.

"Can a mother forget the baby at her breast and have no compassion on the child she has borne?" asks Isaiah. "Though she may forget, I will not forget you! See, I have engraved you on the palms of my hands" (Isaiah 49:15-16).

From his vantage point in history, Isaiah did not know just how that engraving would be accomplished or what it would look like. We do. We know that Christ's palms were engraved with a hammer and a nail. We know the soldier who did it was no artist, and he did a very messy job. We are engraved on the palm of his hands—forever. Nothing can change this. Nothing can sever us from Him.

Yes, a mother may forget. But He will not forget.

From *Great Is Thy Faithfulness* by Thomas O. Chisholm

Better Than Pardon

Pardon for sin and a peace that endureth,
Thine own dear presence to cheer and to guide...

Pardon. It is a term we don't use very often. Vietnam War protesters received pardons at the end of that difficult conflict, and U.S. President Gerald Ford issued a pardon to Richard Nixon after his resignation from the presidency in the wake of the Watergate scandal.

As in these cases, a pardon does not render a person "not guilty," it only deals with the sentence. It means that, for one reason or another, a person does not have to serve the sentence for the offense committed.

Pardon for our sin would be more than any of us deserve, and yet God's grace goes even farther. The prophet put it this way: "Though your sins be as scarlet, they shall be as white as snow; though they are red like crimson, they shall be as wool" (Isaiah 1:18, KJV). God deals with our sins, not just the sentence. He makes it as if our sins were never there in the first place. He washes them away and He removes all the evidence. As far as God is concerned, our sins are not in the picture.

It's not just that we get a break on our sentence. We get a clean record. And this is the way we will meet God.

From *O Lord and Master of Us All* by John G. Whittier

Having and Seeing

We faintly hear, we dimly see,
In differing phrase we pray;
But, dim or clear, we own in Thee
The Life, the Truth, the Way.

Having is one thing, but seeing is quite another. As believers we always have more than we see. I believe this is what Jesus was talking about when He told the disciples why He spoke to the people in parables. "The knowledge of the secrets of the kingdom of heaven has been given to you, but not to them," He said. "Whoever has will be given more, and he will have an abundance. Whoever does not have, even what he has will be taken from him" (Matthew 13:11-12).

This means that the person who has a real relationship with God in Christ will see more and more truth. That person will grow in the understanding of spiritual things. The eyesight, though dim to start with, will improve.

As in so many spiritual things, this is the opposite of what happens with our physical eyes. We start out seeing well, but our sight deteriorates with age. I now have to carry around two pairs of glasses to go along with my contacts. But spiritually, I feel like I am constantly throwing away my glasses. This doesn't necessarily mean I am becoming a better person. It simply means I can see better. The truth I've known for so long is getting clearer every day. Things I had a hard time believing a few years back are getting easier to believe now.

Having and seeing are two different things now. But soon they will be one in the same. Soon, our eyes are opened and we see fully what we have had all along.

From *O Lord and Master of Us All* by John G. Whittier

Sun Shine

The solemn shadow of the cross is better than the sun.

Where I live, people worship the sun. People have moved to southern California for years because it is a place where any day can be warm and sunny. Every day of the calendar year has most likely recorded a near seventy degree high at some time in history.

Who would trade this for the shadow of a gloomy cross? Someone who knew that inside of so many of those beautiful hillside homes overlooking the Pacific Ocean are broken hearts, broken families, broken promises, and broken dreams. Someone who knew that no amount of money, power, or position can buy true and lasting happiness. Someone who knew that sin eats up the appreciable benefits of anyone's earthly treasure. Someone who knew that a cross has freed them from the bondage of sin to serve God with a whole heart and a clear conscience and to love their fellow man with equal abandon. Someone who knew that to love the Lord their God with all their heart, soul, strength, and mind is to bring out a sun that will never stop shining into each and every day, regardless of who or where they are.

That's who.

From *Look, Ye Saints, the Sight Is Glorious* by Thomas Kelly

Once He Was Here

Hark, those bursts of acclamation!
Hark, those loud triumphant chords!
Jesus takes the highest station:
O what joy the sight affords!

Although Jesus has taken the highest station, it's where He has been along the way that is significant to us. That He occupies the highest place should not surprise us. This is where He deserves to be. But we may forget that He occupies the highest place *after* traveling to the lowest. Jesus took the highest place *after* being in our place.

He once was seated with us on earth. He once screamed His way out of a mother's womb. He once learned the Torah in the temple. He once shared dinner around a table with twelve of us. He once cried at one of our graves. He once gave fishing lessons. He once slept in a boat in the middle of a storm. He was tempted in every way we are. He once agonized over a conflict of wills with His Father in heaven. He once was dead and facing what we should all be facing after death—whatever it is. And now, after all of this, He has taken His station in the highest place.

That means everything to us.

From *Sweet Hour of Prayer* by William W. Walford

A Bittersweet Farewell

This robe of flesh I'll drop, and rise
To seize the everlasting prize,
And shout, while passing through the air,
"Farewell, farewell, sweet hour of prayer!"

The regret will last only a moment. How could a moment in His actual presence ever be outdone by an hour of prayer? And yet there is something so sweet in this sentiment. That the passing of a praying era might come with a twinge of sadness on the way to meeting Him face to face only helps us to value more our present opportunity to commune with God.

"Farewell, farewell, sweet hour of prayer!" And to amplify this sentiment: "You are insignificant compared to what I am about to know, and yet for all my life you have been the best part. To know that you will no longer be needed is a bittersweet realization. I know that soon I will be in the presence of the one you led me to, but just now... well, I am surprised that I am a little sad."

Cherish that touch of heaven while you have it, and when prayer is no longer necessary, we will say goodbye to an old friend.

From *Prayer Is the Soul's Sincere Desire* by James Montgomery

Making Angels Sing

Prayer is the contrite sinner's voice
Returning from his ways,
While angels in their songs rejoice,
And cry, "Behold, he prays!"

Yes, angels see you and hear you, and they start singing when they do! Angels are easily excitable. And I'll tell you just what gets them going: It's not a great concert event for God or a national Christian satellite hook-up. It's not the testimony of a famous athlete or the ordination of a new pastor. And it's not a march of thousands for Jesus or a national day of prayer. "I tell you, there is rejoicing in the presence of the angels of God over one sinner who repents" (Luke 15:10). Imagine that! One measly sinner is enough to set the angels off singing! And not only that—"I tell you that in the same way there will be more rejoicing in heaven over one sinner who repents than over ninety-nine righteous persons who do not need to repent" (Luke 15:7).

But wait a minute. Where does that leave us—struggling Joe or Mary Christian trying to do our best to follow God? Don't we get to bring any joy in heaven? The answer is found in the same passage: Are we righteous people who do not need to repent? No, of course not. We need to repent continually of our sin as the Holy Spirit reveals it to us. The contrite sinner's prayer should be a familiar one to Christians.

So you see, we get to make angels sing, after all!

From *Prayer Is the Soul's Sincere Desire* by James Montgomery

Teach Us To Pray

O Thou, by whom we come to God,
The Life, the Truth, the Way,
The path of prayer Thyself hast trod—
Lord, teach us how to pray.

Jesus learned to pray. He had to learn to talk to His Father across the chasm of the universe they had created together. He found out what it was like to talk to someone He couldn't see. He found out what it was like to talk into thin air. When He humbled Himself and became a servant, one of the many things Jesus gave up was His treasured place in heaven with the Father.

"Let us make man in our image, in our likeness..." God had said. And then that eternal "Us" was separated by time and space. The Son was confined to a tiny planet in the vast creation, and divine communication had to go on radar.

It is comforting to know that Jesus had to learn how to pray in much the same way as we do. And once He learned it, He had to depend on it too. Now, we can learn from His example.

For instance, we know it was frequently Jesus' practice to go to a solitary place to pray. He would return from those places focused and often convinced of a change in direction (see Mark 1:35-38). He prayed before major decisions, such as choosing His disciples. And He prayed before major confrontations, such as His famous struggle with God in the Garden of Gethsemane.

If Jesus Himself depended on prayer to this extent, how can we expect to ever get by without it?

From *Prayer Is the Soul's Sincere Desire* by James Montgomery

Praying for the Fire

Prayer is the soul's sincere desire,
Unuttered or expressed;
The motion of a hidden fire
That trembles in the breast.

What makes a person desire God? Where is the hidden fire? How much of this can we do for ourselves and how much can we do for someone else? Can we build the fire? Can we light it, stoke it, or fan it?

It seems to me that we can do everything but light this fire. Like Elijah, who waited for the fire that came from heaven and consumed his offering, we wait on God for the flame.

Too often, we are more concerned about how we look than whether there is a fire. We do this a lot with our children. We try to persuade them to conform to outward standards of spirituality before we are sure the fire of God is in their hearts. This produces a stilted relationship with God, one based on conduct and not on fire. Conduct is never properly placed unless it is driven by fire. Some can conform for a while outwardly, while others may rebel. But sooner or later, outward conformity will crumble if it is not driven by an inward reality.

We need to spend more time on the fire—making sure ours is burning *and* fanning any flame we might see in others. We cannot make a person want to follow God. But like Elijah, we can pray for the fire to come down and consume everything.

From *Come, Thou Almighty King* by Author Unknown

Surprising God

Come, Thou Almighty King,
Help us Thy name to sing...

Sometimes we have trouble motivating ourselves to praise God, and we need His help just to do so. This must be something of a drag to God. It just seems to me that God would get more joy out of praise we initiated, rather than having to prompt it Himself.

I know it is certainly that way with me and my children. There are times when my children's praise is manipulated, such as on Father's Day or Mother's Day. These are days when Hallmark decides it's time for recognitions, prompting children with predetermined poems and appreciative words in card stands everywhere.

But there are also days when my children just thank me out of the blue or follow some impulse of their heart to express love. They might even write their own words in a card made of unevenly cut construction paper. These are the things that bring a parent the greatest joy.

Do you think we might be able to surprise even an all-knowing God in the same way? I can't imagine it would hurt to try. Sometime today, why not stop what you are doing and surprise God with praise.

From *Jesus, the Very Thought of Thee* by Bernard of Clairvaux

No Sweeter Sound

No voice can sing, no heart can frame,
Nor can the memory find
A sweeter sound than Thy blest name...

Jesus. Some people swear by that name. They use it simply because it is powerful. No one ever says "Hare Krishna!" when they hit their thumb with a hammer. Some preachers come dangerously close to taking this name in vain just by the way they say it—sitting on the first syllable and then letting their voices trail off on the second for the desired effect. I often wonder what Jesus thinks about that. I seriously doubt that He likes His name being used to punctuate sermon points.

Even when you know and love Jesus, His name can sound awkward as it comes off your tongue. We're not used to this name. To my knowledge, no one called Him Jesus to his face in the New Testament. They said "Master" or "Teacher" or "Rabbi," but never Jesus this or Jesus that. Maybe it was strange then, too. *Yeshua*, the Hebrew word for Jesus, means "the Lord is salvation."

"Do not be afraid to take Mary home as your wife," the angel told Joseph in a dream, "because what is conceived in her is from the Holy Spirit. She will give birth to a son, and you are to give him the name Jesus, because he will save his people from their sins" (Matthew 1:20-21).

That's when this name becomes the sweetest. Not in power or in punctuation, but in salvation—salvation from *my* sin and *my* guilt. There is no sweeter sound on earth.

From *Take Time to Be Holy* by William D. Longstaff

The Holy and the Common

Take time to be holy—
Speak oft with thy Lord...

Holy is a term that has gotten a bad rap. The first definition in the dictionary implies a morally and spiritually excellent or perfect person—one to be revered. If this is true, then someone who is holy is someone who is perfect and, of necessity, distant from everybody else, as in someone who wears holy clothes and walks slowly. This is someone you wouldn't want to be around. These kinds of holy people make ordinary people feel uncomfortable.

The third dictionary definition, that of being consecrated or sacred, is closer to the word as it is rendered in the Bible. *Holy* doesn't change the nature of a person or a thing as much as it changes its purpose. A regular cup becomes a holy cup, not when it is made into a perfect, gleaming container that looks as if it belongs on a table in the front of the church, but when it holds holy water or holy wine. It's still an ordinary cup, and yet its purpose has been consecrated. This is what happens with you and me when we are consecrated by the presence of the Holy Spirit, who indwells us.

We do not become perfect, nor do we have to move in other circles now that we are "holy." The reality is quite the opposite. As in what happened with Christ, that which is holy comes to dwell among that which is common to remind it of its created purpose. For we were meant to hold God and to speak often with our Lord.

From *The Old Rugged Cross* by George Bennard

Red Badge of Courage

On a hill far away stood an old rugged cross,
The emblem of suffering and shame...

The cross is the believer's emblem—a badge of sorts. People wear various badges of identification, such as pins or arm bands, to show support for certain causes. Our label-oriented society needs some way for people to establish who they are and what they stand for. There are badges of merit and honor with which we decorate our heroes, logos by which we identify major corporations, and flags for various governments in our world.

And then there is the cross. An odd emblem of suffering and shame, indeed. We have tried to take away its shame over the years by making ornate or artistic renditions of it, and these things have served to take us further away from its true meaning.

The cross is not meant to be a pleasant thing. It is a symbol of humiliation and death. Could you imagine people wearing little electric chairs around their necks?

Crosses are currently disappearing from the architecture of many bright new functional churches that don't want the negative aspects of the symbol to drive seekers away.

But in the cross's absence, there is a void where a sacrifice should be. Without a sacrifice, we are left to find other words for sin and other people to blame. Without a sacrifice, we are left with psychiatrists, nutritionists, chiropractors, and recovery groups to try to set us straight.

Without a sacrifice, we are left trying to remove the stain of sin from ourselves, and we don't have anything that can even begin do that.

From *Lead on, O King Eternal* by Ernest W. Shurtlef

It's Not Over Till It's Over

Lead on, O King Eternal,
Till sin's fierce war shall cease,
And holiness shall whisper
The sweet Amen of peace.

We are engaged in a fierce battle, this war with sin. It puts up a relentless front. Just when we think we've got one particular weakness shored up, a hole breaks open on a neglected flank. The assault can come from anywhere, even from something we thought we had under control.

It's an odd battle in that it has already been won in heaven, yet it is not over on earth. The flesh never gets any better. We mature, not because we improve on the flesh, but because we learn how to control it. One of the fruits of the Spirit is self-control, which is also one of the steps toward maturity listed in 2 Peter 1:3.

In spite of our growth, sin will always be crouching at our door like a lion ready to spring when we are most vulnerable. It attacks us after a great victory, or a time when we were greatly used by God. It waits for when we're spiritually exhausted from doing good and we think we deserve a break from holiness.

We can never let down our guard, no matter how strong we think we are. This is a fierce war we are engaged in, and it's not over this side of heaven.

From *Lead On, O King Eternal* by Ernest W. Shurtlef

When We All Get to Heaven

For not with swords loud clashing,
Nor roll of stirring drums;
With deeds of love and mercy,
The heavenly kingdom comes.

God's kingdom comes quietly. It always has. It has not come through military might or political process. God's kingdom has never been ushered in with a patriotic display. It should never be confused with human pomp and circumstance.

The kingdom of God is quiet and real. The undeserving are ushered into it by deeds of love and mercy. The kingdom of God is love in action, and its acts are never trumpeted. In fact, when Jesus told us to give, He suggested we do it secretly so that our right hand wouldn't know what our left hand was doing. This is as much to keep the giver from unnecessary pride as it is to protect the dignity of the receiver.

Beware of the temptation of wanting to bring God on with fanfare. We will have plenty of time for that in heaven, but that's never been His style on earth. When Jesus performed miracles, He told the recipients not to tell anybody who did it, but to go present themselves for the proper cleansing in the temple, and then get back into the stream of life.

God is more interested in the deeds of love and mercy we offer those in need than He is in a lot of fanfare, even on His behalf. Heaven is for fanfares. Our time here is for helping make sure as many get there as possible.

From *Lead on, O King Eternal* by Ernest W. Shurtlef

Friends In Low Places

Thy cross is lifted o'er us;
We journey in its light:
The crown awaits the conquest;
Lead on, O God of might.

The cross is an odd banner to be paraded before us, is it not? Who would champion a symbol of humiliation and death such as this? Some Christians would probably want out of the parade if they knew what they looked like marching behind the cross.

Those who would hold up the cross before them would be those who knew they had nothing else to brag about. They are a surly lot, these believers who follow behind the cross of Christ. They are people in low places who know what it is to find themselves on the short end of the stick. Even the powerful, wealthy, influential people who have managed to find themselves in this group have had to pass through the eye of a needle to get here, and they have learned not to see themselves as different from anyone else.

Those who are uncomfortable being around this gospel crowd should take note of their attitudes now, or they might miss the parade. Heaven is made up of people in low places who were invited to the party. They are people who got in at the last minute, prodigals who came home. Heaven is a lost-and-found department for hungry souls.

July 23

From *Lead on, O King Eternal* by Ernest W. Shurtlef

Nomads

Henceforth in fields of conquest
Thy tents shall be our home.

Christians are tent-dwellers on this earth—spiritual nomads camped on the dusty plains of a world, dry and parched by the curses of sin. God is here, too, but the world does not notice Him. As far as the world is concerned, He doesn't exist.

In 2 Corinthians 5:1-10, Paul says our bodies are tents—temporary and fragile. He says we long to be clothed with our heavenly dwelling, where we will no longer be homeless nomads, but kings and queens in heavenly mansions.

But while we are in this tent, we groan (verse 4). We would prefer to be away from this body and at home with the Lord. But these tents are our homes for now, and Paul says that whether we are at home or away, our goal is the same: to please Him.

This perspective is important for two reasons. First, we must continually be reminded of the temporary nature of this earthly existence. We need to temper our dreams, longings, and aspirations with this truth. We must re-think success and failure in light of the tent we live in. And second, when we focus on pleasing God, Paul tells us we are engaging in something that will turn out to be as good a choice in heaven as it was on earth. This way, we will not be investing in things we will eventually lose. Set your mind on pleasing God and you will be equally ready for earth or heaven.

From *Lead on, O King Eternal* by Ernest W. Shurtlef

Morning Breaks Again

Lead on, O King Eternal,
We follow, not with fears,
For gladness breaks like morning
Where'er Thy face appears.

God's presence comes with gladness. Gladness follows along after Him. It is like the dawning of a new day—a significant recreation event that happens every morning without fail.

What would happen if one day the sun failed to rise? Imagine living in perpetual darkness. All creation must hold its breath each morning as it waits to see what happens. And in that darkest hour before the dawn, fear grabs its tightest hold. But what joy and rejoicing when the sun prevails one more time on each new day! I doubt that creation ever gets over this.

In the same way, our fears spring from the absence of God's face in our lives. His coming is as sure as the dawn. But that dark hour of fear before its light cracks the horizon still grips us. We go through this suspense every time we pass through the darkness, as if we didn't learn enough of a lesson the last time.

His face appears and the sun breaks through, dispelling the darkness one more time, reassuring us that He is truly in control and that we have nothing to fear. You could say we are foolish to not learn this lesson and distrust the darkness. And yet, if we were too casual about the darkness, we wouldn't be so glad when dawn comes.

From *Souls of Men, Why Will Ye Scatter* by Frederick W. Faber

Reckless Love

For the love of God is broader
Than the measures of man's mind...

We can talk about it and analyze it. We can amass volumes in the study of it, discuss it, and paint pictures and write poems and songs about it.

But we cannot fit the height and depth and length and breadth of God's love within the walls of our brains. Nor can we properly define it, draw out its boundaries, or deliberate on its destinations. We are not in charge of it, so we don't control it. We don't know where it belongs and where it doesn't. We have nothing to say about who gets it and who doesn't. If we cannot tell the ocean "Thus far and no farther," then how can we direct the love of God?

Ah, but we can receive it, bask in it, and give it away as freely as it was given to us. We can tell everyone what it is like to know His grace and pour it out on unsuspecting sinners.

We are not experts in understanding the love of God. Only on experiencing it and spreading it around. But then again, no one ever asked us to understand it... only receive.

From *Souls of Men, Why Will Ye Scatter* by Frederick W. Faber

More and Less Desirable

But we make his love too narrow
By false limits of our own;
And we magnify its strictness
With a zeal He will not own.

Jesus saved His harshest words for the Pharisees. He portrayed them as self-appointed gatekeepers to heaven who, thinking they possessed the way in, elected to stand at the door and keep questionable characters out (see Matthew 23:13).

We are not much different. We are always wanting to put restrictions on the love of God. We talk about "God's unconditional love" but we want it to be unconditional for us... and *conditional* for everyone else.

God will have no part of this attitude. In fact, His attitude was the opposite of the Pharisees. Instead of restricting entry into heaven, He threw open the door to anyone.

When very few of the folks He originally invited to the heavenly banquet RSVP'd, He sent a messenger out to the streets and the alleyways and told them to bring in the poor, the crippled, the blind, and the lame. And when there was still room left at the table, He had them go out to the roads and the country lanes and bring in more. Anybody they could find.

This was what the Pharisees could not tolerate about Jesus: He kept opening the door to undesirable people. When the Pharisees find out who's going to be in heaven, they will probably be relieved to know that they don't have to spend eternity with these folks.

From *Souls of Men, Why Will Ye Scatter* by Frederick W. Faber

Running from Love

Souls of men, why will ye scatter
Like a crowd of frightened sheep?
Foolish hearts, why will ye wander
From a love so true and deep?

Why do we run from love? Is it the intimacy? Fear that we will be found out? Or do we lack trust, perhaps because of memories of former rejections that have left a smudge on our hearts?

Are we afraid that if God's love truly found us that we would have to be known in ways we do not want to be known, revealing things about ourselves we do not want to see?

Maybe we prefer the dark and the cold to the warmth and the light of God. The dark hides us, so we need not tremble as we might in the light.

Or maybe we fear having to give up our complaints and relinquish our excuses. (Though by now we've forgotten what it was we're excusing ourselves from!)

Perhaps we have never known a perfect love—a love unearned and unasked for and un-required. We want to believe such a thing could be true. It is so good, and yet so unfamiliar that it terrifies us. It is unsettling. We think it is easier to run and live with what we know than it is to stay and find out if it is true.

What is it to have someone die to save you before you ever even screamed for help?

From *Ye Servants of God, Your Master Proclaim* by Charles Wesley

The Author of Salvation

The great congregation His triumph shall sing,
Ascribing salvation to Jesus our King.

Who but God would have thought of saving us? No religion that humanity has ever devised contains a concept of salvation—of God sacrificing Himself for humankind. Salvation belongs to God. It is uniquely Christ's. And because of this, it tells us something about God's character.

We didn't plead for this. We didn't beg Him to get us off the hook. Salvation isn't God's response to us; it's the other way around. Salvation was His plan from the very beginning. He offered it to us before we could think of it ourselves. (Besides, we're much too proud to admit we were lost.)

So His offer remains a mystery to us. Why would God pardon us at the price of his Son? Why would a just and holy God bother to salvage the wreckage that humanity has become? Why would He ever bother with us in the first place? We're selfish to the core and full of sin. Why didn't He just doom the race with the first sin and start over?

Because He had decided to save us from the very start. He is the author of salvation. How can we help but receive this gift and worship Him.

From *Ye Servants of God, Your Master Proclaim* by Charles Wesley

Go Ahead, Make God's Day

Then let us adore and give Him His right,
All glory and power and wisdom and might.

It is possible to be too impressed with our praise of God. Praise can become so polished that we think we are making God's day when we praise Him. Some teach that praise benefits us. It is a valuable addition to a believer's walk—a way to make things go better. In other words, praise will not only make God's day, it will make our day, too.

Though personal praise is important and corporate praise is essential, it is never a cause-and-effect arrangement. God is not somehow beholden to me because I am giving Him such nice praise. Praise is not a nice-to-do for God. It is His due... His right. It belongs to Him. It always has.

In Scripture, praise is the natural order of all created things. The heavens declare the glory of God; the earth shows forth His handiwork; mountains and hills break forth into singing, and all the trees of the field clap their hands. They don't do this because it's Sunday morning and someone is admonishing them that it would be good for them to give God some attention for a change. They do this because their light in the sky was made to twinkle that way. Their grass was made to wave. Their leaves were made to brush together in the wind and their arms naturally go up.

Should it be any different with us?

From *Ye Servants of God, Your Master Proclaim* by Charles Wesley

Magazine Rack

Ye servants of God, your Master proclaim,
And publish abroad His wonderful name.

God is always in the market for a new publication. The encyclopedia of His creation continues to be widely read, and His major book, the Bible, annually tops the best-seller charts.

But God's not satisfied. He wants coverage in something more current, say a magazine or a periodical—somewhere He can express His immediate concerns on living pages. Paul says that we are kind of like magazines—letters from Christ, known and read by everybody (see 2 Corinthians 3:2-3). Perhaps the magazine of our life would include some articles with fresh approaches to faith... fresh insights into worshiping God. Perhaps a regular column on finding Him in the ordinary, day-to-day routine of our lives. Maybe something on facing the reality of temptation, or the subtle ways sin can creep into our lives.

He also wants to specifically publish His name. This opens up a broad spectrum of themes since He has so many of them—*Wonderful Counselor, Mighty God, Prince of Peace, Everlasting Father, Shepherd of the Sheep*, just to name a few.

What would your magazine be called? And what part of His name would you want to publish?

From *In Christ There Is No East or West* by John Oxenham

Blood Relatives

Who serves my Father as a son
Is surely kin to me.

We are a part of a diverse body... the body of Christ. It's hard to imagine we could all come from the same family, since we have so many different beliefs, different interpretations of truth, and different ways of doing things.

What makes us one is not that we think alike or act alike, and not that we say things in the same way, or agree on all points of doctrine in their ranking importance.

What makes us one is what makes any family one... our blood. We come from the same line. We have been born of God through Christ, and we have the same blood—that blood that washed each of us clean by faith in the death and resurrection of our Father's Son.

All families are diverse. Children all have different personalities, interests, goals, pursuits, and priorities. But their oneness is a given. Their unity never changes. Father to son, mother to daughter, brother to sister... once born, they are always related. Nothing can change this.

It's the same in the body of Christ. It's in the blood—the blood of Jesus.

From *No Other Plea* by Lidie H. Edmunds

No Argument

I need no other argument, I need no other plea;
It is enough that Jesus died, And that he died for me.

I need no defense lawyer, no constitutional rights, no public defender to plead my case. I need no defense strategy to cover the holes in my argument, no alibi to excuse me from the scene of the crime. I need not fear the surprise witness I failed to uncover in advance. I need not try to second guess the prosecution.

I'm guilty. I know it and I make no excuses for myself. I pleaded guilty in the pretrial hearings. It was a true admission and not induced by any plea-bargaining. I'm guilty as charged.

A guilty plea brings relief, especially when you have spent time and effort covering for yourself and presuming innocence. It can be overwhelming trying to keep all the stories and alibis straight. A statement such as "Guilty, your honor," clears the air. It's painful to say, but once said, it takes an enormous weight off your back.

But then comes the real surprise. You find out that you are sentenced to death, but that someone has already been executed on your behalf. In one proceeding you are guilty, sentenced, served, and released. Case closed.

No wonder forgiven sinners have so much to sing about.

From *O How I Love Jesus* by Frederick Whitfield

Picking Up Our Assignment

It [the name of Jesus] *tells me what my Father hath*
In store for every day...

Better not head out the door before stopping and picking up your assignment from the Lord. Jesus is not just a friend to keep us company. He is like a coach or an activities director sending us out with a plan. You can't stand around His presence very long without receiving an assignment. Jesus keeps us busy with plenty to do.

You come to offer Him a gift, and He may tell you to first go straighten out what is wrong with a strained earthly relationship (Matthew 5:23-24). You tell Him you want to follow Him, and He might tell you to go give all you have to the poor (see Matthew 19:21). You ask Him how to know if you have love in your heart, and He tells you the story of the Good Samaritan (see Luke 10:29-37). And when you come even to repent, He asks for fruits of your repentance (see Matthew 3:8).

That we simply hear His voice is not enough for Jesus. He wants us to do what He tells us to do. The foolish man who built his house on sand was the one who heard the word but didn't do anything about it.

So you had better stop by the front desk on your way out this morning and pick up your assignment. Jesus is the one standing next to it with the clipboard and the whistle.

From *Am I a Soldier of the Cross?* by Isaac Watts

Pop Gospel

Is this vile world a friend to grace,
To help me on to God?

We Christians have finally figured out how to market the gospel: It's really becoming so-o-o-o-o comfy being a Christian. The gospel is fitting in so nicely with everything around it. The gospel is even popular. We can draw so many parallels now between the gospel and the world that it seems as if we are almost saying the same things.

For instance, people are trying to feel good about themselves and better their lives. Jesus cared about that, too. He died for us because we were so important—that alone should do a lot for someone's self-esteem. I've even heard it from a reputable source that He would have died for me even if I had been the only person on the face of the earth! Wow! I must be pretty special!

He died on the cross so that I could get more out of life. That's cool too! I heard that in a Christian song. I also heard that He loves me just the way I am. I don't have to change anything! And that's just like the Billy Joel song, *Just The Way You Are*. See how it's all blending together?

Pretty soon, everyone will be Christians and they won't even know it!

From *Am I a Soldier of the Cross?* by Isaac Watts

Bloody Seas

Must I be carried to the skies
On flow'ry beds of ease
While others fought to win the prize,
And sailed through bloody seas?

Sometimes I long for circumstances that would simplify the issue of faith. History has shown that persecution can clear the skies on an otherwise cloudy faith.

Take Shadrach, Meshach, and Abednego, Daniel's three friends who were serving in a pagan king's court. The challenge to their faith was straightforward and blunt: Bow down to the idol or be thrown in the fiery furnace. Would that all our choices were that well defined!

Instead, we live in an age of relative ease and affluence, where faith has shaken hands with culture. Instead of the furnace, we get a book contract and publicity on Christian talk radio. We may bow down to the idol a hundred times a day and not even know it.

I have a hunch that things haven't changed much from biblical times. The "bite" of truth is still there, buried beneath layers of compromise with the world and its philosophy. Isaac Watts must have known the same confusion in his day. He was longing for some bloody seas to navigate.

The way of least resistance is rarely the way of truth.

From *Am I a Soldier of the Cross?* by Isaac Watts

No Peace on Earth

Are there no foes for me to face?
Must I not stem the flood?

The greatest threat to spiritual growth is not the enemy himself, but our oblivion to the war we are in. If I am not fighting a battle with sin or temptation, with undisciplined behavior or selfishness, or with lack of love—if I'm not engaged in a spiritual struggle on any number of fronts at once—I can assume that I am most likely losing ground.

Our society places a priority on the alleviation of pain and conflict. We spend large sums of money and time trying to find peace with ourselves and our world. In this cultural setting, it is easy for us to expect God to become one more pain-reliever. But the angels' message was not an announcement of Jesus as aspirin for the human race.

"I did not come to bring peace," said Jesus, "but a sword" (Matthew 10:34). And suddenly God hands us not only a sword, but also a whole suit of armor. And He ushers us into battle.

We are at war. There are forces of good and forces of evil fighting on our behalf. There are principalities and powers and rulers of darkness in the heavenlies who would love to see us done in. We must stand our ground. And having done everything in our power to equip ourselves for this battle, we must stand and not give in.

From *O Jesus, I Have Promised* by John Ernest Bode

Hearing His Voice

O let me hear Thee speaking,
In accents clear and still,
Above the storms of passion,
The murmurs of self-will...

Let me pick out your voice, O Lord. Let me learn how to tell it from the others. There are so many voices in my head. Some come from my passions—the natural hungers of my body. They often confuse me with their tangled motivations. I might arrange to pursue one relationship over another—to talk to a person with a pretty face versus your direction to speak with a less-attractive, but more open, individual. Or I might choose one direction over another due to temporal reasons, instead of considering how that decision impacts the kingdom of God.

Sometimes I can't even hear your voice over all the murmuring of my selfish will and all its needs and wants and desires. How do I sort it out, Lord? How do I pull your voice out of a garden full of verbal weeds? How will I know it's truly your voice when I hear it?

If this is your prayer, I offer these guidelines for picking out the voice of God: He will always lead you in ways already prescribed in the Scriptures. He cannot contradict His own word. His way will benefit others, not just yourself. It will spring from a heart of compassion and love. He will speak of things from an eternal perspective, not just a temporal one. He will keep you honest by making you face something in your life that needs spiritual attention.

From *More about Jesus* by Eliza E. Hewitt

Sacred Conversation

More about Jesus in His word,
Holding communion with my Lord,
Hearing His voice in every line,
Making each faithful saying mine.

Spending time with God's Word is like no other time spent. To spend time in His Word is to enter into a conversation with the Father, the Son, and the Holy Spirit. That conversation has been going on since before time began.

When we open the Bible, we walk into the conference room. We hear voices and lively discussion. The Bible vibrates with energy. These words are not static; they are truths that come alive as we enter into the dialogue. We commune in sacred conversation.

Other voices meet us as well—voices of prophets and kings and saints and martyrs—voices and lives that have trusted God and also failed to trust Him. We hear from them as they shout encouragement and warning from the rim of heaven.

Hold the Word and treasure it. Open it slowly and watch the lives pop up. Pray that you can be worthy to follow in their footsteps. And then make the words your own. Not by rote memory, but by rote living—by repeatedly following what God is teaching you as it becomes clearer to you each day.

From *More about Jesus* by Eliza E. Hewitt

More About Jesus

More, more about Jesus,
More, more about Jesus...

More, more about Jesus. More facts, more insights, more stories of His reality in more people's lives. You can't seem to get enough. You can't seem to exhaust the subject. The more you find out, the more you want to know.

You hunger for truth and knowledge. You want to know stuff and you want to know it from God, because then you can trust it. You taste absolutes for the first time, and you know you've got solid food for a change, something that isn't going to slip off your plate.

Then after you gather some facts, you hunger to know how to use them. In other words, you long for wisdom. Little by little, you watch godly people and see the truth enter the arena of life. You begin to do this yourself. You act on truth and it becomes sweet in your mouth. You realize you know what to do. What you've learned is something you can apply to your life as you really live it.

Then you suddenly find out that all the knowledge and the wisdom lead you back to Jesus, which is where this all started. Only now you know Him more deeply. You start to see Jesus everywhere. Principles fall away and you are left with Jesus. Laws are fulfilled in Jesus. Steps and procedures all become Jesus. And so, just like before but only deeper, you want more of Jesus. More about Jesus.

More, more about Jesus.

From *Praise Him! Praise Him!* by Fanny J. Crosby

Jesus the Humiliated

He our Rock, our hope of eternal salvation,
Hail Him! Hail Him! Jesus the crucified.

Jesus the Crucified. That's His name and that's what He's known for. He wears the marks of His death forever, even in His name. The wounds are still on His body as a reminder for all eternity of what He did for us.

Jesus the Crucified. If you didn't know the whole story, you might be tempted to take the name as a form of mockery. *Jesus the Executed* or *Jesus the Death Row Inmate* would be likely modern-day renderings. Time has deified the crucifixion because of its relationship to Christ's particular way of dying. But there is certainly nothing honoring about this name. It is a humiliating name, not a name of glory. It is incongruous to hail one who has been executed as a criminal and now wears the name as a sort of medal. But this is part of the mystery of this gospel. Nothing is ever as it seems.

Jesus the Humiliated. This brings home the true meaning of His name. *Hail Him! Hail Him! Jesus the humiliated.* He will wear this name throughout history. The lowering of Himself to a criminal's death is a part of His name now. He wears it like He wears the wounds on His body: with love.

From *Praise Him! Praise Him!* by Fanny J. Crosby

Prophet, Priest, and King

Jesus, Savior, reigneth forever and ever;
Crown Him! Crown Him! Prophet, and Priest, and King.

Jesus is all three: prophet, priest, and king.

Prophets prophesy. Jesus prophesied concerning the temple. He prophesied concerning the end of the age. He prophesied concerning His disciples. He spoke of who would be in charge after He left and how the disciples would die. He did not prophesy just to prophesy, but rather to teach. Most of all, He prophesied concerning His own death and resurrection. And then He pulled it off—He fulfilled His own prophesies.

Priests act on behalf of the people. The priest stands in the place of the people in front of God and offers sacrifices. The priest also goes into the Holy of Holies and talks to God on behalf of the people. Jesus *was* the Holy of Holies. He did not have to go there; He was there all the time. And when it came time to offer up the sacrifice, He was that, too. So He offered up Himself, the final sacrifice, for the last time.

Kings rule. They are the highest and final authority. All power rests with them. They also judge. They settle disputes and punish evildoers. Evil kings are dictators, but kind and wise kings rule over kingdoms marked by peace and order. Jesus is above all other kings. He is a loving and wise king who came in disguise to serve His subjects. When He returns, He will rule over all. Everyone will bow at His feet. For some folks, that will be a big deal because they've never bowed to anyone before. But to us—like Mary Magdalene, who was intent upon anointing His feet—it will be a familiar, treasured posture.

From *Praise Him! Praise Him!* by Fanny J. Crosby

The Good Shepherd

Like a shepherd, Jesus will guard His children,
In His arms He carries them all day long.

The Good Shepherd lays down his life for the sheep (see John 10:11-18). Jesus calls Himself the Good Shepherd. What makes Him good is a unique relationship to His sheep. He is not like a hired hand who bolts at the first sign of trouble—such as a wolf or a wild animal attack. A hired hand has no personal investment in the sheep—no reason to stay when his own life is in danger.

Jesus is different. He has already given up His life for these sheep. He has paid the highest price anyone could ever pay: His own life. He is intimately involved with His sheep, and knows each one by name. He recognizes their voices, and they recognize His. Because He has voluntarily laid down His life for them, He has a reason for His commitment to the sheep. He is bent on caring for them. He is the Shepherd/Owner, so He will personally see that all who are His will be brought into the fold.

Listen for His voice and follow Him. He knows where to lead you, and He will bring you safely through. Never has there been another shepherd like Him.

From *Jesus, Lover of My Soul* by Charles Wesley

Grandma's Lap

Jesus, Lover of my soul,
Let me to Thy bosom fly...

I never liked these type of hymns growing up. They always embarrassed me. They made me think of a grandmother with big flabby arms and a pillowy bosom. Now that I am older, I am not so sure that it is such a bad image after all, even for God.

Everyone should have a loving, comforting grandmother. Someone who, every time you went over to her house, was always pulling something sweet out of the oven. Someone who wrapped you three times around in a welcome hug. Someone who never said a bad thing about anybody. Someone who wanted to know everything there was to know about you. Someone who listened and remembered, and could attach everything new you said to everything you said before and make sense of it all. Someone who has gathered the span of your life into hers and held it for you to see whenever you want a reminder.

A grandmother's love is always there, always ready to be dispensed. It cannot be earned or ended. Grandmothers provide security, warmth, and love. And most of all, grandmothers provide a great big, fluffy lap.

I am certain that somewhere in the great and manifold character of God, there is a grandmother's love for us.

From *Jesus, Lover of My Soul* by Charles Wesley

Desperate Clinging

Other refuge have I none;
Hangs my helpless soul on Thee...

I love this picture: the image of a limp soul, hanging like an old coat somewhere on God. It makes me think of Salvador Dali's famous rendering of watches and clocks draped over rocks and fences like spineless time. It also makes me think of humorous pictures, such as the limp hens hanging around at Gary Larson's boneless chicken farm. But the "Hang In There!" poster, with its image of a startled cat holding onto a bar by only its front paws, is the picture that most closely resembles what the hymn writer had in mind here.

He is talking about a desperate clinging, about having no other refuge and nothing else to hold onto. *All my trust on Thee is stayed*, the hymn goes on the say. *All my help from Thee I bring*. In other words, I am counting on nothing and no one else to hold my life together. I have already determined that I am helpless, that I cannot hold onto myself. All the others I have grabbed onto have let go of me, and now I have finally determined that you, Lord, are all I have. I want you to know I've staked all my claims here. I've let go of everything else. I'm holding onto you, so please, don't let go of me now.

Real faith has immediacy and risk. There are no harnesses or safety loops to catch me. Just the hard ground and a long, long way to fall. Faith isn't faith until we live it this way.

From *Jesus, Lover of My Soul* by Charles Wesley

A Hiding Place

Cover my defenseless head
With the shadow of Thy wing.

We need a covering. Reality is too harsh; life is too cruel. We need a place to run, a place of refuge from the storm. This is not being "chicken." This is life, and this is God, who wants to be there for us. Otherwise, He wouldn't have given us metaphors of Himself as a rock, a city of refuge, a fortress, a strong tower to run to, or a wing under which we can find protection.

Our society tells us to be tough, to stand alone, to take the knocks and get up for more. Football coaches yell at young boys to stop their crying and toughen up. The work place and the professional world give us no sympathy. You either cut it or you don't. We live in a hard, cruel world.

God does not speak this language. To be sure, He disciplines us and He throws us into the fray and the fire. But He does not stand apart. He is not cold, distant, and aloof. If we have that idea of Him, it came from somewhere else, and not from those who have walked with Him and passed on to us a firsthand knowledge of His character. People like the psalmist David, and the hymn writer, Mr. Wesley. They know something else about God and are not ashamed to proclaim it. They know God is a place to run to, a place of protection, a place to come in out of the storm. And for little children like us, who are often caught in an unexpected downpour, that is a good thing to know.

From *How Tedious and Tasteless the Hours* by John Newton

Sweet Prospects

How tedious and tasteless the hours
When Jesus no longer I see!
Sweet prospects, sweet birds, and sweet flowers,
Have all lost their sweetness to me.

The idea of an ordinary day without a vision of Jesus in it holds a number of gloomy prospects for the believer. Lack of direction might be one. An inability to see the true meaning and purpose behind the events of the day could be another. Or how about an irritable nature around others and a lack of patience from not seeing others through the eyes of Jesus? Or worse yet might be a day filled with guilt—forgetting the grace and forgiveness that is available at the cross for all who believe, and living with self-inflicted payment for one's own sins instead.

All of these seem like obvious results of a Jesus-less day. But who would have first come up with general boredom as the fruit of a day without Christ? It would have to be someone who was intimate with God in the first place. It would be someone accustomed to sharing everything with Him: the sunrise, the flowers, the details, the joys, and the sorrows. It would be someone to whom Jesus was a constant companion, someone who would find everyday life without Him a drudgery.

It makes me look at the things in my life that I find tedious and tasteless and wonder if the boredom comes because I have left God out of those areas. If I fail to miss Him in the routines of my life, perhaps it is because I never really believed He was interested.

If He is, that would change everything.

August 16

From *How Tedious and Tasteless the Hours* by John Newton

Who's In Prison?

While blest with a sense of His love,
A palace a toy would appear;
And prisons would palaces prove,
If Jesus would dwell with me there.

Jesus puts everything in a new perspective. He organizes the world by standards other than the ones we naturally go by. Wealth appears insignificant when compared to His glory and beauty, and His presence can turn a prison into a palace.

I have visited prisons and have been rebuked by believers there. In the presence of their radiant inner joy and freedom—in spite of their chains—as I pass in and out of guarded security, I have wondered who was imprisoned and who was truly free.

The systems of the world can entrap us. The wealth of the world can rule us to where our freedom is but a thin facade over a more terrible prison. It is more terrible because we do not see it. And in our blindness, we are not able to benefit from the rehabilitation that can be found in a literal prison. We are not made humble. We are not shamed or made to feel remorse. We do not get a chance to consider the results of our bad choices and resolve to make different ones. We merely keep going, thinking that this charade is the way it is for everyone. And if it is, it makes me think that we could all benefit from a few days in a real prison.

Such a place of truly facing ourselves and being with Jesus—loved and accepted as we are—would be as fine as any palace I could think of.

From *How Tedious and Tasteless the Hours* by John Newton

A Love Affair with God

The midsummer sun shines but dim;
The fields strive in vain to look gay;
But when I am happy in Him,
December's as pleasant as May

This is the song of someone who is in love with Jesus. Such a thing as a love affair with God *is* possible. The poets and the mystics were enraptured by the presence of God. Paul was carried away to the seventh heaven and saw things unutterable. John Newton, who wrote this lyric, loved to contemplate God in his garden, as did St. Augustine, whose famous *Confessions* came to him during one of his garden contemplations.

Many spiritual people today would call this kind of activity into question. Today, spirituality is measured by success in business, in personal relationships, and in self-esteem. Time today is too important to be spent in contemplation. Someone noticing the fields straining to be happy in the bleak month of December is most likely not going to be successful in today's world, and would likely be thought of as a little loony.

In truth, however, there is no spirituality outside of a love affair with God. That is what everything else springs from, and it is possible at all times and in all places. It is the beginning and the end of the matter. "Love the Lord your God with all your heart and with all your soul and with all your strength" (Deuteronomy 6:5). Apart from this love, all hours become tedious and tasteless.

From *I Surrender All* by L. W. van Deventer

Surrender

I surrender all, I surrender all,
All to Thee, my blessed Saviour,
I surrender all.

Give it up. Hand it over. Give up that cherished little sin no one knows about and that person who gives you tangible attention but pulls you away from God. Hand over those old memories that keep you helpless and hopeless and those anniversaries of pain that feed your excuses. Hand over those old tapes that keep you stuck in the same ruts over and over again. Give up those habits that have mastery over you and those compromises that keep you in control. Give up those excuses that keep you out of control when it's convenient. Whatever you hold tightly in your hand, surrender it.

We are selfish and twisted and largely ineffective at satisfying ourselves. And the things we try to satisfy ourselves with are equally ineffective. This is because we were made for God, and we are never satisfied until we rest our weary souls in Him.

Surrendering also means that our hands and arms are empty and open to receive. He has so much He wants to give us. We settle for so much less when we refuse to give up all.

From *Grace Greater than our Sin* by Julia H. Johnston

The Futility of Hiding

Dark is the stain that we cannot hide...

Raising children teaches you many things. My children have shown me that it is not only impossible to hide my sin, but it is silly, too. I have often been caught thinking I was getting away with something only to discover my children looking right through my disguise. This is the way it is with families, isn't it? We all know each other too well.

Lately, I've realized that our families aren't the only ones who see through us. Don't people know intuitively who we are and what we try to hide? Aren't we all capable of deeper discernment than we might give each other credit for?

We are all human. We know ourselves, so we know each other as well. As children, we believed that adults are smarter, stronger, and better than we are. But as we grow up, we find that adults were flawed all along. We learn this when we begin to face our own imperfections as we grow into adulthood.

My children sometimes laugh at me when I get really angry. I used to think this was being disrespectful, but now I know they laugh at me because they can't help it. I finally figured out that I look funny when I'm mad. My voice rises, my veins pop out, my language gets strong, and I lose my composure. When I say I'm not angry when I really am, my children know it is a lie. Everyone knows. If I try to hide my anger, they know that too. This is not to sanction outbursts of anger. But hiding our true feelings is not any better than a temper tantrum.

What's better is the truth and we must come out of hiding in order to see it.

August 20

From *Grace Greater than our Sin* by Julia H. Johnston

Inexhaustible Grace

Marvelous grace of our loving Lord,
Grace that exceeds our sin and our guilt.

The greatest thing about grace is undoubtedly its abundance. There is more than enough to go around and more than any of us can exhaust.

Most of us were brought up by parents who had limited grace as a resource. We could easily tax their patience and use up their good will. Freedoms came with ultimatums, and love had strings attached.

When we met God, we found out that wherever sin abounds, grace abounds all the more. You can't out-sin grace, and some of us have found this out the hard way.

This abundance of grace does not cheapen it, as some fear. Rather, it defines it. Some people are bothered by this. They worry that it can be taken for granted, which is true. It wouldn't be grace if it couldn't be taken for granted.

Yet only those who misunderstand grace take advantage of it. Those who understand it want more and more of God, not less and less.

The law makes you want to find ways around it. Grace makes you want to find a way to live worthy of it. Once you know what grace really is, you don't look for ways to abuse it. Instead, you look for ways to pay God back for what He has done for you that you don't deserve.

From *O Happy Day* by Philip Doddridge

Remedy for a Divided Heart

Now rest my long-divided heart;
Fixed on this blissful center, rest.

Evangelistic appeals often paint the Christian life in bright, happy colors, tantalizing the unbelieving with the hope of a better life. Promises are made about an abundant life, healing and eternal happiness. From many of these messages, one could gather that the Christian life is close to being problem-free. This, however, is misleading.

New Christians are soon introduced to a conflict that they were not even aware of in their pre-Christian days—the conflict of a divided heart. When we enter into a relationship with God through His Holy Spirit, another will is brought into play. Before Christ enters a life, there is only one will—the self-centered one we were all born with.

Though this will is ultimately a destructive one, it makes decisions fairly uncomplicated: Since there's no one around to tell you anything different, do whatever you want to do. But when we become Christians, we receive another will, and now we have two wills in conflict. One that wants to do what God wants, and one that follows the natural course of the flesh. And though we might try, we Christians are never really happy sinning.

Turning your divided heart over to Christ is the only real solution to this conflict—the only rest. Giving ourselves over to His will is our only resolve. And it will also become our greatest joy.

From *My Hope Is Built* by Edward Mote

Standing on the Rock

His oath, His covenant, His blood,
Support me in the whelming flood;
When all around my soul gives way,
He then is all my hope and stay.

There are times when everything around you erodes except for the rock upon which you stand. You step out in one direction and the sand gives way, so you step back to the rock. You step out in another direction and the ground gives way again, so you step back to the rock. Everywhere you try the same thing happens.

You start to wonder if the sinking sand might encroach on your rock. All around you is giving way, so is the rock going to go too? This kind of thing has to happen to our faith once in a while in order for us to trust the rock. This is when you pray, "Lord, you had better be real, because you are all I have right now. If you wash away too, I am gone for sure."

It is in times like these that you find the rock to be solid. This is when you learn to trust not in feelings, but in facts. This is when you go to His promises in Scripture and stand firm on them. Remembering the Word in your mind may not be enough. You will need to open up the Bible and let the words be a place you can stand.

This is when you remember that Jesus Christ has made a covenant with you, a new covenant in His blood. You are His and He is yours. He has bought you, and He will bring you through. His word is His oath, and He will not go back on His promises. He is the ground on which you stand. Everything else is sinking sand. Everything.

From *Faith of Our Fathers! Living Still* by Frederick W. Faber

To Suffer Justly

Our fathers, chained in prisons dark,
Were still in heart and conscience free;
How sweet would be their children's fate,
If they, like them, could die for Thee!

What a different world it would be if Christians were persecuted for their faith. Not persecuted for their political beliefs or their stand on contemporary issues, and not for their boycotting of offensive art. But persecuted for their faith in Jesus Christ as the Son of God who died for the sins of the world and rose again from the grave.

Christianity has always risen to the occasion amidst persecution. It owes its finest moments to the martyrs.

Historically, Christianity has always struggled with its surrounding culture in some way. Too often, though, the struggle moves away from the gospel and into other issues that are more political than spiritual: the Protestant/Catholic conflict in Ireland; the Christians and Muslims in Bosnia; or the current cultural wars in the United States, which have everything to do with conservative moral issues and little to do with what the martyrs died for. If we are going to suffer for being Christians, we should be sure we are suffering for the gospel of Jesus Christ and nothing else.

Fierce loyalties sometimes make it hard to tell what fuels our passions. I wonder if some Christians would be willing to lose their political power to gain Christ. What would happen if we were given the opportunity to win all our political agendas if we simply denounced Christ. If we were forced to make such a choice, the decision would certainly show where our hearts are.

How sweet it would be if we could die for Christ!

From *Go to Dark Gethsemane* by James Montgomery

Just One Bitter Hour

Go to dark Gethsemane,
Ye that feel the tempter's power;
Your Redeemer's conflict see,
Watch with Him one bitter hour.

When we start to come under temptation, when we think we might not be able to resist, when our will seems so weak and the wrong seems so strong, we need to mentally transport ourselves to Gethsemane and wait up with Jesus for just one hour (something that Peter, James, and John were unable to do). If we ever think we have it tough, an hour like this will cure us of our self-pity.

Jesus struggled in the garden with the seed of all our struggles: a conflict of wills. Are we willing to submit our will to the Father's?

I wonder if this works for other things, as well. I wonder if watching Jesus drive out the money changers would help us drive out the compromises in our lives. Or maybe a few minutes with a forgiven prostitute would teach us compassion. Watching Him touch a leper, or seeing Him talk to an outcast Samaritan woman, might help us overcome the prejudice we face in our society and in ourselves. And seeing Him carry His cross would give us new motivation to carry our own.

Yes, there's nothing like a little reflection on the life of Jesus to put our own lives into perspective, no matter what we are facing.

When faith seems difficult, we need to gain strength and humility from what Jesus already went through when He walked in our shoes.

From *All Glory Be to God on High* by Nikolaus Decius

Call Him Friend

All glory be to God on high,
Who hath our race befriended.

How do we think of God as our friend without diminishing His majesty and glory? If we make God our friend, won't we be in danger of casting Him in our image? A friend is someone we are comfortable with, someone we don't have to be self-conscious around. But how can we be comfortable around someone as powerful as God? How can we strike this balance and still have God be God?

One way would be to think of Him as Jesus.

Jesus insisted on being baptized like everybody else at that time: by John the Baptist. Jesus hung out with tax collectors and sinners at Levi's going-away party. Jesus' first miracle kept a party going in high style. Jesus motioned to a group of His followers in a room and called them all His "mother and brothers and sisters," while His earthly family waited impatiently for Him outside. Jesus gathered children in His arms. Jesus met Nicodemus by night and discussed eternal life with him. Jesus likened His Father to a joy-crazed, absent-minded teddy bear at the return of a long-lost son. Jesus allowed a sinful woman to anoint His feet in the home of a religious fanatic. Jesus loved the home of Mary and Martha and wept at the death of their brother Lazarus. Jesus had a breakfast of forgiveness ready for Peter on the shore after the disciple had denied Him three times.

Something tells me, after remembering just a few of these events, that this man Jesus could be my friend.

August 26

From *Lord Jesus, I Long to Be Perfectly Whole* by James Nicholson

De-Animating the Inanimate

Break down every idol,
Cast out every foe...

Idols are always found on the inside, but foes are from without. Foes must be driven back to where they belong, but idols must be crushed. They must fall where they have arisen: in our hearts.

Idols arise in our hearts and minds. They are seeking a throne and thus can be found occupying our innermost being. Idols have no life of their own. (Everyone knows they used to be made of wood and stone.) The danger is not the idols themselves, for they have no power. The danger is the power that we give them. We infuse them with the very power they claim to have over us, and then we fall down and worship. It's a stupid trick we've been performing for a long time.

Idols have no words that we did not give them and no voice we did not devise. Idols are silent. They are merely substitutes for the real God, and we prefer them because they are safer, more predictable and easier to control. I can carry an idol around with me. I can comfort myself with it, rule over others with it, or bury it in a drawer if I get tired of having it around.

Dethroning an idol is a simple thing, really. Since its power came from us in the first place, we simply take our worship somewhere else. An idol only has power over those who worship it. An idol that is not being worshipped is merely a log of wood or a piece of stone. Maybe it's a pile of money or an overblown image of a star like the little guy behind the Wizard of Oz.

From *Lord Jesus, I Long to Be Perfectly Whole* by James Nicholson

Bound Together by Passion

To those who have sought Thee,
Thou never saidst no...

"Seek and you will find," Jesus said in Matthew 7:7. He also said "Whoever comes to me I will never drive away" (John 6:37).

Jesus has never refused anyone who sought Him with a whole heart. God does not consider our station in life as a prerequisite for knowing Him. He promises to cast out no one, and He is bound by His word. He can't say no to someone who comes to Him.

Just as we can't refuse God when we encounter His love, He can't refuse us when we seek Him with all our hearts. Passion binds us together.

In fact, this is the surest proof I know of our relationship with God. That we desire this relationship and are seeking after Him is evidence of our place with Him. We wouldn't do this if we were not already in His sights—if He was not already working in us. That we are seeking Him proves that we have already been found.

From *Lord Jesus, I Long to Be Perfectly Whole* by James Nicholson

Whiter Than Snow

Now wash me and I shall be whiter than snow.

Can you think of anything whiter than snow? Perhaps God made snow just to give us a picture of how He sees our hearts after they are cleansed from sin.

But the comparison doesn't end there. Anyone who has lived in a snow belt knows what happens just before the first big storm catches you unawares. Lost objects from summer play protrude from under bushes and vines that have been stripped bare by autumn winds. That yellow sand bucket everyone thought was left at the beach suddenly appears under the blackberry vines. You find the green frisbee that was embedded deep in the blueberry bush for half a summer. And unraked leaves appear matted in bare flower beds.

And before you can get around to cleaning up the mess, a surprise six-inch November snowfall covers it all with a splendid white blanket. Then the sun comes out and nearly blinds you with its beauty.

That's when you remember that snow is not only the whitest thing you have ever seen, but that it also covers up everything that is ugly and unsightly with a blanket of purity.

From *Lord Jesus, I Long to Be Perfectly Whole* by James Nicholson

Why Righteousness?

Lord Jesus, I long to be perfectly whole;
I want Thee forever to live in my soul.

Our desire for a relationship with God is the reason for our righteousness. Wanting to be whole is noble, but it is not an end in itself.

If God were only in the business of making perfect beings, He could have made robots that would have accomplished His goal without all the trouble we've given Him.

God created us in His image so we could have a relationship with Him. Our righteousness—or wholeness—makes that relationship possible. God cannot have fellowship with darkness, and we are all in darkness without the light of Christ and His salvation.

We long to be whole, not just to be whole, and not so we can say "Hey, look at me, I'm whole!" We long to be whole so He can live in our souls. Only when we are cleansed of our sin through the blood of Jesus can He take up residence in us. Only in our holiness can we share eternity with Him.

Our righteousness has a reason. It is not for us as much as it is for Him. We are made for Him—for a relationship with Him—that we might be to the praise of His glory. Beware of righteousness for its own sake alone. This is not reason enough.

From *Come, We That Love the Lord* by William Hammond

Getting Rid of the Love of Sin

Sing till the love of sin departs,
And grace inspires our songs.

Our love of sin is inversely proportional to our love of God. If we are far away from Him, sin will have a stronger pull on us than if we are close. But in the presence of God, sin becomes undesirable.

Sin almost always comes from our trying to get attention in a wrong way. When we don't believe we are loved by God, we try to get fulfillment and attention some other way. Just see if you are tempted to sin when you are looking at the beauty and loveliness of God and experiencing His unconditional love for you. Sin loses its appeal in the presence of God's affirming love. We sin when we believe an idea of ourselves other than God's. We sin when we do not believe what His grace proclaims about our belovedness.

So sing, then. Sing songs of His forgiveness and His love for you. Remind yourself of God and what He has done and why He did it. Sing songs that remind you of who you are simply because you are loved by Him. And when you've done all that, keep singing until the love of sin starts to fade.

From *Come, We That Love the Lord* by William Hammond

Dry Tears

Then let our songs abound,
And let our tears be dry...

Tears are not always dry where songs abound. For me, the best songs make tears come. To experience the grace of God in a new way is to be overwhelmed and overcome with tears.

I don't know exactly how I feel about "dry tears." That sounds like an oxymoron to me. It may be referring to those times when we are so cried out that there are no more tears left to cry. But I would never want to be rid of tears altogether.

Tears capture our astonishment and amazement at the wonder of the gospel. One day I had lunch with a professor at a Christian college, and he was telling me of his frustration over trying to communicate the gospel to Christian students who want everything spelled out in easy answers. When he told me that the long and short answer was Jesus Himself, his eyes went wet with tears. I knew then that he had been touched by Christ more deeply than words could ever explain.

Those are the tears I never want to go dry. And when I get to heaven, those are the tears I would just as soon not have anyone wipe away—even the Lord Himself. I want to be able to look at Him in all His glory and sing as the tears stream down my face.

From *For the Beauty of the Earth* by Folliott S. Pierpoint

Celebrating the Senses

For the joy of ear and eye,
For the heart and mind's delight,
For the mystic harmony
Linking sense to sound and sight...

How intricately we have been woven together! The human body is one fine piece of work, and the quality of workmanship demands worship in its most elemental form.

"I praise you because I am fearfully and wonderfully made," the psalmist says in Psalm 139:14. This kind of worship is based not on salvation, but on being part of the created order, made in the likeness of God. This is worship of the Creator by the created.

We don't worship this way enough for two reasons: First, we don't really think of it—we take too much for granted. The chemical synapses that link our eyes, ears, hearts, and minds are constantly exploding their messages throughout our bodies, and we hardly notice them unless for some reason one of them gives us a problem.

Second, we have not thought fondly of anything human for at least the last half of a century. For many Christians, celebrating the physical senses isn't considered a spiritual thing to do. On the contrary, most Christians have assumed that the physical senses are the culprit when they sin. "My senses made me do it," some would say. But what a shame to degrade something so wonderfully made. Isn't this a greater sin?

Jesus put the blame for sin on our hearts, not our bodies. When righteousness begins in the heart, then we can glorify God in our bodies. This is when we find out why we were made.

From *The Light of the World Is Jesus* by Phillip P. Bliss

Go Wash

Ye dwellers in darkness with sin-blinded eyes,
The light of the world is Jesus;
Go wash at His bidding, and light will arise...

Just do that one thing He's asking of you, and you will see the miracle.

Jesus sometimes works this way with us. He likes to have us do something first before He shows Himself or His power to us. Quite often it's as simple as, "Go wash in the pool." This is what He told a blind man after placing mud over his eyes (see John 9:7). He could have healed him by a word, like the others, but this man was different. Perhaps he needed the courage to act on the words of the Savior for some future act of faith.

He must have looked silly walking over to the pool with mud on His eyes. He would have looked even sillier if after washing, nothing had happened.

Faith sometimes makes us look silly, and we have to decide which is more important: to look cool, or to do what Jesus says. Walking around trying to find a pool with mud in your eyes is not very cool, but if it meant you might regain your sight, wouldn't you do it?

What is God asking you to do today that might look a little silly? It just might be worth the embarrassment. There could be a miracle in it for you!

From *Fairest Lord Jesus*
(a German hymn adapted by Richard Storrs Willis)

Beautiful Savior

Jesus is fairer, Jesus is purer,
Who makes the woeful heart to sing.

Who sees the beauty of Jesus? Who finds Him fairer than the meadows and the woodlands, even when they are robed in their blooming garb of spring? To whom does He shine brighter and purer than the sun, the moon and the stars put together?

Surely, it wasn't the prophet Isaiah. He called Jesus a Man of Sorrows and acquainted with grief, one who had no form or comeliness that anyone should desire Him, one from whom a person would have to hide his face (see Isaiah 53:2-3).

Nor could it have been John the Revealer, who gave us a picture of the Son of Man as one coming to judge the earth. It was a terrible picture of flaming eyes, feet glowing like bronze in a furnace, and a mouth brandishing a razor-sharp, two-edged sword. That picture threw the prophet to earth as a dead man (see Revelations 1:9-17).

Who, then, can speak of Christ's beauty? Who sees Him as fair and pure and beautiful? Is this someone with special insight? Is it the scholar who has studied Him, or the pastor who has preached His message? Is it the missionary who has taken the message abroad, or is it the famous contemporary Christian singer who has popularized Christ's beauty to thousands?

It may be one of these, but not necessarily so. That is because it will always be the one with the woeful heart who sees the beauty of the Savior. It is the undeserving recipient of the grace of God to whom Christ becomes an object of affection. No one can see His beauty any better than a forgiven sinner.

And what a song the woeful heart sings!

From *Fairest Lord Jesus*
(a German hymn adapted by Richard Storrs Willis)

Friends of Jesus

O Thou of God and man the Son...

Jesus was both Son of God and Son of Man. But of the two, He most often referred to Himself as the Son of Man. "The Son of Man has authority on earth..." "The Son of Man came to save what was lost..." "The Son of Man did not come to be served..." "The Son of Man came eating and drinking..." "The Son of Man must suffer many things..." "The Son of Man is going to be betrayed..." "You will see the Son of Man coming on the clouds of the sky..." "You will see the Son of Man sitting at the right hand of the Mighty One..." and so forth.

Jesus knew He was from God and that some of us would recognize that. But He spent more time trying to get us to see that He was also from man, that He was one of us. He spent eternity with the Father, but now He was spending thirty-three years with us. And you get the impression that He liked that. He enjoyed identifying with His creation. How else would He have gained a reputation as a "glutton and a drunkard, a friend of tax collectors and sinners" (Matthew 11:19)?

Jesus was a friend of sinners because, believe it or not, He was among friends. He did not just *tolerate* these people, He *loved* them. Even while He was dying, He forgave them. He even took one of them—a criminal—along with Him into paradise as they died together side by side.

Looking at Jesus this way makes you want to think twice before you judge another person. Remember, that person is one of His friends!

September 5

From *Fairest Lord Jesus*
(a German hymn adapted by Richard Storrs Willis)

Soul Talk

Thee will I cherish, Thee will I honor,
Thou, my soul's Glory, Joy, and Crown!

The dictionary defines *soul* as "the essential part of anything." The soul is what we feel with. It is what moves us and what makes us alive. A person who has no feeling is said to be a person without a soul. In some ways, the soul is smarter than the mind. Or at least wiser.

As such, the soul is more subconscious than conscious, more intuitive than cognizant. King David addressed his own soul from time to time, as in "Praise the Lord, O my soul" (Psalm 104:1), as if the soul could be engaged in conversation. This is an example of the conscious mind instructing the soul what to do with itself. Sometimes the soul needs to be directed.

Other times, as in this hymn, it's the soul that has it right and everything else in me needs to listen up. More often than not, I find this to be the case. My soul's true joy and glory is the Lord Jesus Himself. My soul knows this best of all. My soul has received the first fruits of the Spirit and will one day be clothed in righteousness and wearing a crown. So it is pure and right and natural for my soul to express itself now and glory in this truth. My body and mind are more easily distracted by lesser things.

This is why the Lord tells us to be still and know. We do know. Our soul knows. But sometimes we forget, because we're listening to everything but our soul.

From *Where Shall My Wondering Soul Begin?* by Charles Wesley

Hell Bound

O how shall I the goodness tell,
Father, which Thou to me hast showed?
That I a child of wrath and hell,
I should be called a child of God?

We don't think of ourselves as once being children of wrath and hell. To be sure, *wrath* and *hell* are words we rarely hear any more, even in church. They are unpleasant words, and we are too busy making church less offensive to people.

But children of wrath and hell is exactly what we are—or were. We were born into this. Our sin sealed our destination. We were hell-bound from the womb until Jesus found us and rescued us from the inevitable plunge.

Hell is a place where we have to pay for all the sinful things we've done. God will not be mocked—whatever we sow, we will have to reap—and to the degree that we still keep sowing, we have to keep reaping, or at least somebody does. If it isn't us, it's Jesus. God has no rug to sweep sin under. He has to deal with it. Sin never was and never will be casual. Sin brings wrath, and wrath brings hell. And hell means you spend all eternity paying, unless someone else pays for you.

This all means that we mustn't get casual about sin when Jesus is paying.

From *Where Shall My Wondering Soul Begin?* by Charles Wesley

His Open Side

Come, O my guilty brethren come,
Groaning beneath your load of sin!
His bleeding heart shall make you room,
His open side shall take you in.

This is a difficult thought, this picture of a wounded savior. But the essence of what Mr. Wesley is saying here is that Jesus was cut open so we could be brought in to God. His pain and suffering opened the way for you and me to enter in and become one with God.

Adam was cut open too. And out of his rib, God made Eve. Could this be a picture of the crucifixion, but in reverse? At the cross was the bride of Christ being brought into oneness with Him through a similar surgery—His own "Eve" brought in through His sacrifice? Certainly, it was a much more painful ordeal for Christ than it was for Adam.

While Adam did not know what was happening to him, Christ did know. Jesus had already counted the cost, and but for a brief moment in the garden, He never hesitated. His Father had already counted this whole enterprise worthy of everything it would cost.

Jesus was acting out the heart of God, and God's heart is big enough to take in the whole world through the pierced side of Christ.

From *O Sacred Head Now Wounded* by Bernard of Clairvaux

Dying Safely

For he who dies believing,
Dies safely through Thy love.

A safe death? I've never heard of such a thing. What could be more dangerous than death? Indeed, death is synonymous with danger. Adventure novels and films count on this. The more dangerous the situation, the closer the hero is to death. And what circus would be complete without two or three "death-defying" acts?

All the more reason to wonder about such a mystery as this: that death could actually be something safe. Why would the hymn writer say this? Only because of God's love. His love has made a way for Jesus to be waiting to meet us on the other side of death.

Indeed, it is a strange turn of events that has us entering the world in terror and exiting in joy. What a switch God pulls on our friends, all celebrating and laughing at the hospital of our birth while we cried our heads off. Then, these are the same folks who cry at the end when we pass on to the safe arms of the Father and the laughter of angels.

To a believer, it's much more dangerous entering this world than it is leaving it.

From *O Sacred Head Now Wounded* by Bernard of Clairvaux

Mine... Forever

O sacred Head, what glory,
What bliss till now was Thine!
Yet though despised and gory,
I joy to call Thee mine.

Jesus shared glory with the Father from the very beginning. The worlds were made in and through His glory. His glory made the moon and the stars and set the earth buzzing with flowers, bees, crashing surf, and rolling thunderheads. His glory made all things, from the vast oceans to the molecular particles that make up the water in them.

And He made man and woman a little lower than the angels, crowning them with glory and honor. And after all this, He became one of them. He was unjustly charged and punished. He endured lashings, mockery, a farce of a trial and a dishonorable death. He made a ghastly picture hanging there with blood dried and caked on His face and pouring out from wounds to his feet, hands, and side. It was a picture few could look at and fewer can imagine.

And yet this sight was a crown of glory for you and me. For glory passed over to us at the moment of His death. Our death became His, His glory became ours. For this, I will look and call Him mine... forever.

From *Purer Yet and Purer*, Author unknown

By and By

Swifter yet and swifter
Ever onward run,
Firmer yet and firmer
Step as I go on...

One good thing about this life of faith: It gets better. Note that I said *life of faith*, not *life* itself. Life doesn't necessarily get better. In some instances—maybe even most—it gets worse. But our faith eventually gets stronger. God gets closer, truth gets clearer, and hope gets firmer.

Faith builds upon itself. Each time you step out in faith, you create a platform of substance that wasn't there before, establishing a newer, stronger place to stand. This is why it's such a joy to be around men and women of God who have lived a long life of faith. In their presence, "Faith is the substance of things hoped for" (Hebrews 11:1, KJV) becomes reality. What's hoped for is sometimes more real than what's tangible.

When I was growing up, my parents and their friends used to sing a gospel song that ended each verse and chorus with the phrase: "and we'll understand it better by and by." That didn't mean much to me then, but it means a lot now.

Maybe I'm starting into my own "by and by." Having a hard time believing? Keep at it. It gets better.

From *Jesus, I My Cross Have Taken* by Henry F. Lyte

"Feelings"

Oh, 'tis not in grief to harm me,
While Thy love is left to me;
Oh 'twere not in joy to charm me,
Were that joy unmixed with Thee.

This hymn reminds me of a haunting statement from the apostle Paul: "From now on those who mourn (should live) as if they did not; those who are happy, as if they were not" (1 Corinthians 7:29-30).

Both the hymn and the verse are speaking about tempering earthly joys and sorrows—what our present culture idolizes as "feelings." To one who worships daily at the First Church of Daytime Soaps, nothing seems more important than the joys and griefs of everyone's twisted, sordid lives.

But a relationship with God stands on more than our feelings. It stands on truth and it puts a floor and a ceiling around our emotions. As Christians, we do not live for our feelings, nor are we ruled by them. We grieve, but not in despair. Grief touches us, but not so deeply that it separates us from the love of God. Our grief has a bottom, just as our joy has a ceiling.

We should never trust in a joy that does not contain the presence of God. It will slam us down faster than it carried us up, and leave us lower than where it found us. This is always the way it is when God is not part of joy.

God, however, shares countless joys and sorrows with us. There are dances to be danced and tears to be shed. But through it all, His presence tethers our emotions to the truth.

From *Jesus, I My Cross Have Taken* by Henry F. Lyte

True Devotion

Let the world despise and leave me—
They have left my Savior, too;
Human hearts and looks deceive me—
Thou art not, like man, untrue.

People can be so fickle, and yet we keep going back to them for what we think we want. People give tangible feedback, and it doesn't matter whether the response is positive or negative. We are all starved for attention, so much so that we will take it even if we know we are being deceived or, in some cases, even abused.

Only God can actually touch our hearts and satisfy our deepest need for love and attention. And He is eminently more desirable because He is true. Still, it is a challenge to be satisfied with a relationship that relies totally on faith.

Lord, you know how powerful these tangible sources of worth and identity are to us, and yet how destructive they can be as well. You know how we can even misuse friends or husbands or wives for our own purposes and cling to them in unhealthy ways. Teach us to wait on you—to learn to make our devotion to you the source of our strength and value. For you will never leave us or forsake us. You will never deceive us or trick us. You will never use us to fill up some lack in yourself, for you lack nothing.

From *All Glory, Laud and Honor* by Theodulph of Orleans

Sweet Hosannas

All glory, laud and honor
To Thee, Redeemer, King,
To whom the lips of children
Made sweet hosannas ring.

Sweet hosannas. There is an unmistakable sweetness in a child's voice. One thinks of laughter, joy, or purity—as in the bell-like tone of a well-trained boys choir. It is a voice unleadened by the weight of the world, a voice that has no ulterior motive but to come out and play.

Children would not have sung Christ's praises had He not gathered them in His arms or knelt to take in their shining eyes, face to face. He noticed them, and when it came time for them to notice Him, they were ready. Most adults never notice them. Children are to be seen and not heard, right?

My children know immediately whether they count to an adult. You can tell it by how long they stay in the room when an adult visits, how long it is before their busy, active minds think of something better to do.

No one sent the children out to honor Jesus that day when they sang their hosannas in the temple (see Matthew 21:15-16). Their joy was a natural response to being important in the eyes of Jesus. Jesus even rebuked the religious leaders who attempted to silence their voices. "Have you never read, 'From the lips of children and infants you have ordained praise'?"

There are some things that children naturally know, but that adults too quickly forget. Perhaps we should listen again today to those childhood impulses.

From *All Glory, Laud and Honor* by Theodulph of Orleans

In the Heavenlies

The company of angels
Are praising Thee on high.

It is enlightening to know that, while I engage myself here on earth with seemingly unimportant tasks such as organizing my time, trying to figure out which bills to pay, answering the phone, logging business calls, watering the plants, getting the children to soccer practice, and getting the next day's events down on paper, there are at the same time a multitude of the heavenly hosts, surrounding the throne of God with endless, continual praise. Something tells me that they, like Mary at the feet of Jesus, have chosen the best part.

Of course, this doesn't change much for me. I still have to go through my average day of comparably mundane activities. But somehow, just knowing they are up there carrying on like that in their praise of God puts a little smile on my face. It helps me put things in perspective because I know that someday I'll be joining them.

It wouldn't hurt to have a little of that angelic praise spill over into my day, either. Why not join in for a chorus or two while I'm on my way somewhere? And if I'm seated in the heavenlies like Paul said (Ephesians 2:6), I should be able to hear them singing even now.

September 15

From *All Glory, Laud and Honor* by Theodulph of Orleans

What Delights God

Thou didst accept their praises,
Accept the praise we bring.
Who in all good delightest,
Thou good and gracious King!

God delights in what is good. What is good has something to do with God. Goodness exists. It is present in the world, and it is present in people. Wherever we encounter it, there is cause to delight.

We are always checking the label first before we can find anything to delight about. We think, "I see good there, but it isn't coming from a died-in-the-wool, justified, sanctified, sanforized, Spirit-filled Christian. It can't be good, then. Must just look like it's good."

Aside from salvation, which is another issue, there is much to delight God on earth. He made everything and He called it *all* good. Though marred by the entrance of sin, the intrinsic nature of what He made is still good. God still delights in His creation, unredeemed as it is.

Why, then, are we so bent on finding what is bad? Why are we so quick to pounce on the innocence of a child, the happiness of an unsaved couple, the achievement of an athlete regardless of his income, or the eventual freedom of a convicted criminal? Why do we first assume the evil motive?

It appears that for most Christians, the Fall has gotten better publicity than Creation. It should be up to the redeemed to see the potential in all that still lies unredeemed and treat it accordingly.

There is much to delight in today. Help me to see it, Lord, as you see it.

From *Jesus, Thy Boundless Love to Me* by Paul Gerhardt

A Thankful Heart

O knit my thankful heart to Thee,
And reign without a rival there.

Thanksgiving binds us to God. Our good works don't, and neither do self-denial or a disciplined walk. Not even our knowledge of Scripture or our time spent in devotion are a guarantee of intimacy with God. All of these will play an important role in the spiritual life. But a thankful heart is at the root of a healthy relationship with God.

All spiritual activity, all discipline, all good works begin in the heart. What makes a thankful heart? The assurance that before we do *anything*, God has already done *everything*. It's also the realization that we have nothing to prove—He has already proved Himself and approved of us before we start.

In this way, a thankful heart is the beginning of all spiritual activity. We have nothing to prove, and we are merely grateful for what He has done for us. Our efforts, including duty and discipline, spring from this glad response.

Nothing spiritual can be accomplished without a spirit of thanksgiving because nothing spiritual can spring from any source other than what He has done for us. A thankful heart is probably the best barometer of the spiritual climate of our souls.

From *I Love to Tell the Story* by A. Catherine Hankey

Heavenly Hits

And when, in scenes of glory,
I sing the new, new, song,
'Twill be the old, old story
That I have loved so long.

Sometimes I wonder if the songs of our salvation might be the only earthly things allowed in heaven. How can we ever forget His grace? Is this not what makes our worship different from that of the angels? Though they are higher and more powerful, they do not know what we know. They have not experienced what we have been saved from. And if grace will continue to be our theme in heaven, does it not stand to reason that some memory of sin will remain as well, just to give meaning to our praise and to make our praise unique, as it were, in the heavens?

I wonder if it might be through songs such as this one that we will remember—earthly songs that remind us of what, in our completeness in heaven, we might be tempted to forget. Wouldn't it be grand to think that we will forever sing not just songs *like* this, but *this song*, carried into heaven by His bride as a trophy of our earthly deliverance and an eternal reminder of how we got there?

We may forget our sin, but how can we ever forget that we once had sin, and that God did a remarkable thing to free us from it? Won't we be telling the story over and over again? And singing it? And something tells me we will never grow tired of it.

From *I Love to Tell the Story* by A. Catherine Hankey

Like the First Time

I love to tell the story;
For those who know it best
Seem hungering and thirsting
To hear it like the rest.

Properly understood, the gospel is hungered for as much by Christians of long standing as it is by those who first come to it, convicted of sin. The passion and resurrection of Jesus rejuvenates even those who have been in the faith for decades. All believers come to the gospel like children with wide eyes.

This defies the normal course of events. If you know something well, you are familiar with all of its ins and outs. You have studied its implications and its details until you are an expert on it. As a result, you are usually somewhat aloof to it. Those who are "in the know" on a certain subject are usually in another camp than those who are coming to it for the first time. Knowledge has a way of creating its own intellectual caste system.

Not so with the story of Jesus and His love. Seminary professors who have been poring over it for decades still weep over it and hunger for it in their own personal lives. Pastors who have taught it over and over again still find it fresh in their own hearts each time they come to the story. Evangelists, when they deliver the gospel for the some hundred thousandth time via satellite hookup to the world, are still hungering and thirsting for it in their own souls—just as much as the young drug addict who comes forward for the first time.

If the story of salvation ever gets old, it's a sure sign that we need to make certain we're in the story.

From *Nothing but the Blood* by Robert Lowry

Miracle Wash

What can wash away my sin?
Nothing but the blood of Jesus;
What can make me whole again?
Nothing but the blood of Jesus.

Sin is particularly vulnerable to blood. In the Old Testament, the blood of bulls and goats effectively cleansed the stains of sin, if only for a season. Daily sin soils the soul's inner garments so that they need repeated washings. The Israelites never seemed to get caught up on the laundry.

But everything changed when the true Lamb of God came. His blood has such cleansing power that it gets sin stains out permanently. Those who are washed in this blood need never wash again. The same wash can be applied by faith over and over for sins so as to keep your garments as white as snow.

This is powerful stuff on sin—powerful enough to get the stain out and keep it out. No need to harm those delicate garments of the soul with harsh detergents. Just one application, and watch those stains disappear. Try this miracle wash today!

From *Nothing but the Blood* by Robert Lowry

It Is Enough

This is all my hope and peace—
Nothing but the blood of Jesus;
This is all my righteousness—
Nothing but the blood of Jesus.

Without the blood of Jesus, we have no hope, no peace, and no righteousness. The blood was the price paid for our sin, which had exacted heavy dues on us. We were in serious debt, and we could never possibly pay for our deeds. The price was just too high. We could have died, but our blood could not have secured heaven for us. We would have been dead, and that would have been the end of it.

His blood is different. It came from God Himself. It was royal blood... holy blood. It was God's blood running through human veins. It was perfect blood—untainted by Adam's race, and with no sin or damaged genes in it to pass on to following generations. This blood meant something, and when it was spilled, a miracle took place. Just as the two loaves and a few fish fed a multitude, so His precious blood kept flowing until it covered the sins of the world.

Apart from this, we have no hope. We are dead in our trespasses and sin. The blood we got from Adam is good for only one short life. But the blood of Christ lasts for all eternity. And there is more than enough to cover anyone who needs it.

From *Rescue the Perishing* by Fanny J. Crosby

Gut Reaction Gospel

Weep o'er the erring one,
Lift up the fallen,
Tell them of Jesus the mighty to save.

Do we weep over someone caught inexorably in the web of sin? Do we weep, or do we wish upon them a swift and lasting judgment? When someone falls, especially from a high place, do we gloat over their demise, or look for a way to lift them up? When we see the obvious fallenness of humanity every day in the newspapers, do we long for the perpetrators to know the saving power of Christ, or do we long for them to know the fires of hell? What's our gut reaction?

What about the pathological killer, the child abuser, the terrorist? Are some people so bad that they are beyond the saving power of Jesus? It is understandable that the normal gut reaction of a person toward those who prey on the innocent is a swift judgment—that they might suffer in a measure equal to the suffering they have caused. But this indignation must quickly be brought under control and blanketed by the gospel and the knowledge that vengeance and judgment belong to God and the state, not to us.

Until the gospel becomes our gut reaction to a world in sin, we will continue to propagate an eye for an eye and a tooth for a tooth. We will probably suffer the loss of our own eyes and teeth in the process, and no one will ever become whole.

From *Rescue the Perishing* by Fanny J. Crosby

Deep in the Heart of Sinners

Down in the human heart,
Crushed by the tempter,
Feelings lie buried that grace can restore;
Touched by a loving heart,
Wakened by kindness,
Chords that were broken will vibrate once more.

No one is outside the scope of the saving power of Jesus Christ. But if it were up to us, certain people would be ineligible for the gospel. Fortunately, for everyone's sake—our own included—this is not the case.

Deep in their hearts, sinners know and long for their Maker. But that longing is only awakened by love and kindness. How a sinner responds to being touched by grace is none of our business. It is only our business to do the touching.

The gospel is not primarily about morality, for it assumes we are all transgressors. The gospel is all about forgiveness and restoration, and it is carried by acts of love and kindness—something no sinner is expecting to receive. When Christians bestow love and kindness on those who don't expect it, it can break open the calloused heart and reach in to pluck the chords of consciousness once again.

"Do not be overcome by evil," wrote Paul in Romans. In other words, do not let evil draw you into the net with evildoers by coercing you to act in an evil way toward them, "... but overcome evil with good" (Romans 12:21).

From *Rescue the Perishing* by Fanny J. Crosby

Care for the Dying

Rescue the perishing, care for the dying;
Snatch them in pity from hell and the grave.

This hymn brings old insight to a new problem, hitting home with surprising accuracy. There is a rise in the world of fatal diseases, in some places reaching epidemic proportions. Some of these diseases are transmitted through promiscuous sexual behavior, thus linking the disease—and its results—directly to sin.

Some will argue that people thus afflicted are receiving in their bodies the judgment of their specific sin, as spoken about in Romans 1:24-32. And if these people are being judged by God, shouldn't we leave them to their judgment?

To answer this, it must be asked: Are we not all dying? Are we not all receiving every day the deterioration of our bodies through the judgment of sin? On what basis do we receive mercy while they don't? Aren't we lucky that God, at least at the present time, does not seem to be distributing deadly diseases for sins such as lying, slander, or envy?

Anyone who quotes the first chapter of Romans must also quote chapter two: "So when you, a mere man, pass judgment on them... do you think you will escape God's judgment? Or do you show contempt for the riches of His kindness, tolerance and patience, not realizing that God's kindness leads you toward repentance?" (Romans 2:3-4).

The opening lines of this hymn speak to how Christians should feel toward those who, for whatever reason, have been afflicted with these or other diseases. In caring for the dying, our kindness may lead someone to repentance.

From *When I Can Read My Title Clear* by Isaac Watts

Last Look

When I can read my title clear
To mansions in the skies,
I'll bid farewell to every fear,
And wipe my weeping eyes.

You'd have to be pretty close to death to be able to read the title on your heavenly mansion. You'd have to be right at the doorway—at the very portals—of heaven. Apparently, when we are this close to the end, we will be able to see into heaven so well that any fear of leaving earth will vanish.

Many who have watched loved ones leave the earth have told stories that bear this out. They say there is a pleasantness, a peace, and joy in the spirit of the departing one that no one can deny or explain.

We can learn a lot from seeing someone watching something else. For instance, watch an audience observe a play or a comedy routine and you will be entertained almost as much as you would be by watching the show. Much of the story shows on their faces. It must be something like this when we watch a believer slip into heaven. I've heard that last look on the face is glorious. Perhaps because someone is meeting that dying person on the other side? Maybe a heavenly lawyer with the title to their mansion in His hand? Close enough to read it?

From *My Saviour's Love* by Charles H. Gabriel

Living and Dying for Someone Else

For me it was in the garden
He prayed, "Not my will, but Thine,"
He had no tears for His own griefs,
But sweat-drops of blood for mine.

Our culture floods us with lies. It even tells us that if we serve ourselves first, we will end up doing what is best for everyone else. This is the basis of our free-market economy, and it is also the basis of a good deal of the pop psychology that has made significant inroads into the church. We are told by some that Jesus' injunction to love our neighbor as ourselves is actually an authorization to put love of self above all else. But that is a big stretch of the words of Jesus.

Jesus' command to love our neighbors as we love ourselves is not, as some teach it today, a command to love oneself. It is a command to love others in a way that assumes a self-love. It is similar to Paul's admonition to husbands: "He who loves his wife loves himself. After all, no one ever hated his own body, but he feeds and cares for it..." (Ephesians 5:28-29). In both cases, self-love is taken for granted.

We do not need to be instructed to love ourselves. Even people with bad self-images look after themselves, albeit in a negative way. Jesus is only saying that we should look after others *at least* as well as we are looking after ourselves.

And then He gives us His own example of His whole life: Living and dying thinking of someone else. Thinking of us. Who are you thinking of today? Only yourself, or someone else?

From *My Hope Is in the Lord* by Norman J. Clayton

Be Sure to R.S.V.P.

His grace has planned it all,
'Tis mine but to believe...

He's taken care of everything. The invitations have gone out, the banquet is planned. The ceremony will be well attended and well heeled, though it's been rumored in the society pages that some of the more distinguished guests may snub the Host and not attend. Too bad for them.

It's a long-standing feud they have with Him—these religious types, steeped more in self-righteousness than in true godliness. They have always disapproved of the way He treats everyone the same, even giving "dishonorable guests" places of honor, while relegating some of them to the background. And after all their years of service to the church! Many of these modern-day Pharisees have announced they have had it with this kind of treatment, and they are not even going to attend.

"Not to worry," says the Host. "There's plenty to go around for everyone." That's what led Him, in fact, to throw an open invitation to people from the streets and the highways and byways of life. It's gotten to where anyone who wants to believe the Host and receive an invitation can come now.

I'm going to be there for sure. I've already given my R.S.V.P. Hope to see you there!

From *How Sweet the Name of Jesus Sounds* by John Newton

First-Name Basis

How sweet the name of Jesus sounds
In a believer's ear!
It soothes his sorrows, heals his wounds,
And drives away his fear.

It's amazing how just one name can do all that... the *sound* of one name. One name that assures me that I am found. One name that reaches across the ages and over the multitudes and picks out *me.*

This name—*Jesus*—defines God. It puts Him in terms I can at least begin to understand. Through the bloody gateway of a mother's womb He came: scrawny, dusted with white, and screaming. He grew and laughed and played the games of childhood. And soon—sooner than any of His friends—he was about doing His father's will.... His Father in heaven, that is. His Father's will would take Him to an early end, when He would die thinking of you and me. He would die unforgotten, that His Father might remember all those the world forgot. And He has assured that I will be among many remembered in paradise.

This name is my ticket to heaven. It is proof that I know someone there—someone important—and He knows me. His sacrifice has put Him and me on a first-name basis. Jesus is His name, and never was there a sweeter sound in my ear than the name of the One who took my sin away and made me right with God. This is the name of Him who sought me before I knew Him—who did for me what I could never do for myself. It's nice to know I'm on a first-name basis with the Ruler of all things, the Giver of life, and the Judge in the judge's chamber—all at the same time.

From *Come, My Soul, Thou Must Be Waking*
by Friedrich R. L. Von Canitz

Our Helpless Hours

For the night has safely ended;
God hath tended
With His care thy helpless hours.

It's morning now. We went to sleep in the darkness and woke up in the light. While we slept, God tended to our helpless hours. Not a bad thought—not as long as we don't forget our dependence on Him when we are awake.

Our helpless hours come in batches of twenty-four a day. Only our pride tells us otherwise. Waking up to the light of day and coming out of a vulnerable sleep makes us feel as if we can have things under control. But danger lurks in this kind of independence. We need God tending to our waking hours as much as to our sleeping ones. Maybe even more so, considering the trouble we can get into when we are awake. Can't get in too much trouble when we're asleep, can we?

Faith is learning to live our waking hours with the same trust we put in God when we sleep. When we are asleep, we don't worry, and that should be our frame of mind when we are awake. This is what the Scriptures call "entering into the rest." It means that while we are awake and working, God is at work in and through us, working out His will for our lives.

From *In the Place of Sorrow, Waiting,* Author unknown

No Self-Interest

Undismayed, his foes forgiving,
To the last for others living,
Lays He down His life for all.

Everything Jesus did, He did for someone other than Himself. He didn't have to come to earth. He came only for us. He was born for us and lived for us. He died and rose again for us. He ascended into heaven for us and is at the right hand of the Father right now. All for us!

Jesus never went to a guidance counselor to find out what career would be best suited for Him. He never considered His options. Jesus never wondered what other people thought about Him—He probably knew, but didn't care. He not only made Himself of no reputation, but reputation was nothing to Him. Jesus had no vested interests to confuse the picture. He never considered Himself. He only considered His Father's will and the lives of those He came to save.

Jesus never cried for Himself, and He never considered His own feelings. He never doubted what He could do, and He never weighed His chances against those of another. Jesus feared no one. He had no self-interest. He held nothing back. And when it came time for Him to give, He gave it all—His whole life... everything He had.

Who could be more trustworthy?

From *In the Place of Sorrow, Waiting,* Author unknown

Two Great Wills

Love heroic, love unshrinking,
Heaven and earth together linking,
Reigns He as the shadows fall.

The lives of millions hung in the balance. The will of the Father was at stake. The plan was now in its most crucial hour. Jesus had to be obedient unto death.

Along the way, Jesus had friends. But in the end, they all left Him. Even when He prayed and struggled over the cup of death, His last three friends slept on, unable to heed His simple request for companionship.

"Father, if it is possible, may this cup be taken from me," He prayed as the angels held their breath. "Yet not as I will, but as you will" (Matthew 26:39). And two Great Wills clashed for an awful moment, before one gave in to the other.

Then all left Him—even His Father turned away. And in the loneliest moment in human history, the Son of Man hung between heaven and earth. And He died in the shadows.

Had He been any less heroic, had He exerted His will over His Father's, we would have had no hope.

From *From Every Stormy Wind that Blows* by Hugh Stowell

Around the Table

There is a scene where spirits blend,
Where friend holds fellowship with friend;
Though sundered far, by faith they meet
Around one common mercy seat.

God has created us for Himself, but He also has made us for each other. He enjoys our quiet moments of devotion, our silent and personal prayers. But it also appears evident that He enjoys us enjoying each other as His creations. Witness His first miracle at a wedding reception and His bent for being found at parties when He was here. Witness the special role that feasts, suppers, and banquets play in the Old and New Testaments, culminated by that great marriage supper of the Lamb that we all have reservations for.

In my mind's eye, I can see the Lord looking around the table at some point during these festivities—at a time when He is not in conversation with anyone, but when everyone around Him is conversing with each other. I can imagine His eyes moving from group to group, reveling in our enjoyment of one another.

John writes: "We proclaim to you what we have seen and heard, so that you also may have fellowship with us. And our fellowship is with the Father and with His Son, Jesus Christ. We write this to make our joy complete" (1 John 1:3-4).

The disciples John refers to here must have had some really good times together. So much so that they wanted to add to the party. We've got to get out and invite as many people as possible to the banquet too. It would be sad for anyone to miss it.

From *The Story of the Cross* by Carrie E. Breck

All of Love

That shining cross shall ever stand
For all of love that man can know.

Think of all the love. Think of family love—husband and wife, parent and child, sibling and sibling. Think not of the rivalries, but the love. Then think of it as the best it can get: a brother who has died for brother on the battlefield, a man who has crossed great barriers for the woman he loves, a family that has fought to stay together.

Think of love that has overcome difficulty, disease, mental retardation, physical ugliness—love that found the loveliness when all was unlovely. Think of all the great stories of human triumph fueled by love at its best—stories chronicled in novels, plays, movies, and television.

Think of love for things familiar—the warmth of a fire, the thump of a dog's wagging tail on the floor, the joy of a new book, the sound of children laughing, or the enjoyment of a fine meal with friends.

Think of love of natural beauty—a sunset, the crash of the ocean, the view from a high mountain in an alpine wilderness, the smell of wild brush being crushed underfoot, the silent blanket of the new-fallen snow.

Think of all the love you can think of, and then realize the cross stands for more. It exceeds the sum of them all. We would trade every earthly joy for the cross if it were required, and yet in it, every earthly joy only deepens.

From *Jesus, Thine All-Victorious Love* by Charles Wesley

The Scattering, Life-Illuminating Gun of God

Refining fire, go through my heart,
Illuminate my soul;
Scatter Thy life through every part,
And sanctify the whole.

Law-enforcement agencies have been trying to outlaw a new bullet that breaks apart upon impact, sending tiny, shrapnel-like pieces of metal ripping through a victim's body. In this hymn, Charles Wesley was looking for something similar to that. He wanted to be shot with the scattering, life-illuminating gun of God. My analogy is shocking, but Wesley's own imagery is so arresting that only something startling could adequately portray it.

Scatter Thy life through every part—the words break up on impact. Pieces of His life lodge themselves in and around vital organs, and suddenly His influence is in us everywhere. This is what it means to be sanctified. It means that every part of me has been touched with the reality of His presence. There is no longer any part of my life He does not share intimately with me. Any hope for a private self, apart from God, has been blown away. Any hope of secret sin is obliterated. He's everywhere. All is sacred now.

No more compartments. No more ability to relegate God to one area of my life that has nothing to do with the rest of me. He has punctured my heart, and His light now illuminates everything.

From *A Shelter in the Time of Storm* by Vernon J. Charlesworth

Strike the Rock

O, Jesus is a rock in a weary land,
A weary land, a weary land;
O, Jesus is a rock in a weary land,
A shelter in the time of storm.

We wander through a weary land, which is what God said this world would be. If this were the promised land, we would be happy and at rest and fulfilled. This was never supposed to be heaven on earth, yet we keep looking for it and trying to procure it. We are constantly surprised at our inability to find it. We are weary over the search. False prophets feed our discomfort by telling us we should have it all now.

I can understand how promises of instant gratification pour forth from our materialistic culture, particularly from those who stand to gain from trying to satisfy our insatiable souls with material possessions. But what I don't understand is how those who are entrusted with the awesome responsibility of bringing the message of God to us can espouse that way of thinking. Ministers of the gospel should not be promising us temporal joys, material satisfactions, or worldly success. Television, radio, newspapers, and magazines continuously promise us these things. But God never made these promises *anywhere* in His Word.

The Bible tells us to suffer and to hope for what we do not see. It tells us to hide our treasures away in heaven and to watch and wait for His appearing. It tells us to endure the discipline of the Lord, to resist temptation, and to postpone pleasure. For now we see through a glass darkly, we know in part and prophesy in part, we hold onto Jesus as we would hold onto a rock in a weary land, for all around us is weariness.

continued

Contrary to what our culture tells us, we were not made for life, liberty, and the pursuit of happiness. We were made to pursue God, and life and liberty only set us free for this purpose. Now, we thirst for Him in a desert where the only water comes from a stricken rock.

From *God the Omnipotent* by John Ellerton and Henry F. Chorley

Two Bad Guys

Falsehood and wrong shall not tarry beside Thee...

The picture I have in my mind when I meditate on this particular hymn lyric is of two guys: Falsehood and Wrong. They're wearing black suits, looking very uncomfortable as they stand beside a man in gleaming white. They nervously check their watches, exchange a few words, tip their hats begrudgingly, and squint in the light of Mr. Gleam as they slip out the back way.

Too many gangster cartoons? Maybe. But in the presence of God, Falsehood and Wrong are out of place. Uninvited guests. They know as well as anybody that they don't belong. They're not even dressed for the occasion.

If I am in God and He is in me, Falsehood and Wrong will want to make a similar exit from my life. Not necessarily because of my effort to find and destroy them, but because in the presence of my permanent Guest, they simply don't belong.

When I go on a crusade against these guys, I usually play into their hand in some way. I give them more attention than they deserve, and they start making plans about moving in. Most people would rather fight than switch.

It may be harder to switch, but it's the only way to get these guys to leave. The more I focus on God within me, the less comfortable Falsehood and Wrong will be around me. They won't tarry long. They've got other more important things to do. And I'm sure they know where the door is.

From *God the Omnipotent* by John Ellerton and Henry F. Chorley

The Sleeping Giant

Let not Thy wrath in its terrors awaken...

"Sinners in the Hands of an Angry God" was a famous sermon by Jonathan Edwards, the Puritan revivalist. History tells us that every great spiritual awakening is accompanied by a great fear of God and a conviction of sin. In some accounts, evangelists needed only to enter a city, and folks would fall on their faces, aware of their uncleanness for the first time.

We don't hear much about the wrath of God anymore. Many preachers would call it spiritual blackmail—not a good way to fill up the pews, they think. To be sure, preachers have misused the wrath of God to scare people into the kingdom, but that's no reason to overreact and drop God's wrath from our vocabulary.

The hymn writers have pictured it well. God's wrath is still in effect, but it's just being restrained for a time. Paul says that the unrepentant are "storing up wrath against (themselves) for the day of God's wrath" (Romans 2:5). While we are not aware of it, God's wrath against sin is building up intensity. Every evil act will have a justifying recompense from a holy God on the appointed day.

We don't have to live in terror of this. But we live in a realization that His wrath is a terrible thing, and that we truly deserve to burn in the heat of it. And were it not for the blood of Jesus, we would.

From *Stand Up, Stand Up for Jesus* by George Duffield

The Arm of Flesh

Stand up, stand up for Jesus!
Stand in His strength alone;
The arm of flesh will fail you;
Ye dare not trust your own.

Self-effort fails every time. While it can initially put on a pretty good show, it never lasts. False ministries rooted in self-effort often fool many genuine people. On camera or on cue, false teachers can in the short-run pull off some pretty impressive displays. But no one stays around long enough to see whether the ministry continues off camera or off stage.

New Year's resolutions and campfire commitments are often like this. We make great promises to ourselves, then try and keep them with the arm of flesh. We always fail when we do this. We let ourselves and our God down, and that puts us in a worse state than before we started. The problem is not in our desire or commitment; it is in the arm of flesh with which we try to make good on our commitments.

Like Moses, who put a veil over his face so that the children of Israel could not see the brightness fading (2 Corinthians 3:13), the arm of flesh—or self-effort based upon law—always fails us. True glory comes from the Spirit inside us, giving us strength to follow Him and keeping us going, even when we fail. Only His strength will never fail us. Trust in Him and Him alone.

From *All Praise to Thee, Eternal Lord* by Martin Luther

Why Did He Do It?

All praise to Thee, eternal Lord,
Who wore the garb of flesh and blood,
And chose a manger for Thy throne,
While worlds on worlds were Thine alone.

He had worlds upon worlds to occupy Him, yet He chose to come to ours. Why would he do that? Coming to this world cost Him dearly. Why not let us rot in hell for all our rebellion? Why bother tangling with Lucifer—that serpent that bruised His heel? Why not just burn him up with all the rest?

Why come to a world that celebrated His coming by putting many of its infant inhabitants to the sword? Why come to a world that welcomed Him with insults, that rejected Him from the beginning. Why come to a world that is *still* trying to explain Him away, even after all He has done to save it? He must have known that this would happen all along, that we would do this to Him. Why bother with it? With us?

Despite all this, he came. He chose to take on human flesh and blood. He chose a manger for His throne. He chose to give up the glories of His universe for an earth-bound home on a hostile planet.

Maybe He did it for love. Or perhaps He did it to save us or to keep us in suspense. Maybe He did it to show us something about Himself or to make possible a real relationship with Him. Maybe it was one of these reasons. Maybe it was all of them.

One thing's for sure: I'm glad He did it for me.

From *Revive Us Again* by William P. MacKay

The Night Scatterer

We praise Thee, O God, for Thy Spirit of light,
Who has shown us our Saviour, and scattered our night.

God the Night Scatterer strikes again! He creates light out of darkness. He makes something out of nothing. This is His specialty. He did it first in the beginning when there was nothing but darkness over the face of the deep. He said "Let there be light," and there it was—light! He brought forth this light out of nothing—out of the very darkness itself.

Today, this same God does the same miracle all over again every time one of us is born of Him. He looks into our dark hearts and says "Let there be light," and there it is—light! God spoke it forth in you. Otherwise, you would not be able to see. You could not see before, but He scattered your night and brought you the light.

God never stops creating. He's always bringing light to dark worlds and dark hearts. He's still doing it, even as you read this. As a matter of fact, right now, somewhere in the world, someone is coming to know Christ. God is causing light to shine in a dark heart. The miracle is happening again. Someone is being born of God. Welcome that person into the family, right now. Pray for them. God will know who it is, and some happy soul is going to get a number of unexpected prayers today.

"For God, who said, 'Let light shine out of darkness,' made His light shine in our hearts to give us the light of the knowledge of the glory of God in the face of Christ" (2 Corinthians 4:6).

From *Be Still, My Soul* by Katharina Von Schlegel

Post-Galileoan Reflections

Leave to Thy God to order and provide;
In every change He faithful will remain.

God stays the same, though everything around Him moves. He is the one constant in the universe—the sun that always shines, the star that never goes out. Lights in the heavens are merely reflections of His glory. He is the fire that burns for us all. We are warm when we face Him, cold when we turn away.

We might talk about the sun coming up and going down, but we know we are the ones who are moving. There was a time when we thought that the earth was the center of the universe and that everything revolved around us and our superior intellect and importance. Galileo proved that perspective wrong.

Spiritually, we need a similar paradigm shift. If we are to know God, we must see that there is one wiser and more important than we are, one around whom all things revolve and for whom they exist. We must relinquish our need to have everything revolve around us. We must turn and make our lives revolve around Him and what He wants for us. It has to be this way. To do otherwise would be like a post-Galileoan claiming that this little, non-glowing, twirling cinder is still the center of the universe.

From *Be Still, My Soul* by Katharina Von Schlegel

O Ye of Little Faith

Be still, my soul: the waves and winds still know
His voice who ruled them while He dwelt below.

So you're tempted to get anxious. You are wondering whether God really cares. You are being tossed about on a stormy sea, and you can't believe that Jesus is asleep in the boat. You try to trust and you try to take it, but you are soon overcome by questions. *What is He thinking? Doesn't He know what danger we are in? Should I wake Him up? Maybe He's just a heavy sleeper.* So you finally lose it and wake Him up, screaming something about how could He possibly fall asleep on you at a time like this. Still half asleep, He begins to rise, mumbling something about your little faith. Then He balances Himself in the middle of the boat and speaks to the winds and the waves, which by now are quite familiar with His voice. All at once, everything calms down. Then He sits back down in the place where He was sleeping and stares at you with those deep, penetrating eyes. You feel like a fool.

He doesn't have to say the next part. It's so obvious that it comes to you while you look at Him. Or maybe it's coming to you *because* you're looking at Him. Did you *really* think that the boat would sink, leaving you to drown? With the Son of God in it?

October 12

From *Now Thank We All Our God* by Martin Rinkart

The Eternal Now

For thus it was, is now,
And shall be evermore.

Early in my songwriting career I wrote the following lines: *When you think you've got to worry/'Cause it seems the thing to do/Remember He ain't in a hurry/He's always got time for you*. When I wrote this, I did not realize it was more than just a figure of speech.

The concept of God always having time for you and me is a way of saying that He has all of eternity to deal with each and every one of us. It is impossible to take up too much of His time since He exists outside of time. God does not fit within the frames of our human minds, and He is not bound by our boundaries. We often forget this, and when we do we fail to treat Him like God.

He is the same yesterday, today, and forever. He is the Alpha and the Omega, the beginning and the end. "Before Abraham was, I AM." God was, He is, and He is to come. Past. Present. Future. He is all of them all at the same time, for He is outside of time. He is the eternal Now, "Who wert and art and evermore shall be."

The eternal "Now" is never in a hurry.

From *My God, I Love Thee,* Author unknown, from the Latin

A Belonging Love

My God, I love Thee, not because I hope for heaven thereby,
Nor yet because who love Thee not must die eternally.
Thou, O my Jesus, Thou didst me upon the cross embrace,
For me didst bear the nails and spear, and manifold disgrace.
Then why, O blessed Jesus Christ, should I not love Thee well?
Not for the hope of winning heaven, or of escaping hell.
Not with the hope of gaining aught, not seeking a reward;
But as Thyself hast loved me, O everlasting Lord!
So would I love Thee, dearest Lord, and in thy praise will sing;
Because Thou art my loving God, and my eternal King.

When we finally love completely, it will be like this. We won't love God in return for all the things He has done for us, though certainly these are reason enough. We will love Him simply because of who He is—our God and King. This is the way He has loved us: We are His children. This love has nothing to do with performance, or even character. It has to do with relationship.

The new covenant reads: "I will be their God and they will be my people." This is family. Fathers love their children and children love their father, regardless. Of course, this is tested regularly and not always expressed, but we all know love binds us together.

In a perfect way, this is how it is with our Father in heaven. It is a belonging love, and everything has already been done to transact the ownership. And we are enjoying the fruits of this relationship today.

From *Trust and Obey* by J.H. Sammis

Faith or Calculation

But we never can prove the delights of His love
Until all on the altar we lay

Unfortunately, faith does not come with a thirty-day trial period or a money-back guarantee. We resist the truth about faith, that you don't prove it until you act on it. This runs against the grain of human nature. We naturally want to prove things first. We want to test the bridge before we walk on it.

Faith never works this way. If it did, it wouldn't be faith. Rather, it would be calculation. Faith calls us to walk on the bridge and believe it will hold us. Faith calls us to believe in words and promises, not in tangible things we can test. It promises us blessings, but only after we give up everything else. The blessing never comes first.

Faith appears foolish to those who don't have it. We cannot talk others into faith because they will never know what we are talking about. We can't compare realities because a person cannot *know* the reality of faith until he or she *acts* in faith.

And the act of faith is to put everything that is important to us on the altar. Until we do that, we just don't get it.

From *Make Me a Captive, Lord* by George Matheson

Give Over and Cling

My will is not my own
Till Thou hast made it Thine...

Nothing becomes ours until we become His.

We are such demanding children—never satisfied, always asking for more, always looking somewhere else, always distracted. Our desires are insatiable. But their satisfaction would be our ruin, because we are not very smart. We think we know what is best for us, but we do not. Our will is so childish, so self-centered. Before we can grow up, everything has to be changed.

God has a solution for these immature demands, and it is found in worshiping Him. It is not just in giving up these lesser desires, but in replacing them with a greater desire. We come to God with an armful of wants, needs and desires—as well as the idols we have satisfied them with for so long. God asks us to give these things up, but we stand there—with our arms loaded—and hesitate. We cannot put our arms around Him until we first empty them.

It is then that we realize the irony of this situation. Until we give up all these little things we thought were so important (indeed, this is no small struggle) we cannot lay hold of God, who already has EVERYTHING. For in becoming His, all He has becomes ours, too.

How silly to keep clinging to such small things.

From *Make Me a Captive, Lord* by George Matheson

You Gotta Serve Somebody

Make me a captive, Lord,
And then I shall be free.

Freedom is not what it is cracked up to be. Americans venerate freedom as if it were the highest value. But freedom is showing its ugly side in the world. Countries where communism once reigned are now caught in the grip of violent civil war. People in those places found their long-sought freedom, only to become immediately enslaved to the unforgiven racial and ethnic hatreds they harbored for generations. In many cases, one has to question whether this "freedom" is better than their former bondage.

Similar struggles are surfacing in America, where freedom has come to be an issue of obtaining rights for certain individuals or groups of individuals banded together for a common cause. In America, freedom is now synonymous with rights, resulting in internal social strife between groups whose rights are in conflict.

True freedom comes only in being a captive of Christ. Ironically, only as a slave to Him can I be finally free of my bondage to sin and self. Only when I serve Him, can I find joy in serving others and use my freedom for the right thing.

From *The Solid Rock* by Edward Mote

Rest on the Facts

When darkness veils His lovely face,
I rest on His unchanging grace...

Many times we can't see His lovely face through the darkness, the clouds, the tears, or the pain. These are the times we must rest on something else. We fall back on His unchanging grace. For this, we rely not on feelings, but on intellect—not on spirit but on soul—not on the present but on the past.

Fact: God is there and He is here.

Fact: God never changes.

Fact: God invaded human history on our behalf.

Fact: God's Son, who is the human embodiment of Himself, died in our place.

Fact: This same Son who died also rose from the dead and is now seated next to His Father in heaven, where He is preparing a place for us.

Fact: God gives forgiveness of sins and eternal life and the presence of His Spirit to all who repent of their sins and believe these facts thus far.

Fact: You believe, so you have all of these things. You couldn't have believed this in the first place if He hadn't been pulling on you.

Fact: You are a marked man or woman. Whatever you are going through has a reason and a purpose and is part of a plan that is more far-reaching than you can see right now—perhaps than you will ever see.

Fact: Although you may not see anything right now, because of all these things that don't change, you can rest on the facts.

From *O Worship the King* by Sir Robert H. Grant

The Roar of God

Thy bountiful care what tongue can recite?
It breathes in the air, it shines in the light.

This is the omnipresence of God that is so often missed by both those who know and love God and those who don't. This is what prompted Paul to say in his address to the Greek intellectuals at the Areopagus in Athens: "The God who made the world and everything in it... gives to all men life and breath and everything else. God did this so that men would seek him and perhaps reach out for him and find him, though he is not far from each one of us. For in him we live and move and have our being" (Acts 17:24-28).

This is the ever-present close proximity of God. This is life on the other side of a very thin veil—the veil of belief and awareness. This is what makes two people look at the same picture and see two different things. One sees the hand of God while the other curses the darkness. One hears the voice of God, the other only silence. One sees only rain falling while the other might be wondering if God is crying.

George Eliot wrote in *Middlemarch*: "If we had a keen vision and feeling of all ordinary human life, it would be like hearing the grass grow and the squirrel's heart beat, and we should die of that roar which lies on the other side of silence."

This is the roar of God.

From *O Worship the King* by Sir Robert H. Grant

My Friend

Our Maker, Defender, Redeemer and Friend.

If I could write this the way it appears to me, I would write it: "Our MAKER, DEFENDER, REDEEMER, and friend." If I could read it, I would use my deepest, biggest voice, reading "MAKER, DEFENDER, REDEEMER," and my warmest, most welcoming voice for "friend." That's the way it reads to me. All of God's mighty resources brought down to my level in the person of a friend.

This is not belittling God. Rather, this is the availability of God. This is the way He wants it. It was His call, not ours. "I no longer call you servants, because a servant does not know his master's business. Instead, I have called you friends" (John 15:15).

That God would come to me in this way—that He would even want to be called my friend—is proof that He loves me and desires fellowship with me. He lets me in on this business—what He is doing in the world. This doesn't make the scary part of Him disappear, for God is all things at all times. But this is the part of God that we can curl up to with a good book, or walk with after a rain, or chat with in the car as we drive. This is the God who laughs at our hand motions and our funny voices when no one else is there.

This is the part that makes me say in a small voice, so not too many people will hear—almost a whisper: *God is my friend.*

From *O Worship the King* by Sir Robert H. Grant

God's Dark Side

His chariots of wrath the deep thunder clouds form,
And dark is His path on the wings of the storm.

There is a dark side to God, similar to the dark side of the moon. It is a holy darkness. Not that God embodies darkness itself, for in Him is no darkness at all. But there is a part of Him that is dark to us—mysterious. This is the God of the storm, the God of thunder, the God of wrath and pain and suffering. And we are called to worship Him.

Just as we can't see the dark side of the moon, we can't always see or understand the hand of God in the dark paths of our lives. But He is there nonetheless, working His will that we might be to the honor and praise of His glory.

This does not mean that every cloud has a silver lining. Nor should we pray for the sunshine and wait out the rain. Rather, every cloud rattles with the power and presence of God Himself. Don't wait for the clouds to go away. He is there. It is Him, rattling.

Worship Him.

From *O Worship the King* by Sir Robert H. Grant

Lost and Found

Our Shield and Defender, the Ancient of Days,
Pavilioned in splendor, and girded with praise.

Don't ever let anyone make you feel sorry for God, for He is to be praised, not pitied. We were made to praise Him as were the earth, the sky, the sea, the sun, the moon, the stars, and countless angelic hosts. Then there are those who have gone before us into heaven and are praising Him right now. Believe me, when it comes to praise, God is doing just fine. He is girded all around with praise.

We praise Him, not because He needs it, but because *we* need it. We praise Him for our own good. Our createdness calls for it. We are not whole outside of praising God, for He is the one for whom we were made. "It is He who made us and not we ourselves" (Psalm 100:3). We did not invent ourselves, and we don't reinvent ourselves.

I just heard my neighbor say that she was "trying to find herself." I thought that was odd, since she was standing right in front of me. I certainly could quite easily find her. But such is the nature of our odd, twisted thinking.

I am more and more convinced that in worshiping God, we will find all we ever needed to know of ourselves. We will see that our wholeness is in Him.

From *The Pilgrims of the Night* by Frederick William Faber

They're Playing Our Song

Cheer up, my soul! Faith's moonbeams softly glisten
Upon the breast of life's most troubled sea;
And it will cheer the drooping heart to listen
To those brave songs which angels mean for Thee.

Have you ever heard them—those brave songs the angels sing to spur us on? You haven't? Well, they are filling up the air around you right now. And they are meant for you!

Why not believe such a thing?

In relation to eternity, I have long thought that we could utilize our imaginations to their fullest extent to picture what life in heaven will be like, and still not imagine even half of it.

Lately, I've been applying that same thinking to angels and their involvement in our lives here on earth. I don't think we've thought up the half of their work and presence in our lives.

I have no proof of any of this. But I have Bible stories and experiences of saints and hymn writers like this one that tell me that angels were around them at all times. I have countless reports of eyewitnesses to their appearances and other unexplainable happenings in the lives of believers, as well as those who are trying hard not to believe.

Is it too hard to imagine that these things could be true? Wouldn't it be an easier way to explain them by believing? And most of all, wouldn't it be more fun?

From *Take My Life and Let It Be* by Frances R. Havergal

Ever, Only, and All

Take myself, and I will be,
Ever, only, all for Thee.

Ever for Thee. This means "for all time." Forever. This is an eternal commitment I have made. I'm not going back on it. I'm not changing in mid-stream. All of my plans are made with this commitment to Christ in mind.

Only for Thee. This means there are no other gods in my life. No one or no thing is vying for first place. No idols. This is harder to pin down than "ever for Thee" because my idols are not as obvious as they used to be. They don't have funny names and they aren't made of wood and stone. They are things like cars, power, money, sex, and self. They are parts of our culture and parts of everybody's lives, even Christians. Contemporary idols are hard to determine and almost impossible to destroy. The test would be to ask: "Am I doing this for Christ, or for some other reason?"

All for Thee. This means all that I have to give. This is about passion. This is about worship. This is about putting guts into my faith. This is about putting all that I have into this relationship with God. My relationship with God is the central reason for my existence, the defining "why" of my life. "All for Thee" gives reason and meaning to my life, and as a result, I am giving all my life back to the one who has given His life for me.

From *Take My Life and Let It Be* by Frances R. Havergal

Impulsive Love

Take my hands and let them move
At the impulse of Thy love.

Imagine being on call for God's love to be impulsively expressed through you. You'd never know when it might strike. You could be suddenly drawn to someone in a crowd who was sick, or you might find yourself picking up and loving an AIDS baby. Or you could suddenly find yourself wondering if a multitude of people around you were hungry.

One thing's for sure: You would start noticing children of all kinds, colors, shapes, and sizes. And the ones who were suffering would claim the deepest part of your soul. You would be rolling up your sleeves and putting your hands to work in whatever way you could to relieve some of their pain. You might even take to task those who caused it. You would be amazed at your boldness.

You would most likely find yourself liking someone who you previously found distasteful. You would see deep into that person's soul and see the person they wanted to be or could become, and you would show love whether he or she became that person or not.

But you would also be surprised at your distaste for—and lack of patience with—religious folks. This would be rather hard, because these would be important, prominent people in your community and in your church. Some of them might even be your friends.

You'd always have to be on guard because you would never know when or where an impulse to love might strike again.

From *Jesus Loves Me* by Anna B. Warner

Unabashed Littleness

Jesus loves me! He who died
Heaven's gates to open wide.
He will wash away my sin,
Let His little child come in.

For the little child in all of us, this hymn was found in an old hymnal listed under *The Life of Christ—Love and Gratitude*. That means it was not always relegated to children's church and Sunday school. At one time it was a regular hymn, like the rest. And well it should be.

If the kingdom of heaven is made up of such as the little ones, then we must never outgrow this song. As children, the Father meets us and affirms His love. As children, we are accepted before any attempts at earning His love. As children, we believe with total trust. As children, we worship in wide-eyed wonder. As His children, we react to our Father with unguarded emotions and uncalculated joy. As children, we cry when we are hurt. And as children, we are comforted.

Little ones to Him belong. Time to revel in our unabashed littleness. In a world of big, it's nice to come to God and be little again.

October 26

From *Being of Beings, God of Love* by Charles Wesley

Asking

The sole return Thy love requires,
Is that we ask for more.

This shouldn't be too difficult. God reaches out to us on the cross and loves us through our sin and shame. And that love requires of us only that we request more of the same.

Asking brings us into a relationship with God. Nothing from Him is automatic, and He does not force Himself on anybody. If we want something from God, we must ask for it. When we ask, He can give.

We often don't understand what God requires of us. We sometimes mix up the old and the new covenants. We come to Christ by grace, but once in His favor we start heaping demands upon ourselves and others.

God's love does have a requirement. It demands that we ask for more—that we take and eat and drink in His life and death for us.

Is that such a difficult demand?

From *Our Great Savior* by J. Wilbur Chapman

Sinners "R" Us

Jesus! What a Friend for sinners!...

It's a good thing Jesus decided to be a friend of sinners, or else He never would have had any friends.

For a while I thought He was my friend because I was such a special little boy. I had a godly family; I had a calling on my life; I knew all the right words to say in church. I even went to a college where they taught me more about God. It was all the right stuff, too!

Then I saw that sinners were falling more in love with Him than I was. I heard them talking about how He had touched their lives and saved them. I heard them write songs and sing about an intimate relationship with a God I was supposed to know better than they did. At least I knew more *about* Him than they did. I became envious—envious of sinners. I felt left out.

Then the most wonderful thing happened: I found out I too was a sinner. It was cause for celebration. My sin was just as hideous as anyone's. Perhaps even more hideous, because it was so well hidden and I was so proud. The day that I realized I was a sinner was the day Jesus became a friend to me.

This is the only way it works. If you want to be a friend of Jesus, you *have* to be a sinner. Forgiven sinners are the only friends He has. The people who know Him well are the ones who accept the fact that they are sinners He has forgiven.

From *Bread of the World, in Mercy Broken* by Reginald Heber

In the Middle of Once and for All

Bread of the world, in mercy broken,
Wine of the soul, in mercy shed,
By whom the words of life were spoken,
And in whose death our sins are dead...

"Our sins are dead." I've heard this before and wondered if a doctor reported this death. Was there a coroner's report? If Christ died to save me from my sins once and for all, why is my sin nature still alive and kicking? Maybe it slipped off the table during the autopsy and crawled away. I've heard of such a thing happening in science fiction novels.

I read phrases in Scripture such as "consider yourself dead to sin" and "put off the old man and put on the new." That sounds so easy. So automatic. But what if the old man is fighting with you while you're trying to put him off. Worse yet, what if he's got you by the throat?

Could it be that even though this death was once and for all, we still have to *live* in the middle of "once and for all"? Maybe that's why the bread of the world was broken in mercy, and in mercy the wine of the soul was shed. Maybe Christ told us to remember His supper because we keep needing it.

What Christ did on the cross was done once and for all, as far as God is concerned. But we are living out that "once and for all" every day. And for us, blood needs to flow, bread needs to break, and sin needs to die *daily* in our lives. When you are living in the middle of "once and for all," you will be experiencing the reasons and the results of that death moment by moment.

From *O Could I Find from Day to Day* by Benjamin Clevland

Uncomplicated Joy

Lord, I desire with Thee to live,
Anew from day to day;
In joys the world can never give
Nor ever take away.

Spiritual joy—joy in the Lord, that is—is a precious possession of the believer. It has nothing to do with the world, so it is impervious to the world's machinations. It can't be won or lost, bought or sold, earned or stolen. Such joy has nothing to do with the circumstances of our lives, be they good or bad. In short, our spiritual joy is not in any way attached to this world.

Most important, spiritual joy has nothing to do with one's social status or power. Employer and employee, rich and poor, slave and free—all can know it equally. But those on the lower rungs of life's social ladder are more likely to find it—to know it when they see it. Their lives have fewer physical joys, so they are more likely to see God's hand in the ones they have.

Jesus issued a blessing on the poor and the hungry (see Luke 6:20-26), and then cursed the rich and the well fed, claiming that those rich in earthly goods already had their blessing. It is a serious warning to check the source of our true joy and happiness.

Real joy comes from being rightly related to God, and anyone and everyone can have and know this joy.

From *Yield Not to Temptation* by Horatio R. Palmer

Life in the Trenches

Yield not to temptation,
For yielding is sin...

Contrary to what many of us may believe, temptation is not the same as sin. Jesus was tempted in every way we are, yet He was without sin (see Hebrews 4:15). Sin is in the yielding to temptation. The minute we yield, the temptation leads us into sin. Jesus was constantly tempted, but He simply said "No" every time.

We need to learn to say "No" more often and more effectively. Learning to say "No" is life in the present-tense struggle—life in the trenches of sin and temptation. We don't accomplish this by some grand commitment—some going forward of our body and will at a Sunday night church service. We do it in the trenches on Monday morning when we say "No" to sin. This is not "I'm going to say 'No' to sin the next time I'm tempted." That doesn't do any good at all. This is saying "No" to the temptation right in front of us.

"And do not swear by your head, for you cannot make even one hair white or black. Simply let your 'Yes' be 'Yes,' and your 'No,' 'No'; anything beyond this comes from the evil one" (Matthew 5:36-37). Jesus was discussing the idea of taking oaths, as in swearing *I will do such and such*, or *I will not do such and such.* We learn from this that anything more than facing temptation head-on and dealing with it in the present-tense trenches of life sets you up for failure.

Don't make promises. Make decisions!

From *O Lord, Who Hast This Table Spread* by Edward A. Collier

Something from the Deli?

Then rich the portion Thou wilt give;
No more the hungering heart can need;
Thyself the bread by which we live,
Thy precious blood our drink indeed.

Once, the disciples came back from town to find Jesus talking with a woman by Jacob's well. They did not know at the time what had transpired during that now-famous conversation where Jesus revealed His messianic identity to a Samaritan woman. They were only concerned about their stomachs. "Rabbi, eat something," they told him. Apparently they had come from the town of Sychar with something from the deli. Jesus responded by saying He had food to eat that they knew nothing about: "'My food is to do the will of Him who sent me and to finish His work'" (see John 4:1-34).

The desire for food pales in the face of someone's desperate life and eternal destiny. Jesus was dealing with a fellow human in the matters of the soul when the disciples burst in upon the scene with sandwiches and matters of the stomach. No wonder Jesus put them off. He was not ready to make the transition from eternal to physical.

It's not that we don't eat and take care of our bodily needs. But like Jesus, our real food is to do the will of the Father. That would mean placing a priority on matters of the soul.

Look for someone to talk to today who might be ready to hear some truth about themselves and some truth about Jesus. You'll never even miss the deli sandwich.

From *Praise the Lord Who Reigns Above* by Charles Wesley

What's Holy There Is Holy Here

Hallowed be His name beneath,
As in heaven on earth adored...

May His name be regarded below in the same way as it is regarded above: as holy. May what is important in heaven be important on earth. May the way things are perceived there be the way they are perceived here. Not necessarily by everybody, but at least by somebody. May there be somebody who cares, who sees it on earth as it is in heaven.

And who is this going to be if it isn't His people—those He has redeemed? Why else did He teach us to pray: "Thy will be done on earth as it is in heaven"? Doesn't this imply that we are to discover His will and do it? We have a mandate here, a responsibility to see things from God's perspective, then figure out what to do.

We are so used to viewing life from our own perspective that any other view is hard for us to consider. We see things first through our own eyes, and only later catch a glimpse of God's view. By then, it's usually too late to do anything about it.

If you saw a car from God's perspective before you went out and bought one, it might affect your choice of purchase. If you saw a job from God's perspective before you went in for the interview, it might affect the way you went about answering the questions.

And if you saw heaven first, it might make earth more sacred.

From *Praise the Lord Who Reigns Above* by Charles Wesley

Wide Hearts; Narrow Minds

Praise Him, every tuneful string,
All the reach of heavenly art
All the powers of music bring,
The music of the heart.

All that is art and all that is music needs to be brought to bear in the praise of God. It will take everything we can muster to begin to capture the music of the heart.

The heart is vaster than the mind and harder to explain. The mind, being full of words, can be described in books and studied and pored over vigorously. But mere words don't do the heart justice. The heart has to be sung or painted or acted out, and then we are only getting a glimpse of what's there.

The wise King Solomon described this as a burden that God purposely placed on us. He put eternity in our hearts and limited our minds so we could not fully know it (see Ecclesiastes 3:10-12). Why would God do such a thing?

Two possible reasons: First, He wants us to search Him out—to try to answer the unexplainable longing in our hearts. And second, He does not want us to know Him only in our minds, because then only smart people would qualify. Instead, this is a gospel for children and old people, the poor and the retarded, the criminal and the oppressed. All the folks with big hearts that open trustingly to the Father, even the wealthy and intelligent who are wise enough to see that this is the only way you know Him.... through the heart.

From *O Christ, What Burdens Bowed Thy Head!* by Annie R. Cousin

An Empty Cup

Death and the curse were in our cup:
O Christ 'twas full for Thee!
But Thou hast drained the last dark drop,
'Tis empty now for me.

He drank the whole thing, down to the last drop. The cup is empty now. When we are ready to face our own death, the enemy will hand us the cup, and it will be an awful thing, indeed. We might even have to encounter his gloating face and take the cup from him, only to get it to our lips and find there's nothing in it. That is when the grave will have no victory and death will have lost its sting.

It was our cup of death that He drained, just as it was our sin He bore, our price He paid, our sword He took in the side, our vinegar He swallowed, and our nails that pierced His hands and feet. He took it all while Satan gloated, though only for a moment.

And now He has left a new cup for us to drink, the cup of His new covenant that continues to flow to all who believe. This cup is full and flowing, this time with His eternal life, His righteousness, His forgiveness, and His love.

From *How Firm a Foundation* in Rippon's *Selection of Hymns*

Never, No, Never, No, Never

"That soul, though all hell should endeavor to shake,
I'll never, no, never, no, never forsake!"

Never, no, never, no, never... I remember singing this as a child and feeling a certain kinship with it. Children repeat words like this in their songs and their sayings. In their minds, the more times they say something, the more they mean it. Children cross their heart and hope to die a hundred times, and the more times they hope to die, the more earnest they are.

The hymn writer is strengthening us with these words and appealing to our need for protection and assurance. Not only will God never forsake us, He will *never, no, never, no, never* forsake us!

These are some of the most comforting words in the Bible: "I will never leave you nor forsake you" (Joshua 1:5). Jesus picks up the theme and wraps up the first gospel with, "And surely I am with you always, to the very end of the age" (Matthew 28:20).

He is a tenacious God. He is with us, and He will never leave. He is also stronger than anyone or anything that might try to pull us away from Him. Even hell itself.

November 5

From *How Firm a Foundation* in Rippon's *Selection of Hymns*

Trial-Welcoming Committee

The flame shall not hurt thee—I only design
Thy dross to consume and thy gold to refine.

"Consider it pure joy, my brothers, whenever you face trials of many kinds, because you know that the testing of your faith develops perseverance. Perseverance must finish its work so that you may be mature and complete, not lacking anything" (James 1:2-4).

I wonder if the first recipients of this letter thought James had lost his mind. They had already experienced great trial and persecution for their faith, and now he was telling them to welcome additional trial as if it were joy personified? I can see him telling them to endure trial—to stick it out with God's strength—but telling them to consider trials as joy?

And if it were true and right and sane, what a philosophy! What a way to look at life! I don't suppose this kind of trial-welcoming attitude comes to us overnight. It comes from seeing the purifying process at work and experiencing the rewards several times over. Then we start to realize that God is working His character deep into our lives this way. It is this process that teaches us to welcome a trial and not resist.

If we could get this, it would be a great way to live. Imagine how this attitude must frustrate the enemy. Here he is, throwing all kinds of stuff at us, and we consider each trial as more opportunity for joy.

What kind of trials are in your life today? Outfox the devil. Consider them joy and throw off his scheme.

From *Amidst Us Our Beloved Stands* by Charles Hadden Spurgeon

Half-Healed

If now, with eyes defiled and dim,
We see the signs, but see not Him,
O may His love the scales displace,
And bid us see Him face to face.

Lord, give us a vision that we might see you face to face. How often it seems we're only seeing signs of you through dim and defiled eyes. We see where you've been and signs pointing to where you are going to be at some time in the future. But right now, our vision is not so good. Like the blind man who after your first touch saw men looking like trees walking, we've been half healed.

We don't want to just know about you; we want you. We don't want to tell people you're coming; we want you here. Now. Signs are not enough. We can't talk to a sign.

Visit us with your presence. Let us sit down in this place and know you are here. Whisper in our ear. Wipe the scales from our eyes. Speak to us, Lord, and let us hear you. And may we somehow know that you are listening.

From *Amidst Us Our Beloved Stands* by Charles Hadden Spurgeon

Sweet and Rich

When Jesus deigns His guests to meet,
The wine how rich, the bread how sweet!

Only the best. That's the way Jesus always did it. The wine He made at the wedding of Cana was better than what the host served—and the host served his best. Jesus saved the best for last, and the host got the credit.

But something tells me that the wine wasn't rich and the bread wasn't sweet on that first night in the upper room. The wine was probably too young—it stung—and the bread was most likely bittersweet. My guess is that those present probably couldn't even taste either one of them that night. It was all too difficult and too confusing. The room must have been spinning even before they had anything to drink.

And while it may have been the Last Supper for the disciples and Jesus, it was the first one for the rest of us as His followers. We've had many suppers with Him since. And for some strange reason the elements, though symbolic of such a cruel cup that the Son of God drank, still keep getting sweeter as the years go by. Sweeter and richer.

And so this dinner goes on through history. I've heard He's saving the best for last again, when we will meet with Him at the Marriage Supper of the Lamb. And there, once again, the Host will get all the credit as well He should.

From *All People That on Earth Do Dwell* by William Kethe

Sure of His Mercy

For why? the Lord our God is good,
His mercy is forever sure...

The mercy of God is one thing we want to be sure of forever. As human beings, we live and breathe and move about on tenuous footing, indeed. Therefore, we should all be quick to choose mercy as the characteristic of God that we regard most highly. Without it, we probably wouldn't be around for the rest of the program.

It says in 2 Peter 3:7 that God is reserving the earth for judgment. He said this in response to claims from mockers who challenged the assertions of Jesus' followers that He was coming back. Peter said that if God was slow at all about His promises ("as some count slowness"), it was because He was holding back His judgment so that more people could have a chance to respond to His offer of salvation. If He hesitates at all, it is because He doesn't want anyone to perish.

So God is damming up his wrath until He is ready. The longer He takes at this, the more compassionate we can see that God is. Imagine the patience required to let so much evil go unpunished, just for the sake of those He is saving.

Every action of man must have a reaction from God. We were told this in the beginning, and that has not changed. It's just that God's reaction is being postponed for now. Counting on God's mercy, then, is like counting on the dam to hold back wrath until the day of judgment.

Thank God His mercy is sure.

From *All People That on Earth Do Dwell* by William Kethe

The Gospel According to Cher

Know that the Lord is God indeed;
Without our aid He did us make...

Does anyone remember God checking with us first about making us? I sure don't. If He did, it seems to have slipped my mind. I'm pretty sure I didn't have any input on this at all. For me, it's been a gradual discovery of what He had in mind when He made me. I don't seem to have too much, if anything, to say about it except for what I can change.

Of course, with all the plastic surgery, sucks and tucks, implants, transplants, and grafting available now, it seems you can redo yourself considerably if you don't happen to like God's original design for some reason.

But I have to wonder, when you are all done moving things around, if you might still be the same person you were before you started? Actually, the outside stuff is easy to change—if you have the money. It's what's inside that's hard to change: attitudes, dysfunctional behavioral patterns, old habits, sins. What I wouldn't pay to have someone suck and tuck a few of these away! These things don't go away easily, and yet they are well within my power to change. My power and God's, that is.

But isn't it a comment on human nature that we will spend an unlimited amount of money on the latest experts and techniques to change what we cannot change by ourselves, while leaving untouched what we can?

From *The Coming of His Feet* by S. Whitney Allen

One Ear Cocked

In the crimson of the morning,
In the whiteness of the moon,
In the amber glory of the day's retreat;
In the midnight robed in darkness,
Or the gleaming of the moon—
I listen for the coming of His feet.

Christ is returning, but He left much behind Him to occupy me while I wait. Besides the tasks He left for us, He left beauty, in which He painted impressions of Himself as the Creator. I can see it in the crimson sunrise and the amber sunset and in the gleaming of the moon and stars that appear as puncture holes in the darkness.

But everywhere I look, I am also listening.

We have a little shelty sheep dog (he looks like a small collie). His breed has been trained to herd sheep, so our dog naturally tries to herd anything that moves. He is also constantly aware of everything around him. When you speak to him, he always has one ear directed to you and one cocked—in case something develops somewhere else, I guess.

Christians should live with one ear cocked. *Look* and *listen*. *Watch* and *wait*. Those were the words Jesus used. He said He would come when no one expected it.

Plan your days as if you had many, but live them as if there were few. And always listen for footsteps.

From *Christian, Dost Thou See Them* by St. Andrew of Crete

Spirit-Breathing

Christian answer boldly,
"While I breathe I pray!"

Prayer is the spirit breathing. Just as we inhale and exhale air, so do our spirits take in the Word of God and exhale a prayer. Meditation on the Word revives the spirit, giving it fresh oxygen for the spiritual life to be healthy. Prayer is the answer-back of the spirit—putting His Word into our words as an offering back to Him. This ebb and flow needs to be constant.

Sometimes this spirit-breathing is conscious, and sometimes it is not. We need to make it conscious as much as possible. But as the habit of prayer grows, it becomes involuntary. It is like sitting in silence with a close friend: Verbal communication is not always necessary.

This is probably close to what Paul meant when he told us to pray without ceasing (1 Thessalonians 5:17, KJV). In other words, be in such a communion with God that your spirit is breathing, even when you might not be conscious of it.

Keep the air passages open. Don't let any blockages form. Give your spirit a fresh breath of truth and pray continually about everything and anything. Nothing is outside the realm of His interest. Nothing is too small or too petty.

From *Still Will We Trust* by W. H. Burleigh

Our Turn

Let us press on, in patient self denial,
Accept the hardship, shrink not from the loss;
Our portion lies beyond the hour of trial,
Our crown beyond the cross.

Part of spiritual growth is choosing pain. Not some pain from outside ourselves—some affliction or suffering that we must endure. Rather, it is the painful process of deciding to say "No" to what we have so selfishly and lazily said "Yes" to for so long. We choose this pain. We enter into it because we want to move on. We want to put this immaturity behind us and grow up.

We are weary of our own problems, and we want to help someone else for a change. We are starting to hear ourselves whine, so we want to grace the world and those around us with some kind words instead. We are tired of taking, and we want to give. We are tired of being the problem, so we want to be the solution. We are ready to leave behind the demanding child in us and become an adult, one who can sacrifice, one who can set self aside for the sake of something higher, and one who can postpone pleasure, reward, and rest.

There's an eternity ahead for us to enjoy all the benefits that have been won on the cross. What a small thing is any hardship now, and how quickly it will be forgotten! What a small thing our little sufferings are compared to His! He denied Himself for us. Isn't it our turn to carry this cross?

From *The Day Is Past and Gone* by John Leland

The Naked Soul

I lay my garments by,
Upon my bed to rest;
So death will soon remove me hence,
And leave my soul undressed.

This body will someday be laid aside like wrinkled bed clothes, leaving my soul naked and open to scrutiny. Though it's been naked to God all along, it hasn't been to me or to anyone else. We use our garments to enhance the presentation of ourselves, but also to hide.

What sobers me about this image is not a future disembodiment. It is the picture of the reality of what my soul must look like right now, for this is the way God sees me all the time. It is an image that gives me second thoughts when I lay my clothes down at night—second thoughts about what my soul has been occupied with that day, and asking whether that is something I want to have undressed.

It's a good question to help guard the inner mind. Looking forward to having our souls undressed each night might make us more careful about what they were busy doing during the day.

From *Come, Let Us Who in Christ Believe* by Charles Wesley

Open Hands

Through grace we harken to Thy voice,
Yield to be saved from sin...

By its very definition, grace is undeserved. But it does have a requirement. It doesn't come to just anyone, only to those who yield—to those who give up. Grace does not come to the unrepentant. The proud, the mighty and those who hold on to what they possess have made a decision to live on their own without submitting to His grace. If they ever found themselves in God's vicinity, they would offer up a closed hand.

But nothing can be placed into a closed hand. You can set something on top of a closed hand, but it will just roll off. Only open hands receive from God. You must yield, and that means giving up possession of something upon claim or demand. God claims His right to us, in such a manner, in that He both created us and died for us. We must decide to yield ourselves to the claim. It is how we participate in this relationship.

Grace is offered freely to us. But that is not enough, because grace given must be received. There needs to be a breaking down—an opening up of the hand. Sometimes our hands, though once open, have closed up. When that happens, we have to go through the process of opening them up all over again.

Yield today. Open your hands, and keep them open. There is so much to receive!

From *The Sands of Time Are Sinking* by Annie R. Cousin

A Patchwork of Paradoxes

With mercy and with judgment my web of time He wove,
And aye the dews of sorrow were lustered by His love.

What strange threads are woven in these tapestries of our lives! What clashing colors make up the warp and woof of this weave of truth! There is mercy in and around judgment, sorrow over and under love. There's forgiveness all around sin, while doubt cuts through the middle of faith. Suffering and glory run side by side and are hardly distinguishable from each other, as are loss and gain.

These seeming contradictions—and many more like them—tie together the threads of truth in a strange patchwork of paradoxes. Though some may wonder at these conflicting themes, they can be seen as more proof of the truth than as a challenge to it.

If we human beings were manufacturing our own version of truth, that version would probably make more sense than this. If the gospel were some human construct, I doubt that it would be so full of paradoxes. Who would think of this? We would have every argument tightly tied up.

Yet paradoxes stack up to the realities of life better than simplistic theories and explanations. An absolute truth that takes into account all of life's experiences would have to be held together by a patchwork of paradoxes in order to hold up to real life. Perhaps this is the biggest proof of all. Our lives are like this.

From *Wonderful Words of Life* by Philip P. Bliss

Waiting for the Bridegroom

All so freely given,
Wooing us to Heaven...
Beautiful words, wonderful words,
Wonderful words of Life.

As Christ's future bride, we want to keep ourselves true to Him while He is away from us.

But waiting is difficult. We have the seal of His intentions and the firstfruits of our union, yet we are only betrothed. He wooed us to Him, even though we have yet to meet face to face. For this reason, His words have become the all-important tangible evidence of His promises that we cling to. Through His words, we have come to know Him.

We love to hear them—even the sound of them. We keep them ever before us, because there are other lovers—with selfish intent—vying for our attention. They tempt us with their false promises and tell us there is no bridegroom and that the wedding is a hoax.

But we know better. We have eyewitness accounts of His first coming. And we have His words promising His return. We have the seal of the Holy Spirit, who confirms all this in our hearts. So we wait patiently for His promised return, our lamps trimmed and our hearts pure. Oh, may we be found faithful when He comes.

From *Amazing Grace* by John Newton

Choose Your Fear

'Twas grace that taught my heart to fear,
And grace my fears relieved...

We really don't have too much choice in this matter: We either fear God, or we fear everything else.

"Do not be afraid of those who kill the body but cannot kill the soul. Rather, be afraid of the one who can destroy both soul and body in hell" (Matthew 10:28).

Fear is common to us as human beings because we are not omnipotent. We have limited power, and there are plenty of forces—some of them of our own making—that are bigger than even the strongest of us. It's not that brave men and women have no fear. It's just that they cover up their fear better than others. No one lives completely free of fear.

But when we fear God, all other fears diminish. God is omnipotent, and He becomes our personal possession. "If God is for us," said John, "who can be against us?" Who is there to step up and challenge God? No one but a fool.

And then we find out the big surprise: We actually find favor in coming before God, the only one we really should fear.

We find God favorable to us because of His grace. We come to God trembling, and He tells us the same thing His angels have been telling us for centuries every time they tried to give us a message from Him: "Fear not!"

Ironically, the only one we should fear—the only one *worth* fearing—is the very one who relieves our fears.

From *Brethren We Have Met to Worship* by George Atkins

Hard-To-Get

Tell them all about the Savior—
Tell them that He will be found...

He will be found, though He has a penchant for hiding. God originated playing "hard-to-get." He doesn't do this to get away from us. He does it because He wants to make us look for Him. He likes being found. God desires a relationship with us, but He wants it to be mutual. We will never find ourselves being put upon by God.

This is why He attached Himself to a small, insignificant nation, was born in "O Little Town," spoke in parables, and died like a run-of-the-mill criminal. After a few brief appearances to a handful of people following His resurrection, He left the enterprise in the hands of a few common folk who had no clue about what to do next.

We have to dig for God in all of this, dig in history to find Jesus. We must dig in our Bible and in our minds to figure out His words. We must dig through the lethargy of our souls to fan the fire and dig through a catalog of culturally hip Christian paraphernalia to find a true faith. We must dig through volumes of books to find Him revealed.

But in all of this, with some effort, we will find Him. He likes us to come after Him. He doesn't make Himself too hard to get—just hard enough to force the casual believer to either work harder or give up.

From *Immortal, Invisible* by Walter Chalmers Smith

Quiet Intensity

Unresting, unhasting, and silent as light...

God is never in a hurry. He doesn't need to be. Think of the things that make us hurry, and you will discover why He doesn't have our problem. Our limitations hurry us. We are bound by the hours in a day, the days in a week, the weeks in a month, the months in a year, and the years of our lives. And these come to their own end far too soon. God is not bound by any of these things. He exists outside of time—He thought time up. He has already set the times and the seasons for all things.

But don't think He is lying around, doing nothing. He never rests. He set up the universe, and now He acts intimately in it. He does so primarily in, through, and with us. This is why we were created: to have fellowship with Him and cooperate with His plan.

We should remember this when we start hurrying around trying to make up for lost time. God never loses time. When Christ stepped into our time, He accomplished what He set out to do in a mere thirty-three years—a shortened life span by anyone's standard. And He changed the course of human history, then said "It is finished."

May we find the same grace to live our lives with quiet intensity, and may we know when we are done.

From *O For That Flame of Living Fire* by William H. Bathurst

The Miracle of Grace

Is not Thy grace as mighty now
As when Elijah felt its power?

The men and women in the Old Testament appear capable of acts of faith beyond the realm of our abilities. We sometimes write them off as having a faith for another age—another dispensation, as theologians call it. But our God is the same as always, and His grace has not lost its power. Jesus even said we would do greater things than He did, because He was going to sit next to His Father in heaven and talk to Him about us.

What we often fail to see is that the greatest acts we can do are acts of love and mercy. No, this is not calling fire from heaven or raising anyone from the dead. But it is something greater. What can be greater than introducing one more soul to the kingdom of heaven? What can be greater than a heart that's been changed? What can be greater than love? If we speak with other tongues and even move mountains but don't have love, we are nothing and we gain nothing.

What can be greater than human acts of kindness in the name of Jesus in the midst of a hostile world? What could be greater than treating every person we meet as one for whom Christ died?

From *Jesus Paid It All* by Elvina M. Hall

Undeserved Deservedness

For nothing good have I
Whereby Thy grace to claim...

There is a new grace that is making inroads into the late twentieth century Christian consciousness. Unlike the grace referred to in this hymn, this "grace" comes to those who have worth. It is based on our value, rather than on God's prerogative. God appears almost obligated to display this grace because His subjects are so deserving of value and self-esteem. This grace says, in essence: *God will always be nice to us.* Or, *If I'm OK and you're OK, then God's OK too.*

This newly defined neo-grace is easy to take for granted. Attitudes such as humility, confession, and repentance do not necessarily accompany it. The only way to explain this new slant on grace is to call it an "undeserved deservedness." By definition, grace is undeserved favor. But this neo-grace is given out as if we were deserving of it, making it a contradiction in terms at best. How can you live as if you deserved something that you don't deserve?

What's missing here is the sense that there is something wrong with us that desperately needs attention. What's missing is the fear of God—the knowledge that He is obligated by nothing and no one. What's missing is the realization that His grace is completely undeserved and makes no sense to the rational mind. What's missing is that we have no claim on this grace.

What's missing is sheer astonishment in the presence of God that He would allow us to share His grace in the first place!

From *I Am Thine, O Lord* by Fanny J. Crosby

Too Busy

O the pure delight of a single hour
That before thy throne I spend,
When I kneel in prayer, and with Thee, my God,
I commune as friend with friend!

How things have changed. In 1875, Fanny Crosby felt that a single hour with God was a small amount of time to be infused with such a holy—yet personal—presence. For most of us today, however, an hour alone with God would be an excruciatingly long time.

I once was led in meditation by an evangelical Catholic who was familiar with the lifestyle of contemplation. Among the afternoon plans this person had for me was to spend an hour alone with God in a private place. I found that extremely difficult. I fidgeted and checked my watch every five minutes. He had given us directions for organizing our thoughts during this time, but I completed those simple tasks in the first few minutes.

My biggest struggle during that hour was what I was supposed to be accomplishing: nothing. Nothing outside of simply spending time alone with God. That's what he told us to do ahead of time, but I could not handle that. I had to be *doing* something.

Our society rewards doing, proving, achieving goals, and assessing information. It does not reward being, wondering, contemplating truth, or processing information through reflection. An hour alone with God would be a frightening thing for most of us. That's exactly why it's time we learned a discipline of which the rewards are not tangible.

We also need to learn that if we are too busy to spend an hour with the Lord without an agenda, then we are too busy.

From *Oh, Could I Speak the Matchless Worth* by Samuel Medley

God's Wardrobe

I'd sing the characters He bears,
And all the forms of love He wears...

We can lose ourselves—and well we should—in the study and praise of the multi-faceted character of God. We run out of adjectives when we try to explain who He is and what He is like. But when we talk of His love, He ceases to be in a textbook or a sermon. In His love, all of who God is comes to us. His love wears many different forms.

God's love is unconditional. Nothing we can do can earn it or drive it away. It is a friend's love: "I no longer call you servants," Jesus said to His disciples. "Instead, I have called you friends" (John 15:15). It is a lover's love—an eros, or passionate love, as a bridegroom loves his bride (Song of Songs).

His love is a father's love: He disciplines us as sons (see Hebrews 12). His love is a mother's love. He cares and nurtures and feeds us, and He deals tenderly with us: "A bruised reed He will not break, and a smoldering wick He will not snuff out" (Isaiah 42:3).

God's love is a martyr's love—one that lays down its life for the life of a friend. God caught the bullet; He fell on the grenade; He threw Himself in the path of the train that our lives might be spared.

And His love is forgiving. Even while they killed Him, He asked His father that the killers might be forgiven.

These are just a few of the many different clothes found in the wardrobe of God's love. And yet all of them together do not begin to contain the glory of Him who is love.

From *O Master Let Me Walk with Thee* by Washington Gladden

Purveyor of the Unseen

Tell me Thy secret; help me bear
The strain of toil, the fret of care.

Knowing the secrets of the heavenly kingdom will help us endure difficulty here on earth.

Jesus delivered truth through secrets. He did this through parables, irony, sarcasm and riddles. He was even known to trick the Pharisees on occasion, so as to avoid letting them in on the secrets of the kingdom.

"The knowledge of the secrets of the kingdom of heaven has been given to you, but not to them," Jesus said to the disciples (Matthew 13:11), making it clear that this truth was not to be common knowledge. For the same reason, casting pearls before pigs was not to be done (see Matthew 7:6). Clearly, Jesus' words were not for everybody.

What does this have to do with getting us through difficult times? If you know the secrets of the kingdom of heaven, then you know something about the reasons behind things. You are a purveyor of the unseen. So when you suffer, you know there is more to your suffering than meets the eye. When you are tempted to worry, you know God's will is bigger than your fear. When you strain to reach the mark, you know there is a crown waiting for you.

You know these things because Jesus told you, and these secrets are just another part of what keeps you going.

From *See How the Rising Sun* by Elizabeth Scott

A Long Eternity

My life I would anew
Devote, O Lord, to Thee;
And in Thy presence I would spend
A long eternity.

Yes, this is poor English. But how else can you say it? How else can you capture what eternity is without breaking some rules? Eternity itself is going to break them all anyway!

Yes, it's redundant. Eternity is already forever—you can't make forever any longer—and yet it is impossible for us to grasp what forever is. "A long eternity" seems quite appropriate, don't you think? To me, that means that however long I can possibly imagine eternity being, it will be a million times longer.

We need to constantly keep eternity in view. Far from being "pie in the sky, by and by," eternity actually lends a proper perspective to the present. If there were no eternity, then we would have time to waste, because time would mean nothing. Death would erase it all and leave us with no significance and nothing but silence. But eternity gives time significance. It says that what happens *now* has ramifications *then*. And since it's going to be such a long eternity, I think we will want to have good memories of what we did with our time here while we had it.

From *Awake, My Soul, to Joyful Lays* by Samuel Medley

A Song from Me

He justly claims a song from me...

So you don't think you have a voice to sing with? Do you let other people carry the tune? You would never be caught dead even humming something in your car or in the shower, would you?

The Lord claims a song from you, and justly so. After all He's done for you, a song is due—your own song. Come on, it would gladden His heart!

This will be nothing like a performance, so don't worry. It might be just something you make up as you go along. It might be a certain phrase over and over, or a theme that only you and God would understand—something special to you both.

Remember, He made you, gave you breath and went to the hill for you. He got your attention and He narrowed your choices until you had no choice but Him. And then He gave you everything you really wanted. That deserves a song—at least!

Go ahead. He's the only one who can hear you anyway. Monotone, halftone, sweet tone, sour tone—it doesn't matter to Him. He will joy in any sound you make, because He joys in you.

November 27

From *Awake, My Soul, and with the Sun* by Thomas Ken

Working with God

Direct, control, suggest, this day,
All I design, or do, or say;
That all my powers, with all their might,
In Thy sole glory may unite.

We can have as much of God's presence in our lives as we want. Since He's already promised to work everything out in the end for those who love Him, we might as well work with Him at the beginning, don't you think? Probably makes for an easier time of it all around.

Work with Him or work against Him—these seem to be our choices. Some people fight Him all their lives, then finally give in at the end. Of course they never accomplish much. All their energies are spent in merely getting to the point of giving up. Whereas if they gave up in the first place, all that wasted energy could go toward completing His will for their lives.

Why don't we work with God instead of against Him? Why not put our energies toward His purposes in the world, thus getting ourselves into something bigger?

Someone once said that a Christian working against the will of God was a little like someone walking backwards on a train. They're still going to get there, but they'll just be the last one off, and probably the most unhappy.

Why not get your small will going in the same direction as His big one? Why not ask Him to direct and control your day—and then be sure to listen in once you're up and going?

From *Awake, My Soul, And With the Sun* by Thomas Ken

Just One Day

Shake off dull sloth, and joyful rise
To pay thy morning sacrifice.

Some days it is a sacrifice just to get up. Why is it that sometimes our difficulties roll themselves up in a big ball and hit us over the head, first thing in the morning? Those are the days we want to crawl back under the covers like a child and wish the world away.

On days like this, we need to consider getting up as our morning sacrifice in and of itself. The seeming impossibilities that sometimes face us will not go away until we face them. Nor will God's strength be made available to us until we do. His power is useless when we are slothful.

We could imagine what Jesus woke up to every day and still see only a fraction of the sorrow and despair He saw. But He got up every day and faced a threatening world all the way to a cross. Regardless of the burden He has placed on us, it is not too great to bear. He will be our strength and our reason for overcoming. We can do it with His help. It's just one day, and they're all important.

So shake off sleep. Throw off laziness like a blanket. Get out of your bed, and make it quickly so it won't call you back when you look at it. Open your eyes. Have a cup of coffee if you like. Get your things in order for the day. Prepare to meet your Maker with joy. He is the reason you are alive.

From *Almost Persuaded* by Philip P. Bliss

The Almost

"Almost" cannot avail:
"Almost" is but to fail!
Sad, sad that bitter wail—
"Almost—but lost!"

The almost promises but never delivers. It tries to give us the benefits of commitment without having to pay the price. The almost is everywhere. It creeps into our projects and makes us stop too soon. It finds its way into our resolve and makes us obedient only to a point. The almost takes us right up to a needed confrontation only to accept a lame excuse for backing down. The almost has led some to the very gates of heaven, but never through.

Almost persuaded. Almost delivered. Almost free. Almost done. "I almost called." "I meant to write." "I knew you would wonder." "I thought about it." "I meant to do it... I really did." "If you only knew what I was up against." The almost loves words and phrases like these, and herein lies its greatest danger. The almost is worse than nothing at all, because it gives the illusion of delivering on a promise or an action. It makes you think you've done something or that you're about to do something, when you've done nothing and have no intentions of doing anything. If you faced that you were really doing nothing, you might have to wake up to that fact. The almost fools you into thinking you have what you don't have.

Take it all the way. Finish it. It's the only way to defeat the almost.

From *God from His Throne with Piercing Eye* by Joseph Steward

No Secrets

God from His throne with piercing eye,
Naked does every heart behold,
But never till we come to die,
To us will such a view unfold.

God sees everything, and I often think it's a good thing that we don't. There are times when I don't mind being kept in the dark.

There are two schools of thought on this subject: One, which is more in the tradition of many of these old hymns, is the belief that our whole lives will be put on view in the last day, not only to us, but to everyone. The other is the belief that God has removed our transgressions so far from us that no one will ever be able to find them, even if they tried. He is not only the forgiver, but the forgetter.

There is biblical basis for both of these points of view, and that leads me to believe that, in different ways, both will be true. This is the case with many of the apparent "conflicts" in Scripture. We simply do not have all the information in—or the means by which to interpret it.

In light of this, I would suggest we not take chances. It probably wouldn't be a good idea to do something wrong intentionally, counting on God's magnanimous character to forgive and forget. We just might end up, in spite of His forgiveness, being the star in a movie we'd rather not watch.

Secrets do not exist for the believer. Someone's always watching. God is, for sure. And someday, maybe everybody else will be watching, too.

From *It Is Well with My Soul* by H. G. Spafford

The Big Silence

My sin not in part but the whole,
Is nailed to the cross and I bear it no more...

One of the most shocking statements in the New Testament for those who are well acquainted with their own sin is found in the announcement that Jesus Christ, who knew no sin, "became sin for us." Whose sin did He become, if it wasn't yours and mine? I don't know about you, but I don't relish the idea of Jesus embracing any of my "more colorful" moments.

Does He really have to take on my sins? Couldn't I just write them down on a piece of paper and nail them to the cross? Remember when we used to do that at camp? We'd write down our sins and nail them to a wooden beam or throw them in the fire.

But why does this have to be so personal?

Because abstract sins can't be nailed to a cross. A Savior must be nailed there. The nails have to go through hands and feet, not paper and pulp. Flesh has to be torn and blood has to be spilled. You have to nail a man there, and He has to be the Son of God. He had to have every one of the sins of the world on Him when He died, so that no one will have their sins unwashed by His blood when they come before His Father.

This was the way God willed it. Christ had to live in the world before He could die for it. He had to take on our sins before He could put them away. I'm sure if there had been another way, God would have allowed it. Jesus even requested that He pass up the impending cup of death if there was another way. But He received no answer. Like me sometimes when I pray.

That must have been the biggest silence ever.

From *It Is Well with My Soul* by H. G. Spafford

When Faith Grows Up

And Lord, haste the day when the faith shall be sight...

As believers, we place our hope almost entirely on what is not seen. Christ, the Holy Spirit, heaven, angels, what God has done in history, and the saints and martyrs are all well beyond visual verification.

Yet the Bible says that "faith is the substance of things not seen, the evidence of things hoped for." That means that faith itself needs to be thought of as something solid. It is the tangible evidence of these things we can't see.

"Wait a minute," I can hear the skeptic say. "First you tell me faith hinges on the unseen, and then you tell me that faith itself (something also unseen) is the solid evidence of what I can't verify with my eyes. This is the same as saying, 'what I can't see is evidence of what I can't see.' Okay... And you try and tell me Christians aren't crazy?"

No, Christians are not crazy. We have simply experienced a faith that is real.

In light of eternal glory, our faith is perhaps the most solid possession we have, given the fact that everything we see now will ultimately burn up and be gone.

Faith gives us eyes into the future. When our faith becomes sight, we will see and hold what we have already come to know by faith. Our faith is not a means to something; it is the thing itself. Our faith will *change* to sight, and that by which we now believe will be that by which we see.

At that time, our eyes will finally agree with what our faith has been telling us for some time. We will be familiar with angels and they with us. We will know Christ as we are known. The material world we now experience as being so "solid" will tear away like a thin paper bag, revealing that which God has been doing behind the scenes from the beginning.

That is one bag I would not want to be left holding.

From *It Is Well with My Soul* by H. G. Spafford

He Noticed

That Christ hath regarded my helpless estate,
And hath shed His own blood for my soul.

He noticed. The heavenly Father looked down from His lofty place in heaven and noticed me. And what did He see? He saw my helpless state. He took note that I was in trouble and, most important, that there was nothing I could do about it. So He did something about it Himself.

Helplessness doesn't fare well in this take-charge, grab-for-the-gusto, just-do-it world. Not that God doesn't give us responsibilities, but this first one, this most important one, we cannot do for ourselves. We cannot save ourselves.

And Christ has regarded this. He did something about it. This is love in action. It is not merely a love I hear about, it is a love I experience. This is God forgiving me and filling my heart with His peace. This is the enabling presence of God's Spirit within me that His death and resurrection secured. And the personal knowledge of this amazes me still: that God Himself would regard my humble state enough to do something about it. In an over-populated and increasingly frightening world of lonely, alienated people, it is always nice to be noticed.

From *It Is Well with My Soul* by H. G. Spafford

A Deep-Seated Wellness

Whatever my lot, thou hast taught me to say:
"It is well, it is well with my soul."

This is what I have learned, says the hymn writer. Not merely that I have decided to give my consent to a bad lot in life, should that be the luck of my draw. That would be lesson enough, but this is more than that. This is saying that at any time, the state of my soul has nothing to do with the circumstances in my life. My soul and the life around it are on two different planes. The peace in my soul has no connection to my situation. Suffering and poverty cannot rob me of it; affluence and ease cannot take its place.

This is a deep-seated wellness. It is not a casual "Fine" to the obligatory "How are you?" It is something that is further into the recesses of my soul, so far in that it is out of reach of the perturbations of life. No joy or sorrow associated with this life can unseat it; no arms are long enough to wrestle it from me.

Yet I laugh and I cry. I am sure of some things and unsure of others. I buy and sell and fear the loss of what I have. I both long for and embrace the warmth of human love. But underneath all this, in another realm, in a voice that is all mine, I say, "It is well, it is well with my soul."

From *What a Friend We Have in Jesus* by Joseph Scriven

Taking the Wind Out of Worry

O what peace we often forfeit,
O what needless pain we bear,
All because we do not carry
Everything to God in prayer!

Peace is provided, but we don't avail ourselves of it. Comfort is available, and yet we hold onto our pain. We must like this misery we live in when we don't pray, since prayer is so readily available.

We often worry and fret simply because we are trying to solve our problems all by ourselves. This might be because we forgot to pray, or it might be because we do not want any help.

Once, when making a number of phone calls in a hurry, I dialed the wrong number. The lady who answered wasn't so sure it was a wrong number. At least, she didn't believe it was an accident that I dialed it. She asked if I was a Christian. Dumbfounded, I said I was. She proceeded to give me these words as a message: *Don't fret, God's grace is sufficient, serve Him with gladness.*

I remember feeling at the time that this encounter took the wind out of my worry sail. It made me stop all my rushed activities, which at the time were going nowhere, and pray. And I came out of that prayer rested, comforted, and better able to think clearly and act appropriately.

I once heard the sermon title, *Why Pray When You Can Worry?* That says it all, doesn't it? It's pretty much one or the other.

From *O Come, All Ye Faithful* by John Francis Wade

The Word Doing Things

Word of the Father, now in flesh appearing...

Word, words, words. Christians are experts on words. We hear sermons and read books and attend seminars and get all excited when someone says something in a way we haven't heard before. We also get upset when someone says it in a way we think is wrong. We judge a person's commitment or lack of it by their words.

Imagine if God had chosen to come to us in the form of a seminar or a notebook. Following Him would then have to do with how well we could take notes.

But instead, He came in the flesh, and through the firsthand accounts of those who walked with Him, we can watch Him and touch Him as much as we can listen to Him. We can follow the stories of those who followed Him and get a feeling for what kind of person He is and what He would do in certain situations. We can hear about Him doing things as much as we can hear what He said.

John said that what they had heard with their ears about Christ they had also seen with their eyes and handled with their hands. This was not just made up of words; this was the Word made flesh—the Word in action, the Word doing things.

From *We Three Kings* by John H. Hopkins, Jr.

Born to Die

Myrrh is mine: its bitter perfume
Breathes a life of gathering gloom—
Sorrowing, sighing, bleeding, dying,
Sealed in the stone-cold tomb.

Three gifts the wise men brought. Two were fit for royalty, but the third was a bitter omen. In Jesus' day, bodies were wrapped in myrrh for burial. Myrrh's pungent odor neutralized the smell of decomposing flesh. And thus, even the gifts that were brought to the Christ child announced His ultimate purpose. This was not some cruel joke—the wise men understood the purpose of His coming.

Death is usually the furthest thing from anyone's mind upon a baby's birth. Someone who would even bring up the subject would be thought of as unkind, insensitive, and unfit to join in the celebration. And yet these wise men had traveled long and far to see this child and bestow these gifts upon Him. They knew this was to be no ordinary life and no ordinary death. This life embraced its bleak destiny from the beginning. For it would be in the stone-cold grip of the grave that this child's greatest work would be accomplished.

From *Angels, from the Realms of Glory* by James Montgomery

The Big Event

Ye who sang creation's story,
Now proclaim Messiah's birth.

The universe was buzzing. This was The Big Event. Nothing like it since creation. The angels had something new to sing about. This is the event upon which all of history would turn. Everything before it looked forward to its coming. Everything after would look back upon its implications. And all history—before and after—would be forever altered by it.

This event would forever put God's dealings with humankind on a different basis. It would fulfill the law and make possible His grace. It would forgive the sins of all and restore the fellowship He wanted in the first place. It would make possible a new people, holy and set apart for Him, to be His Bride and live with Him eternally.

No wonder the angels were in a huff. This was the biggest thing since the heavens rang and all the morning stars sang together. Glory to God in the highest and all the way down to earth: Glory!

From *Angels, from the Realms of Glory* by James Montgomery

Following the Star

Sages, leave your contemplations,
Brighter visions beam afar;
Seek the great Desire of nations,
Ye have seen His natal star.

Meeting up with the real Jesus always gets us out of the books and off on camels. The sages from the East had been poring over the stars and their celestial maps for a lifetime, comparing them with prophetic records—even Hebrew scrolls. But never had they seen anything like this. All signs pointed to a major event of historic proportions. They could not stay in their laboratories any longer, and they could not merely gaze at the stars and take notes. They had to gather up their gifts and their possessions and see for themselves, for this star was moving. It was going somewhere.

Even when He was just a baby, Jesus got people up and moving. He got Mary and Joseph to Bethlehem just in time for His birth. He got the shepherds to the manger by morning. The wise men from the East took a little longer. And even though they were very wealthy, their trip was in no way easy. They left everything familiar behind them, except the star. When the star they had seen in the East stopped over Bethlehem, their joy was unspeakable.

Most Christians I know are like me. We have been looking at the Book long enough, studied and dissected it from front to back. Now, it's time to get up and start following. Where is He leading you today? Don't keep your camel waiting!

December 10

From *The First Noel* (Traditional English carol)

Wise Men Still Seek Him

And by the light of that same star
Three wise men came from country far;
To seek for a king was their intent,
And to follow the star wherever it went.

We always hear about the poor guys at the stable—the shepherds who got the message in the fields. They weren't seeking anything; they only got surprised on a quiet night by one of the most elaborate invitations in history.

But there were rich guys who made it to the Christ child, too... and smart. They never received an announcement; *they were already looking*. When they saw the star moving unlike anything they had seen in the sky before—or in recorded history—they knew something was up. Unlike the shepherds, they had a long way to go. But then again, these guys could afford it.

We have made so much of the humble shepherds and the humble birth that we tend to forget about these noble men who came with their entourage and their camels, bearing gifts for the Christ child.

These wise men show us that true pride and humility are not always measured by one's state. Intelligence need not always make one haughty, and wealth need not always corrupt.

Sometimes we assume that everyone who comes to Christ has to stop what they are doing and turn around. But there are some people who were heading in the right direction all along. These are not people who need to be hit over the head by a choir of angels. Just show them the star. It's right there in the sky, where they were already looking anyway.

Where are you looking?

From *The First Noel* (Traditional English carol)

A Deep Night

...On a cold winter's night that was so deep.

I wonder what was "so deep" about that cold winter's night. When we think of Christmas, we immediately think of snow. Snow can be deep. But snow is not mentioned here; only the night. Was it a deep winter—mid-winter—the dead center of the season of long, cold nights? Was it a deep cold—the kind that works its way to the bone?

All of these interpretations work and actually make more sense than the one that is grammatically correct. As the grammar would have it, though, it is the night that was deep. Rather odd, don't you think? I've never heard of a deep night before. And yet there is no better way to explain what it was that the Christ child entered. He came into a deep night. The world without Him is a deep night.

The hymn writer found this quite by accident, I'm sure. Being a lyricist myself, I know how this can happen. He may have started with the word "deep" simply as a rhyme with "sheep." And he may have had snow on his mind, because he had "cold" and "winter" in the line. But he ran out of room to put snow in and found, by accident or by intuition, that he had stumbled upon a deep night that was even better than what he thought he was going to say.

The Christ child came to a world trapped in a deep night—a darkness of sin, confusion, futility, and hopelessness that was ruled by the forces of power and greed. It was a darkness so deep that only the Son of God could penetrate it, and only the angels could drive it back. And though the world without Him is still a deep night, there is light shining now wherever He dwells in the human heart.

From *God Rest Ye Merry Gentlemen,* Author unknown

Can You Be Counted On?

In Bethlehem, in Jewry, the blessed babe was born,
And laid within a manger upon that Christmas morn;
To which the mother Mary did nothing hold in scorn...

But Mary had so much to complain about. There was the trip to Bethlehem at full term, the less-than-desirable accommodations, the bringing forth of a child outside the ordinary securities of matrimony (a midwife, a supporting community...), not to mention the scandal this pregnancy had undoubtedly created. (Yes, Mary and Joseph had both received angelic visits that explained this birth, but the angels couldn't bother visiting everybody in town, now could they!) Yet Mary had borne up so well through it all.

Scripture says she carried all these things and pondered them in her heart. It must have been a ponderous heart at times. And it must have been a glorious release to find her labors rewarded by a male child and confirmed by shepherds who had been directed there by an even stranger holy light. Mary came through with incredible strength. It was not all her own strength, to be sure. But she had to be willing to receive it and to be counted on.

God is always counting on us for something. What is He counting on you for today? And what is it going to cost you?

From *Joy to the World!* by Isaac Watts

Rearranging the Furniture

Let every heart prepare Him room...

Ever notice how a new decoration or piece of furniture can make you rearrange a whole room? Sometimes it might be nothing more than a new flower arrangement that gets it started. With my wife, merely the thought of something different in our home can start us both pulling the couch across the room, dragging the rocking chair here and there, trying it every which way, until we finally settle on what we want... even if it happens to be what we had before!

When Jesus comes into our lives, everything has to be rearranged. Sometimes we forget this and center our lives around the wrong things. Suddenly we realize everything's out of whack.

Christmas is a great time to make sure the Savior is in His rightful place. It may mean rearranging the furniture of our lives. But that's a joyful task—hardly a task at all. Some things will have to go. The rest you'll want to move around until everything is properly around Him.

From *Joy to the World!* by Isaac Watts

Paradise Found

He comes to make His blessings flow
Far as the curse is found...

Blessings reach as far as the curse. Forgiveness covers all of the sins. Grace does everything the law couldn't. And light swallows up the darkness. These are the ways of God. On one hand, we are tempted to ask why the curse, the law, sin and darkness were necessary in the first place. Why weren't we simply created to live in peace and harmony with God and each other? But on the other hand, we will gladly receive the provision. Questions such as this one are ours to ask, but not to answer.

There is no curse that His blessing has not covered and no sin that He cannot forgive. There is no requirement of the law that His grace cannot give us sufficiency to fulfill and no darkness that can put out His light. In fact, in every case, God's recovery process seems to recover more than what was lost in the first place. Paradise found always exceeds paradise lost.

Who wouldn't choose heaven over the Garden of Eden?

From *Hark! the Herald Angels Sing* by Charles Wesley

Taking Joy!

Pleased as man with men to dwell,
Jesus, our Emmanuel.

Jesus was pleased to dwell with us. We will never completely understand this. Yes, He had a task to perform, but there were times He seemed to draw pleasure from life. We are often so focused on the major events: His birth, passion, and death—that we do not allow Him any of this.

We all know that God came down, that He humbled Himself and took on the form of a servant, being made in our likeness. But has anyone ever considered that He might have actually *liked* anything about this? It might be that Jesus was pleased just to hang out with us for a few years. Could Jesus have relished being at Simon's home, watching his Pharisee friends squirm while a prostitute anointed His feet with her hair? Could it be that her touch was something that pleased Him in and of itself? Do we ever allow Him this?

Could Jesus as a small boy have enjoyed skipping rocks? Did He ever lay in the grass and try and find the shapes of animals in the slow-moving clouds overhead?

We rarely think of Him as enjoying His humanity. It's true He was a man of sorrows and acquainted with grief, but He must have had moments that brought Him pleasure—the simple human pleasures we all find at times, even when we are trying hard to be miserable.

Once, when the disciples came back from town with lunch for Jesus, they found Him more stimulated by a conversation with a woman than by the prospect of food.

It pleased Him to see her joy. It pleased Him to interact with her. Just like it pleased Him to dwell with us.

From *It Came upon the Midnight Clear* by Edmund H. Sears

Listen to the Silence

The world in solemn stillness lay
To hear the angels sing.

It was a silent night. The silent stars crept by overhead as the sleeping town of Bethlehem lay unawares. Christ's coming happened during the quietest time of the night, when dew on the pristine hillside garnished everything with a thin frost and the lamps of the little town flickered along with the twinkling stars. It was into this silence that the angels sang.

The hymn writers have made much of this silence, probably because it was so like God (and so unlike us) to do it this way. We would have organized some sort of bombastic display, and we would have planned it at prime time. Certainly not the middle of the night.

There's something silent about holiness, and something holy about the silence. God works in our lives in a similar way. His beginnings are small but with huge ramifications. You can hardly notice the change at first, but the ultimate destiny wrought by the unassuming beginning of His Spirit in us is to set us on a course that will place us 180 degrees and an eternity away from where we started.

Paul says that the Spirit is transforming us from one degree of glory to the next, meaning that our beginning must have been a lot like Christ's—so quiet that it was hardly noticed by anyone but the likes of a few shepherds and a handful of wise men.

From *It Came upon the Midnight Clear* by Edmund H. Sears

Angels All around Us

Still through the cloven skies they come
With peaceful wings unfurled,
And still their heav'nly music floats
O'er all the weary world.

They're still around—those angels, that is. They didn't leave. After delivering their message to the shepherds, they didn't go to some distant place in the heavens. They came from the far corners of the earth to make the announcement. This meeting of angels marked the most significant event in human history. The company of angels might have had a brief reception after the concert, but I doubt they stayed around Bethlehem very long. Angels cannot leave their posts vulnerable to the dark presence of their demonic kin.

And so their song goes on. It is being sung right now. If only we could hear it! Those who see angels are not necessarily getting a special visit as much as they are having their eyes opened to another dimension that has been there all along.

There are angels all around us right now. If there were not, we would know about it all too soon. We can take comfort and take heart from knowing this: God has His agents, and they are working behind the scenes on His behalf—and thus on ours, if we are walking in His will.

I talk to God about this often, especially when I am afraid. And I have been known to request back-ups.

From *It Came upon the Midnight Clear* by Edmund H. Sears

Better Than Reindeer on the Roof

O rest beside the weary road
And hear the angels sing.

Sometimes we need to stop along the road and listen for angels. Sometimes we have to allow God's realm to break in on ours, even if only to remember that it is there.

The Christmas season is important for this. Angels become real to us at Christmas time. Miracles seem more plausible. The mind is more willing to live with mystery. The secular mind would call it magic, and even adults entertain childhood fantasies of reindeer on the roof and a visit from the right jolly old elf himself. This is the season when the ballet celebrates toys coming to life and the implausible conversion of the miserly Mr. Scrooge seems somehow plausible in story after story told in everything from cartoons to Broadway to film.

And why not? What's at the bottom of all this wonder anyway? It's the fact that it actually *did* happen, at least the part about the angels. Why not give in to the joy and the surprise of it all? Why not believe the angels *really* sang that night? Why not hear them now? Come on, let's stop by the road here just for a bit of a rest, and listen....

From *I Heard the Bells on Christmas Day* by Henry W. Longfellow

Peacemakers

Yet pealed the bells more loud and deep:
"God is not dead, nor doth He sleep;
The wrong shall fail, the right prevail,
With peace on earth, good will to men."

The hardest thing about believing that God has entered the world is knowing that things here have continued on pretty much the same course as they were before He came. If anything, things have gotten worse. Shouldn't it have made more of a difference that this baby was born? Shouldn't there be more peace on earth to go along with the proclamation? Has not the state of the world made a mockery of angels?

Yes and no. Yes, in that there needs to be more bearers of peace in the world. No, in that this proclamation was not for everybody. It is only the King James translation that has it as a blanket "good will towards men" (Luke 2:14). Most other responsible translations render a selective peace. Peace on earth "to men on whom His favor rests," says the New International Version. Or peace on earth "to those with whom He is pleased," as Today's English Version has it. It's clearly a qualified statement in the original text. It has to be, or the angels lied. History bears this out.

In other words, there is a realm in which peace has come and one where it has not. And believe it or not, you and I are responsible for this. Regardless of the state of the world, the peace of God is ours to bring into that part of the world in which we have an influence. This is not only a proclamation of Christmas, it is a personal responsibility for all believers every day.

From *Silent Night! Holy Night!* by Joseph Mohr

The Dawn of a Very Long Day

Radiant beams from Thy holy face,
With the dawn of redeeming grace...

Dawn. That magical moment when the darkness has lifted, but the sun is not yet up. It is a moment of promise, that in-between time just before the sun dries the dew on the rose and melts the frost that still clings to shadows on roof tops.

Dawn is a time of hope. The day is fresh. The air has not yet been soiled by pollution or pierced by the sounds of human activity. And the dawn celebrated here is the dawn of a long day of grace. We call it an age. It began two thousand years ago and continues to the present and into the future. It is the Age of Grace, and it dawned on that morning in Bethlehem when Christ our Savior was born.

This dawn lasted thirty-three years, while the universe held its breath. Would He die like all the rest? Would the grave hold Him? Would the sun go back, the darkness return, and the frost turn to ice?

But when He walked out of that grave, the sun came up for good.

From *Silent Night! Holy Night!* by Joseph Mohr

Little Baby Lord

Jesus, Lord at Thy birth,
Jesus, Lord at Thy birth.

Little baby Lord. He never stopped being Lord. The universe would have flown apart if He had, since He was and is the one holding it all together (see Colossians 1:17). Yet somehow, through the most amazing of all mysteries, Jesus was able to be both God and baby at the same time.

We don't imagine Him very often in these stages—it is too much of a stretch for our feeble imaginations. Yet it is in imagining these things that the wonder of the incarnation comes home to us. He had to grow up like one of us in order to be a perfect sacrifice.

Imagine how He hears our prayers now, how He understands our feelings. We can never accuse Him of not being able to empathize with us. He even understands our temptations, for He was tempted in every way we are, yet remained without sin (see Hebrews 4:15).

And now He sits at the right hand of God the Father, pleading our case. God, the God-man, the little baby Lord, our Savior and our friend.

From *O Little Town of Bethlehem* by Phillip Brooks

Hopes and Fears

The hopes and fears of all the years
Are met in Thee tonight.

A lot came together that cold December night.

Fear: We are nothing but a chance collision of molecules—a huge cosmic mistake. It is truly a cruel joke that rendered us personalities and a consciousness with which to contemplate our nothingness.

Hope: We have a past and a future in the mind of one who created us in His image. We mean something to somebody. We have life and good company beyond the grave.

Fear: There are no miracles; there is only science. Life goes on. We live and we die, trying for one small piece of happiness that we most likely already had and missed.

Hope: God can and does break in on our human affairs. Choirs of angels sing and a star breaks out of its ancient course and sets a path of its own. A virgin Jewish girl bears a child from God.

Fear: We messed up and we'll have hell to pay one day *or* we messed up and there is no hell. It will just be over.

Hope: It won't be over, and the Judge will be merciful. There is a way and we can walk in it.

Fear: We are alone.

Hope: God is with us. Emmanuel!

A lot came together that cold December night...

From *O Little Town of Bethlehem* by Phillip Brooks

Starry, Starry Night

Above thy deep and dreamless sleep
The silent stars go by.

Have you ever stared into the heavens for a long time on a dark, moonless night, far away from the glare of city lights? The stars can seem so dense that they almost shut out the blackness of space altogether.

We know that many of these points of light are actually burning balls of exploding gasses, energy sources far brighter than our own sun. Yet to us, they appear as tiny, silent stars creeping across the heavens.

The longer we look, the smaller we feel. How insignificant we are! How vast the heavens! How small He made Himself in order to come to earth! What a wonder that He could even find the place!

It's a little town, Bethlehem. It's in a little nation on a little cinder of a planet that doesn't even shine.

I wonder what the boy Jesus had in His mind when he looked up at a starry night. Don't you wonder, sometimes, how much He knew?

December 24

From *O Little Town of Bethlehem* by Phillip Brooks

Silent Night

How silently, how silently
The wondrous gift is giv'n!

The Virgin Mary conceives of the Holy Spirit. There is no sound. The baby grows inside her womb. Still no sound. She and her betrothed are instructed in dreams as to the significance of this great event. Yet no one hears the messenger, except for the dreamers. They talk excitedly, but whom can they tell?

For months, they cling to faith, hope, and sanity amidst certain doubt and the talk of the town. That was silent, too. Most likely, it was the kind of silence that Joseph felt more as eyes boring into the back of his head than as words to his face.

Then, the trek to Bethlehem to be taxed. Joseph might have protested, Mary being as far along as she was, except that he already saw it unfolding. He had surely found it by then in the Scriptures: "But you, Bethlehem Ephrathah, though you are small among the clans of Judah, out of you will come for me one who will be ruler over Israel" (Micah 5:2).

So they made their way quietly to a small town bursting with wanted and unwanted guests—relatives, home by decree.

And the baby waited until the dead of night to want out. And suddenly, the quiet night—the *stille nacht* we've heard so much about—was pierced by three cries: The shrieks of a mother in labor, the cry of a newborn, and a chorus of angels heard only by a few shepherds keeping watch over their flocks. No pomp. No circumstance. No parade.

But the shepherds got an earful, to be sure!

From *O Little Town of Bethlehem* by Phillip Brooks

Humble Beginnings

No ear may hear His coming,
But in this world of sin,
Where meek souls will receive Him still
The dear Christ enters in.

Humble and unassuming, Christ's birth indicated how He enters a human heart for the first time. Quietly, without fanfare, He steals His way in. He's been doing this ever since He came the first time—stealing His way back. He just can't stay away.

I'm sure there was a design in this, like there is in everything He does. God purposely chose a little town and a humble beginning as a preview of His coming in us, lest we somehow rule ourselves out as unfit birthing places for His Spirit. There is even significance to it being a bed of straw in a damp and smelly barn. Could this be a statement about the nature of our hearts when He first arrives? If a stall in Bethlehem was good enough for Him, we can take courage from that fact alone. If it had been the finest room in the inn He came to, then who would have been worthy to welcome Him?

As it is, we can all welcome Him, from the least of us to the greatest—all who are willing to receive Him into the damp stall of their heart.

From *Day Of Wrath, O Dreadful Day* from the Latin, 13th Century

With Him in Paradise

Thou, who to the dying thief
Spakest pardon and relief—

Two similar lives. Two drastically different endings. I often think of those two thieves dying on either side of Jesus as He hung on the cross. Did these men have a clue they played a part in the most celebrated death in history? Did they realize the significance of the moment of their own demise? Were they too overcome with their own pain and grief to notice His? Did they feel any sense of wonder when they heard His words and His cries as He was the first of the three of them to die?

Somehow, in the midst of his own pain, one of these criminals got the message. Who knows how he figured it out—but he did. Maybe he had followed Jesus from a distance. Maybe he had heard Him preach somewhere along the way and wondered. Maybe all the information came to Him right then and there as they both hung on crosses. He could have gotten Jesus' message in any of these ways. But I can't imagine a greater way to die: right there next to Jesus. And I can't imagine a greater way to walk into heaven than to be accompanied by the Lord Himself.

And when I think of this, I wonder if entering into heaven might be the same for all of us. Could it not be that we will all be ushered into heaven just like this thief? Could it be that we will be welcomed in with Jesus, fresh from His own death? And will He whisper to each of us: "Today you will be with me in paradise"?

From *Awake, My Soul, Stretch Every Nerve* by Phillip Doddridge

Run to Win

Awake, my soul, stretch every nerve,
And press with vigor on;
A heavenly race demands thy zeal,
And an immortal crown.

The runner crouches at the starting block, muscle and sinew wound like a toy airplane's rubber band engine, waiting to be released. Eyes are straight ahead, focused on the goal. Knuckles rock in the dirt. The starting gun comes up, and the hips go down slowly like a cat's.

Bang! And with an explosion of power, the body springs upright and the chest thrusts forward as arms and legs churn piston-like in rhythm. Every fiber of muscle is now engaged, stretched to its maximum level, ignoring the pain.

We need to think of our heavenly race in images such as these. We have been given no less of a demanding course. It is full of challenges to faithfulness, obedience, and commitment. These are challenges that take the determination of a runner. "Do you not know that in a race all the runners run," wrote Paul, "but only one gets the prize. Run in such a way as to get the prize" (1 Corinthians 9:24).

Do you want to just be a runner in the pack somewhere? Is that good enough for you? Or do you want to win? All runners run, but some runners win. Run to win!

From *Praise to the Lord, the Almighty* by Joachim Neander

Getting What You Want

Has thou not seen
How thy desires e'er have been
Granted in what He ordaineth?

It takes time and reshaping, but sooner or later we discover that what we have wanted all along is to be fulfilled in Jesus. It's just that is usually doesn't happen the way we thought it would.

Spoiled children never grow up. They get used to easily getting what they want. Children who have been raised like this become selfish, demanding adults.

God is not some doting parent, catering to the whims of His children. God is a wise, all-powerful God who changes our desires over time, rather than fulfilling them at our bidding. He is much more likely to change us to fit His will than to alter His will to fit what we want.

But He's not a demanding father or drill sergeant, interested only in pressing us into conformity. He works on us from the inside, lovingly building in us the desire to want what He wants. This is a slow process of maturity. It comes through sacrifice and self-denial. It comes through obedience. But at some point, as we mature, we realize our desires already have been granted in what He has planned ahead of time. We find ourselves conforming to His will—wanting what He is already accomplishing on our behalf.

Sooner or later we find that, as we step into our life with God, we are stepping into the very thing we want the most.

From *Praise To The Lord, The Almighty* by Joachim Neander

Friend of God

Ponder anew
What the Almighty can do,
If with His love He befriend thee.

Think about this: You and God are friends. Think about your problems in relation to this. Think about your dark days, your depression, your stress, your addictions, your dysfunctions, and your dependencies in light of the fact that God has befriended you with His love. What does this mean?

It means you are loved regardless. It means that whatever you do, you are loved before you start. It also means that you have as your friend the most powerful force on earth, the Almighty God. He is your friend. He is on your side. Ponder what this means. This seems unbelievable.

This also means that whatever happens to you, you will never be alone. He has promised never to leave you or forsake you. Whatever happens, you're His friend. He is not going to forget about you or leave you behind.

Remember, you are with Him. The two of you are stuck together. Whatever happens to you happens to Him. Think about that before you drag Him into something you know He wouldn't like. But also think about this: Wherever He is, you will be with Him, and when you think about the future, there is no better place to be.

December 30

From *The Love of God* by F.M. Lehman

The Love of God

(*AUTHOR'S NOTE:* I am departing from the format I have set up for this book today and putting the reflection before the hymn selection. Actually, I simply want to leave the selection alone and let it be the meditation for this day. It stands alone as one of the most complete and profound and beautiful lyrics I have ever encountered. There is nothing more to be said about this matter that has not been contained in the final stanza of this great hymn.)

Could we with ink the ocean fill,
And were the skies of parchment made.
Were every stalk on earth a quill,
And every man a scribe by trade,
To write the love of God above
Would drain the ocean dry.
Nor could the scroll contain the whole,
Though stretched from sky to sky.

From *The Love of God* by F.M. Lehman

One up on God?

The love of God is greater far
Than tongue or pen can ever tell;
It goes beyond the highest star,
And reaches to the lowest hell.

I don't know how low the lowest hell is, or where the depths of Sheol can take a person. But I know this: You and I won't have to find out. However low we can go, Jesus has gone lower. It is impossible to outdo Him in this.

It is incomprehensible to imagine God's Son in hell, but there is no mistaking it. Psalm 139 clearly states that there is no place accessible to man that God has not been to first.

God not only knows the crime, He knows the punishment. No one can pull anything over on Him. No one, not even the most evil minded being in the universe, can outsmart God.

Nor can anyone accuse Him of being removed or aloof to the human situation. If God were merely all good and holy and righteous and just, we could pass Him off as being out of range—holy and perfect, but irrelevant to the human situation. No one can lay such a claim against Him any longer—not since the cross. You name the place, and He's been there. A trick? He knows it. Perversion? He's seen it. Can we shock him? Never!

Were it not for the cross and Christ's visit to hell, we could actually have one up on God. We could know something He doesn't know. We could even say that there is no hope for us, that no one knows what we've been through. We could leave Him in heaven and suffer here in our self-pity.

So much for that excuse.

Index, by author

Index, by hymn title